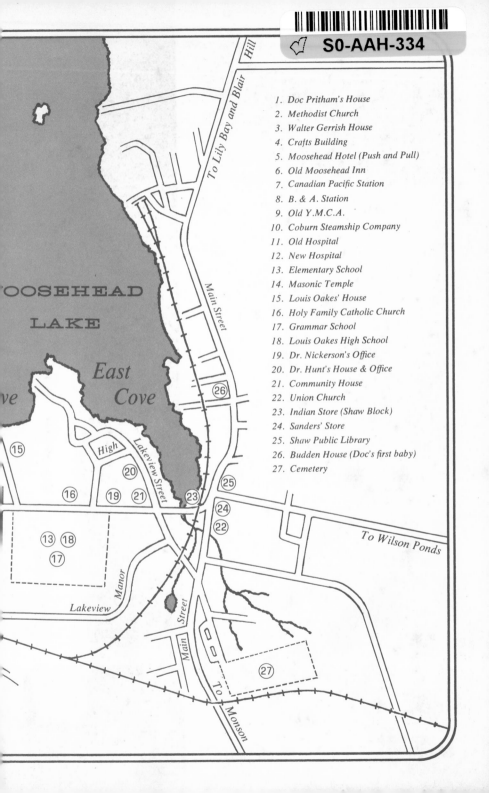

1. Doc Pritham's House
2. Methodist Church
3. Walter Gerrish House
4. Crafts Building
5. Moosehead Hotel (Push and Pull)
6. Old Moosehead Inn
7. Canadian Pacific Station
8. B. & A. Station
9. Old Y.M.C.A.
10. Coburn Steamship Company
11. Old Hospital
12. New Hospital
13. Elementary School
14. Masonic Temple
15. Louis Oakes' House
16. Holy Family Catholic Church
17. Grammar School
18. Louis Oakes High School
19. Dr. Nickerson's Office
20. Dr. Hunt's House & Office
21. Community House
22. Union Church
23. Indian Store (Shaw Block)
24. Sanders' Store
25. Shaw Public Library
26. Budden House (Doc's first baby)
27. Cemetery

To Lily Bay and Blair Hill

Main Street

MOOSEHEAD LAKE

East Cove

High

Lakeview Street

Manor

Lakeview

Main Street

To Monson

To Wilson Ponds

THE
BIG-LITTLE
WORLD
OF
DOC PRITHAM

THE
BIG-LITTLE
WORLD
OF
DOC
PRITHAM

Dorothy Clarke Wilson

Mc GRAW-HILL BOOK COMPANY
New York   St. Louis   San Francisco
Düsseldorf   Mexico   Sydney   Toronto

THE BIG-LITTLE WORLD OF DOC PRITHAM

Copyright © 1971 by Dorothy Clarke Wilson.
Design: Christine Aulicino

Library of Congress Catalog Card Number: 75-154241

First Edition

07-070751-0

Acknowledgments

The author wishes to make the following grateful acknowledgments:

To Dr. and Mrs. Fred J. Pritham and members of their family, chiefly their son, Dr. Howard C. Pritham, and their grandson and his wife, Dr. Howard G. and Ellen Pritham, for their generous sharing of source materials. Other family contributors include Mrs. Pritham's sisters, Viola Redmond and Hallie Greeley. The author is especially indebted to "Doc" for the use of a large notebook, written by him some years ago and chronicling, in great detail, many of his adventures. Most of the incidents and personal details related in this book were derived either from this notebook or from tapes recorded by the doctor in the author's presence.

To numerous friends of the Prithams, many of whom contributed information, anecdotes, and pictures. Chief among these are Miss Ella Gerrish and Rev. Manfred Carter. Others include Rev. Alfred Hempstead, Mrs. Dorothy Ashe, Mrs. Ruth Vickery, Rev. Chauncey D. Wentworth, Gertrude L. Shaw, Rev. and Mrs. Ralph Barron, Mrs. Elsie A. Phillips, Mrs. Edna Gunn, Mr. Hugh Desmond, Miss Erma Budden, Mr. David Ward, Mrs. Anne Howe, Rev. and Mrs. George Bullens, Mr. Charles Sawyer, Rev. and Mrs. John Tolman, Mr. Henry Perley.

To medical associates of Dr. Pritham for invaluable reminiscences, especially Miss Henrietta Bigney, R.N., Mrs. Nellie Morrell, R.N., Dr. Norman Nickerson, Mrs.

Leon Bradley, R.N., Mrs. Bernice Smith, R.N., also to the
Maine Medical Association and Dr. Daniel Hanley, its
Executive Secretary, for statistics relating to medicine in
Maine.

To librarians, curators, and editors, including Mrs. Ruth
Anderson, librarian, Greenville Public Library; Mr.
Robert L. Volz, curator, Special Collections, Bowdoin Col-
lege Library; Mr. Russell Gerould, editor of the *Moose-
head Gazette;* also to Mrs. Rodney Brett of the Greenville
Information Center.

To Mr. Albion Ende, artist, for permission to reprint a
copy of his portrait of Dr. Pritham.

To the James W. Sewall Company, Old Town, Maine,
for help in constructing maps of the Greenville area.

To Dodd, Mead and Company, Inc., New York, for
permission to quote four lines from Holman Day's
"O'Connor From the Drive," contained in his *Pine Tree
Ballads.*

To source materials found in many newspapers, pamphlets, magazines, and books, including:

NEWSPAPERS:

The *Bangor Daily News* (especially articles on the Onawa
    Train Wreck, December 22–24, 1919)
The *Moosehead Gazette* (many news items and articles)
The *Portland Press Herald* and the *Portland Sunday Tele-
    gram* (series of ten articles titled "North Country
    Doctor," November to January, 1963)

PAMPHLETS:

Annual Catalogues of Bowdoin College, 1900–1905
Medical School of Maine, the Medical Department of
    Bowdoin College, 85th Year, Session of 1904–1905
Bowdoin College Bulletin, Number 105, Medical School
    Centennial 1820–1920, October, 1920

MAGAZINES:

Eldon, Alfred, *Motor Boat*, "Moosehead's Motor Boat MD," February 25, 1928

Knowlton, Deputy Sheriff David L., as told to John N. Makris, *Detective*, "Sinister Secret of the Draft Dodging Killer," Fall, 1944

Moran, John W., and Herbert Asbury, *Collier's*, "The Little Doctor," April 29, 1944

The Northern (numerous articles on Moosehead, Greenville, lumbering, the Maine woods)

BOOKS:

Barry, Phillips, *The Maine Woods Songster*, Powell Printing Company, Cambridge, Massachusetts, 1939

Beck, Horace P., *The Folklore of Maine*, J. B. Lippincott Company, Philadelphia, 1957

Coolidge, Philip T., *History of the Maine Woods*, Furbush-Roberts Printing Co., Bangor, Maine, 1963

Eckstorm, Fannie Hardy, *The Penobscot Man*, Houghton Mifflin Company, Boston, 1904.

Hatch, Louis C., *History of Bowdoin College*, Loring, Short, and Harmon, Portland, Maine, 1927

Hempstead, Alfred Geer, *The Penobscot Boom*, University of Maine Press, Maine, 1931

Historical Collections of Piscataquis County, Maine, Observer Press, Dover, Maine, 1910

Holbrook, Stewart H., *Holy Old Mackinaw*, The Macmillan Company, New York, 1956

Holbrook, Stewart H., *Yankee Loggers*, International Paper Company, New York, 1961

Pike, Robert E., *Tall Trees, Tough Men*, W. W. Norton & Company, Inc., New York, 1967

Thoreau, Henry David, *The Maine Woods*, reprint, W. W. Norton & Company, Inc., New York, 1950

The Big-Little World of Doc Pritham

COME WITH ME and explore the big-little world of Doc Pritham.

The little world is not hard to find. Take any road into Maine. Follow Route 15 to Greenville. If you are a beauty hound, stop about seven miles out of town and feast your eyes on twenty-two mountains marching along the horizon. Stop again at Indian Hill Farm for your first view of Moosehead Lake, which Thoreau described nearly 120 years ago as "a suitably wild-looking sheet of water, sprinkled with small, low islands, covered with shaggy spruce and other wild wood." Though its wildness may be somewhat tempered, its pristine beauty remains unchanged, its blue-clear waters unpolluted. Remember later to climb Blair Hill and revel in the view at sunset.

In Greenville turn left at the Indian Store and travel

for about a mile. You will pass the fine high school built in 1935 by Louis Oakes, the town benefactor, and farther along, on your left, the splendid new hospital beside its gray-shingled predecessor, now a convalescent home. At the foot of the hill, on your right, just before you get to a small Methodist church, you will see a square, rather austere house with pyramidal roof, double bay windows in front at either side, its outer walls covered by gray asphalt shingles. Beside the front door, small but visible from your car, is a weather-beaten sign depicting an ancient horse and buggy, under it the words, "F. J. Pritham, M.D."

Don't stop now, but go on down the street. Note the rambling red wooden building with great long porches on your left, now labeled "The Moosehead Lake Hotel." You will meet it again in less distinguished guise as the old "Push and Pull." The square white building on the left beyond the overpass is Crafts' store, where in the southeast corner, upstairs, Doc had his first office. On Bog Brook just beyond, a rushing torrent in springtime, he saw his first river drive.

Follow the stream to its outlet at West Cove. You'll see planes and yachts anchored there now, but try to imagine big gaily painted steamers, fleets of loggers' and fishermen's boats, and anchored somewhere in the medley, ready for instant use, a long, perilously narrow craft called the *Noname*.

That big brick building around the corner and under the railroad overpass is the old Y.M.C.A., empty now except for boat services in the basement. If you find David Ward in charge, he will be glad to take you inside, through the huge barren rooms and up two flights of stairs, where he will show you the dusty, littered, brick-walled corner which was Doc's first operating room. Outside, on the bare land toward the lake, you might see, as I did, a dilapidated red sleigh, a bit of flotsam washed up, apparently, out of this same remote past.

Now . . . go back to the square, austere house beside the church. Mount the huge slabs of stone steps, and push the old-fashioned bell. If you're lucky, a slight, stooped gnome-like figure will appear in the door, ruddy cheeks and keen eyes belying his more than ninety years. Look at him well, for he is one of a fast-vanishing breed, the all-purpose, all-hours doctor who believes it's his job to come to your aid anytime, anywhere, whatever your physical need.

He will invite you in, for his house is always open. On the left you can see the two rooms which for sixty-five years have been his office, contents almost unchanged: the low couch bought from the Methodist minister for seventy-five cents; the table made out of a medical supply box, Lilla Clark's oilcloth still covering it; the big rolltop desk; the medicine cabinet made by Wendell Hubbard. You can sit in one of the "cussed uncomfortable" chairs, admire the new one of shining Moosehead maple, look at the treasured band trophies, perhaps explore the mysteries of the big battered black bag and the back-pack which facilitated the jumping of trains and the treks through mud and slush, over snow and ice. And, if you're very lucky indeed, as I was, you might get him started talking so you could hear firsthand some of those almost incredible tales which make up the substance of this book.

Yes, it's easy enough to find the little world. But the big world—that's another matter.

You can try. Go to the top of Squaw Mountain. You can take the ski lift, as I did, as far as it goes, then climb the rest of the way. Look in all directions, over the dozens of lakes, miles of unbroken forest. As far as you can see, this is Doc's big world.

But you haven't seen it all. Hire one of the small planes down there at the edge of the lake. Ask the pilot to run you north, over Moosehead to Seboomook, over the West Branch of the Penobscot and Chesuncook Lake, over Umbazooksus and Chamberlain and Eagle until you see

Soper Mountain below on the right; then south again
through the Allagash country to Pine Stream and west to
the Canadian border, circling southward past Sandy Stream
Mountain, the town of Jackman pin points of houses
seen on your left, over Attean Mountain and Moose
River, east and south again, looking down on scattered
villages—Blanchard, Parkman, Sangerville, with Dover-
Foxcroft quite a way to the right; east and north around
Brownville and up above the long uninhabited wilderness
to the Kennebec; northwest again over Millinocket Lake
with Katahdin's peak at eye level on your right, over the
majesty and thunder of Ripogenus Dam and gorge; back
again to Greenville. There! You have circled his big world,
an area of more than 5,000 square miles.

But still you haven't really seen it. As well try to sense
the wonder of the Taj Mahal through the monocle of an
airplane window! For it's not just a vast expanse of little
towns, blue lakes, and green forests. It's depth as well as
length and breadth, time as well as space, the terror and
beauty of changing seasons, the passing of eras. In fact, it's
almost a century of a man's life. The only way we can
really see it is to try to live that life with him.

So come with me and explore the big-little world of Doc
Pritham.

Greenville, Maine
October, 1970

CHAPTER ONE

Dress Rehearsal

· 1 ·

THOUGH DOC WOULD scoff at the idea, his first twenty-five years were a dress rehearsal for the epic role he was to play for the next sixty-five.

"Epic role hogwash!" he would hoot derisively. "Judas priest! Is a man a play-acting hero just because he does his job as well as he knows how?"

The stage for his life drama was set long before his birth, at least ten thousand years.

The lakes were there, scooped and scoured by the glaciers out of stubborn granite, the big one shaped like a moose's head, the hundred and more others scattered about it like bits of broken crystal. The rivers and streams flowed peacefully or raced like foaming steeds, unchoked by logs

I

and unbridled by man-made dams. The mountains were in place, the highest one with twin crests standing guard at the big lake's foot, to its east the one shaped like a kneeling elephant, at its narrowest part the stark headland crouching like a petrified monster. The forests were there, their virginity unviolated. Props, lighting, sound effects, backdrops, all were ready—dawns and sunsets, exquisite greens and ineffable blues, flaming autumns, the thunder of waters, the screamings, honkings, crashings, snarlings, carolings, splashings of birds, beasts, and fishes—aeons before there was human eye to see or ear to hear.

But the rehearsal took place on another stage more than a hundred miles away.

It was an apt coincidence that Fred Pritham should have been born and reared in a town called Freeport, for independence was as native to his small wiry body as to the wild birds which rode the airways over Casco Bay. And, though his father's farm, five miles to the east of the village, seemed remote, it was in reality a sally port for high adventure. Back in the eighties, when he was growing from one to ten, he could look across the mussel shoals and see the four- and five-masted schooners riding in and out of Portland Harbor, sails rigged to the winds of far places. It was a breeding place for self-reliant, untrammeled, free-moving life.

For hardness and toughness, too. Even for small boys farm workdays started while the stars were still bright and lasted long after sunset. Hay was the principal crop to feed the twenty-five or thirty head of cattle and, in the eighties, the two oxen. A boy of five or six was not too young to spread the swaths of hay and, a more pleasant task, to run behind the mowing machine or the hand scythe after it had passed through a patch of wild strawberries. Gathering them by the severed stems, he would quickly fill a milk pail, then sit in the shade to hull them before taking them to the house for supper. Before each of them was seven, both Fred and his brother Henry Charles, two years older, had their own cows to milk; and long before the age of ten they were taking turns staying out of school to drive the oxen while Dad held the plow, for with danger of the hayfields becoming winter killed, fifteen or twenty acres had to be plowed each fall to maintain a good head of grass.

But Fred found this more fun than hard work. Even the necessity of tempering his natural swiftness to the plodding rhythm of the big, powerful animals aroused content rather than impatience. The fevered rush of summer was over. Drowsily wrapped in the golden October haze, the world was calm and slow, and he was as much a part of it as the earth flowing in rich brown ribbons from the gleaming share. It was so still he could hear the town clock strike the hours in Brunswick nine miles away. When the oxen became winded so that their tongues hung out, Dad would call a halt and they would sit on the plow beam and listen to the guns banging away at coots over on the bay shore.

It was Dad who became restless. He would push his old felt hat back over his black unruly hair, wipe the sweat from his forehead and his drooping mustache, and stare up into the sky or out over the bay, his short lean body all the time taut as a bowstring ready to let loose. One time especially the boy watched him curiously. Looking for scoters, perhaps? Wishing he could be down on the shore shooting? No. The eyes under the heavy lids were looking farther, even a small boy could see that. To that mythical ancestral castle over in England, maybe, rumored to bear the name of Pritham? More likely to those Grand Banks where Dad had gone at sixteen, following the seafaring bent of the descendants of those three Pritham brothers who had first come to America. He had had to give up the sea to come home and take care of his parents. Did regrets still haunt him?

"Gosh A'mighty, a man shouldn't have to spend all his

time plowin' in weather like this!" The mild expletive was followed by one of those more pungent relics of the Grand Banks which the refined Elinor Merrill had never been quite able to expurgate from her husband's vocabulary. "I wish—I wish—" The high wide gaze wavered, reluctantly shortened its focus. "Godfreys, if a man could just have a week this time o' year to get way up around Moosehead Lake, say, and hunt!"

Moosehead Lake! Though the boy knew it was in Maine somewhere, it seemed far away as the Grand Banks. He felt a strong ache and urge. "You will, Pop," he said earnestly. "Just wait'll Harry'n me get big enough to run the farm."

The man laughed indulgently, then sobered. "No, son. You won't be runnin' no farm, I hope. It's a hard life for a man, leastways this small stuff here in Maine. No, I want you boys should learn a trade, somethin' you don't have to work at from dawn to dark. Not farmin'," then as he caught the flicker of the boy's eyes toward the bay, "no, by thunder, and not sailin', neither."

Dad spat a rich brown stream of tobacco juice and again bent his thin short body to the plow handles. His grip was iron-strong, for the slightness of body was deceptive. Later, when the plowed field had burgeoned and ripened into hay, he would grind his hand scythe to a keen edge and mow swift broad swaths which were the envy of his sons and neighbors. The boy picked up his goad stick and went through the familiar sounds and motions: "Hi-up, there!" with a poke of the broad end in the tough flanks to get the lazy beasts moving, a sharp "Haw, there! Wo-hish!" and a clip on the nose of the near ox to make the team turn at the end of the field, an occasional nudge in the ribs with the long stick to keep the off ox plodding straight in the furrow. But he moved and mouthed automatically. The delicious calm had been shattered, the soft haze had become a portent of bewilderment, uncertainty. Life, heretofore simple, had turned problematic. He felt trapped.

"Hey, there! Gosh A'mighty, boy, you asleep?"

"Gee-off!" yelled the boy, and gave the near ox a smart clip just in time to veer the team right before the plow skittered out of the furrow. But even the yell was absent-minded. Not be a farmer—or a seaman? What, then? And *how?* The specter of choice, of inevitable and painful preparation, had reared its ugly head. He could not know that each day of his young life was one of preparation.

He performed his first surgery at the age of four, when he and Harry, aged six, were helping to chop pumpkins for the cows' supper, and he managed to amputate the end of his brother's forefinger. There followed a great hull-aballoo, a rush trip to Dr. Herbert Twitchell in the village, and keen remorse tinctured with curiosity as to the process by which the doctor had to shorten the bone a bit to obtain flap to cover the end of the finger.

Harry provided other object lessons through their tender years, for he was accident-prone. There was the time at school when he was struck in the eye by the pointed end of a board serving as musket for a group playing "Indian raid." The resulting ulcer required many trips to Portland. Then while trying to hit a swallow with a pole as it flew about the barn rafters, he stepped on a vacant spot between boards and scaffolding and plunged to the barn floor eighteen feet below, striking the wheel of an empty hay-rack on the way. Hastily sliding down off the hay-mow and following their unspoken code that "what Mother doesn't know doesn't hurt," Fred sneaked into the house, smuggled out some clean handkerchiefs, led his brother to the pump, and did quite a creditable job mopping up the blood where some of the front teeth had been knocked clear through the lip. Warned by some sixth sense, however, Mother appeared and with her usual competence took over. Fred rushed again for handkerchiefs when a jagged rock, surely a four-pounder, which he aimed from a high ledge at a squirrel hurtled down and cut a ragged hole in his brother's head. He was a good sprinter, a proficiency acquired partially through expert maneuvers in escaping the farm's animated Jersey bull, but now fear, hot and choking, pumped frantic speed into his thin legs. He was sure that, like Cain, he had killed his brother. But Harry somehow survived.

Survived often, in fact, by superior mental as well as physical stamina. Whereas Fred would rely on sprinting to get him under the bottom wire of the fence on time, Harry would match wits with the bull or the antagonistic old long-horned cow which had a yen for chasing them. One day the latter caught them in mid-pasture near a pile of old stringers that had been dragged out of the tie-up at the time of replacements. When the cow set off after the scampering Fred, Harry stood his ground and lifted one of the stringers, perhaps twelve feet by four inches, on end.

"Hollo!" he yelled. "Look here."

Out of the tail of his eye Fred caught the idea. Taking a quick double-back, he ran past the old cow, which, infuriated by her inability to turn as swiftly, came tearing after him in a blind effort to retrieve lost time. The stringer landed across her back with an ear-splitting bang. The old bovine had had enough. That day they didn't have to race to get over or under the fence.

Fred provided his own first demonstration in anatomy at the age of six. One summer day in that year of 1886 he and his brother were playing in the loft of the shed, which was in the ell at right angles to the house, jutting up against the barn but not attached to it. The loft was a treasure house of old iron, ancient hardware, stored grain, broken snaths, scythes, rusted or outmoded tools, a long unused cider mill, and odds and ends that "might come in handy sometime." When interest in one of their favorite sports, sniping at an unwary rat, waned for lack of victims, they looked about for other attractions.

"I know!" It was usually Harry who got the ideas. "I'll bet we could rig us up some hand scythes all our own. What say?"

Fred agreed. At six mowing was still exciting privilege rather than drudgery. He picked his snath, found a blade that seemed less rusty and chipped than the others, and set to work. Even in the semidarkness of the loft his fingers moved with the swiftness and precision of the born mechanic who, a farm boy, has seen things taken apart and put together almost from birth, and he soon had the task completed. Harry, more skilled with head than hands, was having difficulties. The nut on the snath he had chosen was rusted fast.

"Hold it! I'll come and help."

Darting across the dusky loft, the boy did not see that his brother had stood his old scythe against a barrel of oats. Feeling a stab of pain, he crumpled and slid the whole length of the scythe. Though badly rusted from cutting thatch and black grass, the blade was sharp. For once, heedless of whether Mother discovered his mischief or not, he screamed.

Mother dropped the dash of the churn and came running. In the shed below the loft she saw streams of red liquid dripping through the cracks overhead. Cider, she thought with indulgent annoyance, those foolish boys have tried to make cider with the old press! But it was not cider. Stumbling over her long skirts, she climbed the steep narrow stairs.

"There, there, son, it's all right. Mother's here."

"I—I—" The boy choked and gasped.

"Don't talk. Later."

Somehow, competently, she got everything down the stairs—boy, skirts, blood—and into the kitchen.

"There! Sit here, son, just for a minute. Hold him by

the shoulders, Harry, he's likely to feel faint. Now—I'll just spread these newspapers on the table." She turned to her daughter, the boy's half-sister. "Get a pillow, Frankie, for his head, then you can take over the churn. It's just where it oughn't be left, butter almost come."

From sheer weakness the boy lay still, his world reduced to sound and feeling, for his eyelids were clamped so tight-shut they felt glued together. The throbbing pain, the strangling thickness in his throat, the arms gently lifting, the slap-slap of the dash in the churn . . . Smells, too, Mother and kitchen smells, bread freshly baked, the tangy-fresh smell of butter in all its successive stages from sour cream to moist dewy pats, a queer rank smell like after the pig had been stuck and drawn . . . The calm crooning voice.

"There! Steady now. This will hurt, but I have to clean it out. I'll try not to hurt more'n I have to."

He did not cry out. The sound caught in a strangling knot in his throat. He opened his eyes a crack, surprised to find them unblurred by tears. The first thing he saw was Mother's pink-checked calico dress, which he had watched her hemming, marveling at the neat fine stitches, and was dismayed to see it all blotched with red. She moved away. Gingerly, then, with horrible foreboding, he looked down at his leg. Relief, to find it was still there —or horror to see what a mess he had made of it? Or— curiosity? Rearing his head, he stared at the long gaping ridges of flesh and the queer little valley between. He could see straight into the wound. So that was what a leg looked like inside! He stared. Years later he would re- member the exact pattern of what he saw and ascribe to each detail its correct name. There was a deep gash from the inner anklebone up across the leg beyond the head of the fibula. The tibia lay completely exposed, and he could look into the cavity and clearly see the hollow shaft.

The sight attracted as well as repelled. It was a lesson in anatomy he would never forget.

Mother returned. She carried a needle and a long stout thread. Body tensing, he reared his head. Gently she pushed it back. Her face was as always, eyes clear and serene under the neatly parted hair, lips smiling, nose rather prominent and slightly arched, like his own.

"No, don't watch, dear. Look out the window at the chickens. See if you can count as many as I can make stitches. One—two—three—four—"

Somehow they reached twenty-five or thirty. Both lost count. With a rebound of youthful spirits the boy critically inspected the job. Not bad! The stitches were almost as neat and even as in the calico hem, though, looking at her trembling hands, he wondered how she could have done it. The leg healed without incident, and within three weeks he was able to go to the garden to pick peas for dinner.

But the scar would be there always, and the vivid memory. Fifteen years later he would use the same technique in sewing the hind leg of a beloved spaniel which had jumped in front of the cutter bar of the mowing machine and severed everything but the Achilles tendon. A hundred times in the next three-quarters of a century he would recall the incident when he took needle and thread in hand to perform a suture. And every nurse who worked with him would marvel at his neat, even stitches.

. 2 .

EXCEPT FOR its bitter taste, its salt-laden mists, its marshes and clam flats and seaweed, the bay might have been a big inland lake. Certainly it was a good training school for one. It taught a boy to swim, to skate if the water froze thick enough where the fresh streams flowed into it, to contend with fog and darkness and high waves and rotten ice, to rig and handle boats of all kinds, and, if his father was a sportsman, to instill a passion for the study and pursuit of wildlife.

"Run down to the shore, Fred," Dad would sometimes suggest between morning chores and the day's other farm work, "and look for birds."

The boy would be off like a shot toward Little River Bay, blessing the faster legwork which excused him instead of his brother from the tailend of pumping drinking water for the stock. Scampering to the shore, he would crawl behind a tree on a projecting point to look for game, then crawl back into the open field and wave his hat wildly if a flock was in evidence. But he had better know his ducks! Woe to the scout if the disgusted parent found the birds were only a flock of sheldrake or whistlers instead of the preferred black ducks or geese!

He was initiated into the gunning game by the time he was seven. Dad had a homemade boat called a "float," shaped like a half-filled-out peapod, bow pointed, stern square, round as a barrel in the middle, very much like a kayak. He had other boats, a skiff and a dory, but the float was the most valued asset, almost as much a daily necessity for a seacoast family as the automobile would be for future generations. As children the boys would take turns lying in the front, concealed by a camouflage of grass, seaweed, or ice blocks, while Dad sculled the craft noiselessly into shooting range. But this early float with its square stern was no good for sculling if a little sea was running, for it split the dressing off its deck. Later Dad had Gus Holbrook build them a beautiful big float that was easy to scull and also a good sailing boat, that could be used not only for gunning but for shore and deep-sea fishing, family picnics, and berrying expeditions.

Though Fred did not have a gun of his own until he was nine, he had shot his father's ten-gauge double-barreled Parker long before that. One morning of the summer before he was eight he glimpsed a huge old cat which had been stealing chickens in the act of climbing a rock pile to jump the wire fence. Rushing into the house and grabbing the gun and two duck loads, he loaded it in the shed, then crawled to the shelter of a luxuriant growth of rhubarb, reared up enough to spot the cat, sighted, and squeezed the trigger. Hurled flat on his back, the gun knocked from his hands, he had no chance to shoot again. He didn't need to. The enormous old cat had fallen flatter than he, all nine lives extinguished. A better shot at age seven than the hired man, Mitchell, who had fired half a butterbox of shells to kill a skunk!

His first gun was an old muzzle-loader nearly twice as tall as he was, a murderous-looking weapon, but he handled it efficiently, wreaking damage on nothing more costly than crows, partridge, rabbits, and woodchucks. Not so with another muzzle-loader, not his! Early one morning he was hunting crows, a worthy enterprise for crop protection, with Harry and a chum, Leon Banks. Leon had a muzzle-loader even older and rustier than Fred's. Spotting a flock of crows in a tree, they crawled behind a bank. Each picked his target, took aim.

"Ready," muttered Harry. "Fire!"

Fred thought his head was blown off. The explosion lifted his scalp, blasted, reverberated through his whole small body, settled finally with a shrill ringing in his left ear. He was too dazed to be frightened, but the other two were terrified.

"Wh—what happened? . . . Is—is everybody all here? . . . Gee whillikers, what a blast! . . . You all right, Fred? You look—funny!"

"Yeah. I—I'm all right, I—guess. My—ear feels queer—"

"No wonder." Leon was examining his gun. "Look, it
blew the nipple clean out. The rust inside, maybe. It must
have cleared your ear, Fred, by a fraction of an inch." His
tall huskiness seemed to shrink and pale, and he choked.
"It's lucky you're—still alive!"

Fred's ear was still ringing when he returned home, and
it kept on all through the rest of that day and until he
managed to get to sleep that night. It was ringing when he
awoke the next morning. He could hear all right with the
ear; he covered up the other one to make sure. But all
that day and night and the next day and night the ringing
continued, a steady persistent sound like the distant
jangling of an alarm clock which somebody had forgotten
to shut off. Not exactly, however, for in time the clock
would shut itself off. This ringing didn't. In fact, it was to
continue without cessation, day and night, for the next
forty-five years.

But the accident by no means made him gun-shy or
dampened his zeal for hunting. As he grew older bay shooting had more and more appeal, and he was finally able to
buy himself a double-barreled ten-gauge shotgun. His
hunting bouts did not interfere with farm work or school,
for one of the best times to decoy birds was early in the
morning, just as, he had discovered, one of the best times
to mow a field was late at night, with the heat of the day
over and the cool, salt-laden mists drifting in from the
mussel shoals. Darkness was no problem, for he had always
been blessed with night vision. When Dad left his pipe
out on a bench in the shed or somewhere else, it was
always Fred who was asked to run and get it in the dark.
He could find it as easily as in the daytime. Often after
working late into the evening he would be up again at
three in the morning sculling the float into good position
to take off if birds were in sight when it became light.
Sometimes he hunted with Harry or Leon or both. Occa-

sionally they were joined by the Holbrook boys, Fred and Will and Charles, who lived on Wolf's Neck. And often he went alone.

It was during these times that he became used to loneliness, grew even to welcome it. Silence, he discovered, was not just a device, valuable as a decoy, for bagging game. It was a sharpening hone for all one's senses, intensifying every stimulus: the white flash of a gull, the moist caress of fog, the *kuk-kuk-kuk-kuk* of a coot, the smell of sun-dried seaweed, the taste of the fried-egg sandwich and doughnut Mother had wrapped. The lonely sorties had another by-product. They taught him self-reliance. Little chance to ask advice as to whether rotten ice was navigable, whether the black ducks were more likely to be flushed on the tidal flats between Flying Point and Sow and Pigs or toward the mouth of the Harraseeket. And when advice was given he did not often follow it.

"Ain't no sense goin' out today," one of the neighbors told him on an October Saturday when the boy had finished work and was dressing the float. "Just wastin' your time."

"Maybe," said Fred pleasantly. "But no harm trying. I thought I might work up to some of those dippers. There's a flock of about two hundred here in the bay."

"No use. Your father tried 'em yest'd'y and couldn't get near 'em. Think you're a better sculler'n he is, do yer?"

"I don't think. I know." It was not a boast, merely a statement of fact. Dad might be able to hunt all around him on land, but stretched in the bottom of a float Fred could out-scull him any day.

The neighbor obviously resented having his advice flouted, especially by a chit of a teenager. "Young upstart!" he muttered as he returned to his task of pitching seaweed on a horse cart to haul home for banking his buildings.

Fred launched his float. Sure enough, there were birds

off in the bay, a good couple of hundred, their small black and white bodies floating, upending, diving. "Dippers" they called them, these buffleheads. Keeping down in the float as far as possible and scarcely ruffling the water with his paddle, he worked along the shore close to the thatch bed.

Well up in the upper end of a cove were nine birds, all "dipping" as fast as they could, too busy to notice his approach. Good! He worked his way slowly along. Now if they would only come together so the whole nine would be within shooting range! But to his disappointment they continued in two groups about sixty yards apart. All right, so there was no use waiting. He stayed tense and watchful, poised for the right moment. Then when both bunches of birds dove at the same time, with a few swift motions he drove the float in between them. Sitting up, he seized his gun and aimed it. When the bunch on the left side broke water, he was ready. He bagged them with one shot. Swiftly he squirmed over on his knees and was ready for the other bunch when it appeared. He got all those with the other barrel. Picking his game from the water, he tossed them under the deck and paddled back to the wharf. The neighbor stuck his pitchfork into the ground and sauntered down to meet him. As Fred tied his float to its stake, he peered into the bottom. No birds were in evidence.

"Hah! Told you so. Next time maybe you won't be so goldanged cocksure—"

His mouth fell open as Fred lifted the nine fat "dippers" one by one and laid them on the wharf. "Well, I'll be—!"

If the boy grew up preferring to make and follow his own decisions rather than rely on the advice of others, it was probably because more often than not he turned out to be right.

Hunting birds was not all recreational. It was almost as

necessary to the family's subsistence as was haying to the cattle's. Money was scarce, deriving largely from eggs and the mountains of butter which Mother churned, worked, and packed into molds. Food, except for staples like sugar, flour, and molasses, came from the land and the sea. The ocean supplied a varied diet all the year around: clams, lobsters, a dozen kinds of fish, ducks, geese—yes, and eels.

The latter were also a commercial asset. In the fall they swam up the creeks and bedded in the mud to sleep all winter. Dad and Fred Litchfield, who owned the other side of the creek, put eelpots into the stream each fall to catch them as they ascended. Nights during a heavy rain they might catch a half ton of eels at a time. Others outwitted their captors. One could see well beaten runways where they had gone ashore and overland to the water above the trap and so saved their lives for future spearers. The captured eels were stored in a cage until a propitious time came in which to skin them out for shipping to market. This was usually done in Mr. Litchfield's blacksmith shop, and the Holbrooks and other neighbors were employed in the process. Old Gus Holbrook was an artist at the job. One of Fred's favorite diversions was watching old Gus expertly peel off a skin, then with a quick slap of his hand send it twirling up in a grand arc to land with a thud in the rafters. By the time two or three tons had been skinned out the loft looked like a bandstand festooned for the Fourth of July.

Like eeling and hunting ducks, many of the projects for providing family provender were more fun than work. Berrying, for instance. The expeditions, often by boat to one of the many islands, were big family picnics, with huge lunches of ham and chicken, biscuits, pies, and other goodies. It was Mother who bore the brunt of labor, transforming the big water pails of raspberries, blueberries, blackberries into the endless jars of preserves, jams, and jellies lining the cellar shelves. And now that Frankie, nine years older than Fred, was married to Frank True and living at Flying Point, Mother had no one to help. To appease his uneasy conscience Fred got up before chore time one morning and made a johnny cake, combining lard, meal, soda, and molasses until it looked reasonably like Mother's batter, plopped it into a pan, and shoved it into the oven. It was a moderate success, and he improved with practice. To his surprise he found cooking as much fun as farm work, and he was soon concocting his favorite biscuits and gingerbread.

In fact, the lines between work and play, poverty and affluence were scarcely discernible. Unlike Harry, who was more studious, Fred liked farming, and with the years there came a few improvements to make work easier. In the nineties horses replaced the lumbering oxen, and some new equipment was purchased. The day Dad's new team of Western horses arrived from Portland, a neighbor came to help him hitch them up and show him how to use them.

"A pity your brand-new disk harrow came knocked down," the neighbor lamented as they started out with the team and a plow. "We could see how that works, too. I never seen one workin', but I've read about 'em in the papers."

Fred overheard and, with his usual self-confidence and brash optimism, took a wrench and set to work on the harrow. When they returned they found it put together, ready to be hitched to the team. Dad was surprised, and the neighbor, less used to ingenious adolescents, was dumbfounded. "Well, I'll be goldarned! How in tarnation did you know how that thing worked? Ever seen one before?"

"No," replied the boy. "I just thought it looked like it ought to go this way."

It did.

Horses were certainly faster and better for drawing a mowing machine, but Fred missed the oxen. For twitching out logs, plowing, hauling seaweed and rockweed from tidal water up onto the land, give him the cattle every time! Carrying the heavy whiffletrees and spreader about, he longed more than once for the days when he simply had to hook a chain. Oxen were contented, too, where there was no work for them, while horses were forever kicking the barn to pieces or becoming ill when not at work. But the horse was a sign of progress, and the boy was all for it.

It was fortunate that he liked farming, for during the months and years following his first year of high school, in 1895, it looked as if he would be a farmer for the rest of his life.

· 3 ·

OF ALL IRONIES, the boy who during most of his fifteen years had jumped in hay, mowed it, tossed it, bunched it, stored it in the barn, fed it to cattle, came down with a severe attack of hay fever.

It was not a mild, brief case of the sniffles. It was a deluge, continuous, unending. Handkerchiefs, even the largest of the male variety, were useless. It took one or two towels to sop up the water that ran out of his eyes and nose every morning. Of course, school that fall was out of the question, and it continued to be the next, and the next. The ailment was not a seasonal affliction. It lasted with more or less severity throughout the year.

And now he gained cursory introduction into the world of medicine. Everybody had some pet remedy to suggest. Obligingly Fred tried them all, from smoking powdered cube berries to inhaling one of Genthner's formaldehyde tubes. No use. Unless nature and time developed their own remedy, he was apparently doomed to uncomfortable sequences of sniffling, mopping, and blurred vision.

But he accepted the fate with resignation. The sacrifice or postponement of his education seemed not too important. He was not like Harry, who rushed through his chores so he could spend the evening poring over books under the kerosene lamp. One could milk cows and cut hay and raise chickens—yes, and hunt ducks!—without a knowledge of Latin and algebra. It was rather a relief not to take the five-mile trek to Freeport and back every day, one of three ways depending on the season: walking, driving the team, or going a mile to Banks' Wharf, then by boat to Porter's Landing, then walking another mile to the school.

There were variations from the daily routine: hauling ice which the Holbrooks had cut by hand on a nearby pond; cutting pine, some of it two or three feet through, and carting it to the mill; helping to build a road over on Bustin's Island; digging clams for bait. The latter was a stand-by job for anyone with stamina and gumption. A bushel of clams would cut out a bucket of bait. By the time he had hoed two bushels, shucked them out, rowed with them seven miles to Chebeague Island, receiving fifty cents a bucket, not in money but in store goods, rowed back, he had learned the full value of a dollar.

The road building was more to his liking. At first he went over to Bustin's with a regular road crew, but later he did the work alone after the summer's tasks were over. The island was one big hummock after another. One cleared away the ferns, bayberry, and other small growth from the right of way, then set fire to it, timing the lighting so it would burn down to a nice hotbed of coals by noon, to toast one's dinner on. One simply dug the tops off the hummocks with a mattock, filling the depression with the turfs, and when it was all level got Henry Merrill's horse and carted ground-up clamshells from the beach to spread on the earth. When a culvert was necessary, he went down to the shore with his crowbar, split off a covering stone from a ledge, upended it over the bank, then found side stones to support it. After thirty-five years he would find some of them still intact, far more durable than the hastily installed metal culverts of later years.

It was 1897, the boy's seventeenth year, and he had been out of high school three years, when a sequence of events changed his life. It started with hauling ice from the pond a mile away without knowing that he was coming down with measles. The constant exposure to cold and wet sent him to bed with lobar pneumonia. For three weeks he was near unconsciousness, with no more nourishment than an occasional sip of milk doctored by a splash of brandy. His short wiry body shrank to a wisp. Dr. Gray, who had followed Dr. Twitchell as the family physician, drove the five miles from Freeport to visit him many times. Once, as he tapped the bony chest, tender from the applications of strong onion poultices, Fred eyed the stethoscope curiously.

"What—do I sound like?" he croaked.

Good-naturedly the doctor plugged the rubber tips into the boy's ears and applied the bowl to his lower ribs. "How about it? Hear anything?"

The boy's eyes widened. Above the constant ringing there was another sound, a steady beat-*beat* which reminded him of drums at a parade. "My heart!" He exclaimed weakly. "But"—he looked perplexed "—it beats double! Why?"

Amused, the doctor explained the rhythmic contraction and relaxation of the heart. The boy listened intently, nodding his head. "Systole," he repeated. "Diastole." In spite of his weakness and discomfort he felt the same excitement as when he had looked into his gashed leg and marveled at the complex structure of bone and veins and muscle. "But—what's all that tapping for?"

Still amused, the doctor applied the bowl higher on the bony chest, first to one side, then to the other. "I was listening to your lungs. This is called 'percussion.'" He renewed the tapping motion. "And when you listen, it's called 'auscultation.' "

The boy repeated the words solemnly, then listened intently. Luckily, it didn't require energy to listen.

"Notice any difference on this side—and on this?"

Fred frowned. "It—it sounds sort of—duller on this side."

Dr. Gray no longer looked amused. "It does, indeed. That's because you have congestion in that lung. Do you know, my boy," he said soberly, "I think you'd make a good doctor."

Days passed, and recovery was slow. When he took his first solid food, the fricassee of an old rooster, on Washington's Birthday, he was so weak that Mother, with tears of both thankfulness and pity, had to feed him. Dr. Gray, making his last visit, shared her relief.

"Good! You had us worried for a while, boy. But we'll have you out sculling for dippers again before you know it. Only don't try sitting on any more ice cakes, remember what I say." Fred remembered, not these words so much as others the doctor had spoken.

You'd make a good doctor . . . you'd make a good doctor . . .

The words became the pulsebeat of that spring and summer, a systole and diastole which ebbed and flowed in ever-recurring sequence. A silly idea, of course he was going to be a farmer! . . . A wonderful, exciting idea, exploring all the marvels of the human body! . . . Impossible without long years of study, and with a nose and eyes that wept buckets, how could he even get through high school? . . . But here he was almost seventeen years old, and all his chums on the way to graduation! Bad enough to have them outstrip him in stature, without remaining a runt in knowledge! . . . Expensive, out of the question. . . . But there was the medical school at Bowdoin, only nine miles away, within walking distance. . . .

The idea germinated, throve, ripened along with the hay, beans, and tomatoes. Harry graduated from high school that spring and took a job on the electric railroad running from Portland to Yarmouth, apparently as uncertain of future plans and ambitions as Fred, except that he was vigorously courting Stella, the Freeport girl whom he had adored for at least a year, and attempting to eliminate an equally zealous rival. Still weak from his bout with pneumonia, Fred was devoid of both energy and purpose. Even the new float which he had bought that spring from Will Holbrook did little to temper his restlessness. It was a beautiful light craft ten-and-a-half-feet long, planked six inches deep, its decks and sides all painted a dull color and daubed with mud for camouflage, and Will had shot twenty-two black ducks and several geese with it that spring. But suddenly the pursuit of ducks, though pleasurable, seemed of less importance.

Then came a day in early September when Dad and Fred and Harry were down in the field digging potatoes. Suddenly Harry straightened. He looked at his father.

"I think," he announced, "that I'll go to the University of Maine."

Fred stared at his brother. When in tarnation had he come up with that idea! Been mulling it all summer, had he, and not once letting on? Of course he'd been keen on chemistry and such things in high school, never on farming. But—college! Then he stared even harder at his father.

"Good." Dad spoke as calmly as if his son had proposed a trip to the barn for more burlap sacks. "You go pack your trunk right off, and I'll take you to the train this afternoon."

Just like that! Harry slapped the dust off his hands, wiped them on his overalls, and set off on the run toward the house. Dad went on digging potatoes and, after standing for some moments open-mouthed and speechless, Fred

joined him. They continued working in silence. Presently
a neighbor sauntered toward them across the field. Where
was Harry, he inquired curiously. Harry, Dad informed
him with unmistakable pride and satisfaction, was going
to the University of Maine. The visitor drew himself up,
snorted, cast a disgusted glance at Dad.

"Ho, ho, friend Charles! Sendin' a two-cent boy to college, are ye?"

Perhaps it was the helpless anger unloosed by this speech
which swept Fred into sudden reckless decision. Two-cent
boys, were they? Or, rather, if Harry was two-cent, what
was he? Harry would show the neighbors and everybody
else. Yes, and he, Fred, would show them. Hay fever or no
hay fever, he would go back to high school this fall. And—
yes—*he would be a doctor!*

When finally he summoned courage to broach the pos-
sibility to his father, the reaction was as unexpected as it
had been to his brother's announcement. "Not a bad idea.
I've always thought you boys should learn a trade. Thought
maybe you'd take up carpentering, you're so handy makin'
floats and such. If you stayed on the farm, you might make
a thousand a year maybe, no more."

"Then—you wouldn't mind? You could get along without me?"

"Why not? Got along before you boys come along. Guess
I can again."

Chemistry, carpentering, doctoring . . . all were trades to
Dad.

Others were even less impressed by the profession.

"What are you going to do?" asked Jim Rodick, who
was helping one year with the annual threshing of oats.

"Be a doctor," replied Fred.

For a moment Jim looked blank. "Oh, well," he said
finally, "a doctor is like the weeds in the garden. A necessary evil."

The adjustment to high school was not too difficult. He might be older, but at least he was no taller than even the youngest of his new classmates! The five-mile walk or drive or part walk, part boat ride, soon became routine again. And he discovered that by keeping out of the barn he could study as much as there was time for, which wasn't much. After three years of lying fallow, his mind was stubborn soil for Latin, Greek, and English. There were chores at home and at school and only one twenty-minute study period. But he learned to pick out the essentials and make synopses of his courses. Then he would go over and over them during his five-mile walk.

Someone suggested that mountain air was good for hay fever. By a happy coincidence Dr. Nathan Hyde stopped him one day in the street and offered to get him a job in a New Hampshire hotel for the summer. As soon as school was over he packed the small trunk discarded by his brother and set off on the Grand Trunk train for Randolph, New Hampshire. His pay of fifty cents per sixteen-hour day and board as extra gardener at Labion Watson's were the least of the summer's profit.

"If you want to stand in well with the family," he was told, "take good care of Grammy Watson's geraniums."

He did, all forty of them. But his distinction as a horticulturist derived from even happier skills. In a prolonged drought he was able to keep the boarders exclaiming over crisp fresh lettuce with plenty left over for the hogs. Returning from a three-week trip to Rangeley with a buckboard full of lodgers, Mr. Watson was amazed by the thick sward of deep emerald lawn. How come, he demanded. He had worried for fear there would not be enough water for the hotel. It had taken no water, Fred assured him, only a monkey wrench to the mower. It was a simple matter to mow the grass tall so the sun wouldn't strike and dry the roots.

But his uncanny flair for detail aroused even more amazement. One day Mr. Watson was ready to start for the Summit House on Mount Washington with his four-horse buckboard filled with sixteen people. With the same bold precipitation which enabled him to drive the same filled buckboard from the Summit House to the foot of the mountain, eight miles, in just thirty-two minutes, a world record, he jumped to the seat and seized the reins.

"Look out there, Freddie," he warned. "Get out of the way of the horses."

Fred shook his head. "You don't want to go that way, Mr. Watson."

"No? I'd like to know why not."

"Well—there's no nut on your off whiffletree, none on the right-hand rear spring, none on the bolt holding the left brake shoe, and half a dozen missing on the body. That's dangerous, sir."

The man's eyes opened wide. "You—you mean you can see all that?"

"Yes, sir."

"Then you've got yourself a new job. You just come in here every morning and look this contraption all over."

But summer in New Hampshire yielded a bonus more valuable than pleasure and experience. The moment Fred arrived the hay fever vanished, never to return.

· 4 ·

IT WAS A transition period in the study of medicine. The procedure by which students received most of their practical training under the tutelage of a "preceptor," though rapidly passing, was still commonly accepted. Dr. Gray became Fred Pritham's preceptor. During his high-school years the youth frequently stayed at the doctor's house in

Freeport, accompanied him on calls, absorbed some of the elements of medicine. He learned to give ether, administering it to a John Cox of Durham the day after the *Maine* was sunk in Havana Harbor. His duties were as much menial as professional. More than once when the roads were drifted, he helped right the overturned sleigh. And at least once his know-how as a seaman proved fully as essential as obstetric skill.

Dr. Gray had gone to Bustin's to see a sick child and, because there was a stormy southeast gale, had remained there for the night. Mrs. Gray roused Fred about one in the morning. A neighbor woman was in labor. Would he go home and get his gunning float and go to the island for the doctor? Unfortunately it was low tide, and he could not launch the float.

"But as soon as it's light," he promised, "I'll go to Porter's Landing and take a yacht belonging to an undertaker friend. He'd be glad for me to use it." He would have to wait for dawn, he explained, to see what boat he was taking. Some people wouldn't relish having their boat taken without permission.

He got under way about five o'clock. The rain had stopped and the wind died, but the yacht was a shambles, ropes snarled in every part of the craft. He managed to get sail on her and with a light wind astern slid slowly down the Harraseeket. Just above South Freeport wharf he met John Kelsey coming in with his *Xanadu,* which had dragged its moorings and kept him up most of the night.

"Watch out," he yelled. "It looks squally."

But the wind continued light, and Fred made good time to Bustin's. In answer to his shouts the doctor emerged from the Alcazar, the cottage where he was staying, was rowed out, and put on board the yacht. Fred placed him at the tiller, telling him to steer toward Chebeague while he overhauled the rigging in order to beat to windward.

While working busily at this, he suddenly felt the deck slant steadily. Doc has her rap full, he thought, and must feel in a hurry. But when the doctor shouted, "What do I do next?" he realized with a shock that he had a greenhorn aboard. At that moment he looked up and saw the squall coming. It carried a crest of white water on top of a green roller six feet high!

"Grab the jib sheet!" he yelled, running aft and seizing the helm. At least Doc knew what a jib sheet was! He held it steady while Fred luffed to tack, trying to get a turn around the deckhouse coaming to hold that jib trimmed to windward, in order to swing the craft onto its other tack. He also tried to swing it with an oar to windward, but the first pull took the oarlock cleat off the deck, and the boat fell away again on its old tack, heading away from the island and toward Portland. And, though the doctor got the sheet and held it secure, the rope was rotten and parted when the wind struck it. But, hanging fast to the jib, the rotten rope quickly wound itself about the other sheet, and the doctor managed to seize the double strands.

Now Fred really had to act fast. Realizing that they must have good headway in order to tack, he held her off, filling the mainsail completely. But this heeled the boat over so her mast was halfway down to the water, and seas came in past the mast and washed over the tiller head. With grim desperation he pushed the tiller down to luff, putting his forearm into the elbow. This time, thank heaven, the sheets held. The wind caught in the jib and swung them about. He managed to nurse the boat back toward the island three miles away.

When he was about a quarter of a mile from it and in calm waters a couple of fishermen came out in a skiff and dropped the peak of the yacht's mainsail, then rowed back and, to Fred's disgust, boasted that they had saved his and the doctor's lives. Senseless, since he was already under the shelter of the island! But Henry Merrill, who had seen the whole action, soon squelched that. Fred anchored in the cove, and the doctor went up to Freeport on the steamboat from Portland.

The wind raged all day. The streets in Freeport were strewn with branches from trees which had stood firm for a hundred years. At noon Fred went to the upper end of the island, picked himself a mess of corn from Dada Swett's patch, roasted it over a small fire, and enjoyed a good dinner. That afternoon Henry Merrill helped him ferry enough rocks for ballast to sink the red paint of the yacht four inches below the surface.

"Now," said Henry, "we'll reef her mainsail, put her jib on, and see."

They saw. The first gust snapped the main boom in the middle. When Henry saw that it was nothing but a knotty stick of dry pine, his comments were blistering. "Hold her there, Fred, and I'll go ashore and get a stick that will fix 'er." Presently he came rowing back with a green spruce six inches thick, which they lashed fast to the stump of the old boom. "There, old girl, you won't bust that!" She didn't. They took a short sail, and the boat behaved like an old fisherman.

Before leaving, Fred enjoyed a rich lobster stew at Henry's. Then he could not resist sauntering down toward the wharf, where the erstwhile life-saving pair were huddled under the shelter of a ledge, watching to see that their anchored yacht did not drag ashore. He was going across to Porter's Landing directly, he told them with airy nonchalance, and would be glad to give them a ride. The muttered refusal and sheepish looks gave him immense satisfaction.

Henry rowed him to the yacht and wished him well. Fred hauled the sheets down tight and headed the yacht out past Little Bustin's, where the flood tide was setting in against the wind and the combers looked as high as a two-story house. Putting on an old slicker and a so'wester that he found, he sat on the windward rail, held her rap full, and watched the water fly. She would ride up over a big roller, then plunge down to stick her bowsprit under the next one, then come up tossing while water poured clear over the masthead and poured off the sail by the barrel. It was dark when he made the mouth of the river, maneuvering warily through the narrows between Pound of Tea and Stockbridge Point. Then, with the tide covering the flats a foot deep, only the hills against the sky to steer by, and the wind blowing forty miles an hour, it required neat tacking to follow the ninety-foot channel. Three times in the mile strip he felt the bowsprit grate on the perches (the brush stuck on the side of the channel to mark it by high water). Arrived at Porter's Landing, he fastened the borrowed craft to its mooring. Next Saturday he would have to come over home and make it a new boom, a good spruce stick this time instead of a knotty hunk of pine.

Driven by an even stronger urgency than the gale at his back, he ran the half mile to Freeport Village. Only when assured that the doctor had arrived in time to properly deliver his patient was he fully satisfied. The episode taught him an axiom which, with certain amendments, would govern the next seventy years of his life: *It's a doctor's business to go where he's called, come hell or high water!*

All of his boat trips were not duty calls. He seized every leisure moment to launch his float, plant his hand-carved decoys, and scull for geese, divers, and dippers. No weather was too inclement, no obstacle too great. For the thrill of dropping a single duck or goose he would gladly counter clogging mists and soupy fogs, freezing dawns, darkness, rotten ice. One day—it was March 13, 1899—the ice was out up to Little Flying Point in Maquoit Bay. He was watching for geese near Pettengill Island when Fred Holbrook came around Flying Point in his twelve-foot float. Soon a flock of geese alighted up near Little Flying Point, and they decided to try for them together. Leaving his float in the cove, Fred got in the bow of Holbrook's. It was a bleak day with a northeast wind. Off the upper end of Bucknam's the float was sticking her nose under every sea, and the water washing in over the headboard was sweeping off the ice they had piled on for dressing, leaving them exposed to view.

"Botheration! Not much use going on," complained Holbrook.

"Oh, you never can tell." Fred was not one to give up. "Birds might be tired and go to sleep on the ice. We might work up near enough to get one or two."

No such luck. The birds were an alert bunch. And by the time they had flown away both young hunters were soaked. They paddled under the shelter of Little Flying Point, dumped the water from the float, made a fire to dry out, and ate lunch.

"When the tide ebbs," predicted Holbrook, "I'll bet the ice will go out clear to Bunganuck Rock. That open hole around the rock will be full of birds."

When it happened as he predicted, they were ready and promptly started up the bay among the loosened ice cakes. Then a float came out from Merepoint about a mile behind them and tried to outscull them.

"The rotten sports!" hissed Fred. All the hunters knew that once a man was well ahead of another, the custom was for the one behind to lie back and not disturb him. Holbrook was a strong sculler, and the pursuer could not gain on them. Then what did he do but sit upright so he could scull harder, and of course he frightened all the birds! Hundreds of ducks and geese flew up and away. However, a small flock of about twenty alighted on an ice cake down toward Cistern Island. All might not yet be lost. Fred and his companion slid past each other in the bottom of the float, and Fred took the paddle, driving down toward the birds. But the other boat was a bit closer, and it looked as if the Merepointers might get a shot. After the dirty trick they had played, Fred wasn't going to let that happen. "O.K?" he muttered through clenched teeth, and Holbrook nodded. Fred fired a load of T-ts straight onto the ice cake, and the birds rose with a great whooshing and honking. The Merepointers were furious. Bearing down on the other float, they threatened to sink it then and there.

"Go ahead," Fred tossed back coolly, "any time you feel like it."

He wasn't worrying. He carried two ten gauges, and Holbrook had a seven-shot ten gauge, a double twelve, and a repeating 38-calibre rifle with a magazine of nine shells, all ready for action. Any such display of poor sportsmanship aroused anger as well as disgust. If the other parties had followed the rules, both floats could have sculled to the geese on the ice cake and gotten a chance for one good shot apiece. They deserved to have their goose cooked— yes, and served to them hot!

He was treated to another exhibition of poor sportsmanship when he graduated from high school in 1900, to his amazement the valedictorian of the class. He neither sought nor desired the honor. One of his classmates did. She even dug back into the records of his first year, discovering to her chagrin that even then his ranks had been a bit higher than hers. It was a severe blow to the villagers that one of the "dumb farm boys" from outside should carry off honors presumably reserved for their superior intellects. His valedictory speech delivered in the Baptist church on June 15 was titled "A Nebular Hypothesis."

He could not go to college that fall. His brother, majoring in chemistry, had another year at Maine, and there was no money for two students. But he made good use of the interim. A natural disaster that winter proved a personal blessing. A terrible blizzard of snow isolated the town of Brunswick, leaving all its inhabitants without hay for their horses. A call went out for help, and Fred began hauling hay from the farm. Before the emergency was over he had hauled fifty-five loads and earned enough money —more than a thousand dollars—to buy all his college equipment and pay for much of his medical course.

It was about this time also that his attention focused on a certain young woman. He must have seen her many times before, for Sarah Ring lived only a couple of miles away on the Brunswick road. He well remembered when the family had bought the farm next to her grandfather's and moved there from Charlestown, Massachusetts, where her father, it was reported, had driven a four-horse team for the United Fruit Company. At age five the image of a dashing equipage piled high with tropical succulence had seemed to Fred splendidly romantic, far more so than Mr. Ring's new job of cutting stone in the quarry, with farming on the side.

Now, after being her neighbor for some fifteen years, Fred actually noticed Sarah Ring for the first time. He wondered why. She must be about seventeen, the right age to have been in his high-school class. Her older brother Charles and sister Laura, a little younger, he knew well. But this slender—much too slender—grave-eyed girl who wore the puffed sleeves and billowing skirts of her newly acquired womanhood with such grace and dignity—where had she been keeping herself? Now, suddenly, he was conscious of her presence everywhere, at Sunday school, at the singing school and literary club they both attended, at the church Christmas party. He soon discovered why they had not met more frequently. Sarah had suffered from anemia since the age of twelve and had been out of school for long periods, acquiring much of her education through the help of understanding teachers. His obvious interest aroused comment in the family, much of it disapproving.

"You can do better than that," the college-wise Harry sniffed. "The girl hasn't even a high school diploma."

"Sickly," Frankie warned. "A doctor needs a strong healthy wife."

"Her father's strong enough," commented Dad. "He can work from seven in the morning to six at night and then dance half the night."

"It's an unlucky family," reminded Mother. "Remember that gravestone in the cemetery, half of it plastered with the names of their children that have died? Diphtheria, scarlet fever, I don't know what all."

Fred listened, polite but unmoved.

· 5 ·

THE MEDICAL SCHOOL OF MAINE, established in 1820 by the first legislature of the state and placed under the control of Bowdoin College, had kept pace with the evolution of medical education. At first its course had lasted only a single term of three months, its early lecturers, like most doctors of their time, men who had merely "studied with a doctor," a procedure which often meant little more than filling their preceptors' saddle bags with their favorite medicines and currying their horses. Even Nathan Smith, founder of the medical schools at both Dartmouth and Bowdoin, and later distinguished professor at Yale, practiced for many years without a diploma. But they were men of no mean scholarship, the three first lecturers, Smith and John Doane Wells and Parker Cleaveland, of whom Longfellow wrote, "For him the teacher's chair became a throne." A less poetic analogy was voiced by Dr. Alfred Mitchell, dean of the college in Fred's time and professor of pathology, who remarked dryly that his own chair was a three-legged stool.

Slowly through the decades, as in other medical schools, progress was made. But only after 1880, when there were still only two courses of sixteen weeks each, the second substantially a repetition of the first, was the training period lengthened, first to three years, then to a graded course of four years of six months each, and the number of instructors increased from ten to twenty-three. By the time Fred registered for the eighty-second annual course beginning on December 26, 1901, requirements for admission had been stiffened from "evidence of a good English education" to a thorough high-school course including Latin, physics, and chemistry.

"Fred John Pritham," the record read. "J. E. Gray, Freeport, sponsor."

He paid his matriculation fee of $5, plus $5 each for his first year's courses: anatomy, histology, chemistry, physiology, personal hygiene. An additional $2.50 paid for materials used in the chemistry laboratory. Another hundred dollars would be due at the end of the first year, for examinations. Board and lodging cost him from three to five dollars a week. Bless the blizzard!

Bowdoin had already graduated a generation of students before the Medical School was founded. Just before Fred started his second year, the institution celebrated its first hundred years of actual service. On the campus he felt immersed in history. As he emerged from Seth Adams Hall, built in 1861 to house the Medical School, there just to the right was old Massachusetts Hall, the first building of the college and for forty-one years the school's "temporary" home. As he walked under the towering elms or the famous Thorndike oak, grown from an acorn planted by one of the college's first students, he felt the awesome presence of ghosts—Hawthorne, whose birth centennial would be celebrated in just three years; Longfellow, whose sonnet to Parker Cleaveland hung on the wall of the stairway in Massachusetts Hall; Harriet Stowe, who had written much of *Uncle Tom's Cabin* in a little room in Appleton, just down the Mall.

The first two years were spent on the Bowdoin campus. There were forty-four men in his class, all but four of them from Maine, many like himself from small towns. The second year the number shrank to twenty-one, which was the average graduating class. Fred found lodgings in a house just across the street from the campus. His roommate, Guthrie, unfortunately flunked all his subjects. The next year Fred moved into the house of a clairvoyant on Main Street, rooming with Daniel Russell of Leeds and Harris Ilsley of Limington. Russell was a plugger. Every night it was the same, plug, plug, plug. Not so, Fred. He had learned how to study in high school. Now, trudging the nine miles home and back each weekend, he used the same technique. There were no cobwebs in his head after a nine-mile walk! His first year he went home every Tuesday or Wednesday as well as on Saturday and baked a fresh batch of biscuits for his father. That year Mother was confined to a hospital with a temporary nervous disorder.

He liked his courses and teachers, even Dr. Henry Gerrish, the dour and strict professor of anatomy, a fascinating study with all its casts and models, fresh and preserved specimens, especially Azoux's complete model of a man given to the school by John Fremont Hill, the governor of Maine and a graduate of 1877. Fred was not in awe of Gerrish. One day he rode down from Brunswick to Portland with him.

"What about this roommate of yours, Russell?" asked Gerrish. "How is he doing?"

"He studies too hard," replied Fred with his usual bluntness. "Stays up every night until two. He can recite everything in the books backward and forward. Me, I'd rather have less on my tongue and more in my head."

A farm boy had an advantage in Gerrish's class, which encouraged the dissection of lower animals before coming to college. Ducks and rabbits and woodchucks had furnished excellent practice material. And the recognition of muscles required in the second year before work on cadavers was permitted had been elementary knowledge with Fred since the age of six.

He did well in his subjects. One of his classmates was Charles Hunt, son of the physiology professor and superintendent of the Maine General Hospital. Charles sat on the opposite side of the aisle from Fred. If a question started on Fred's side of the room, it was likely to go unanswered until it reached him. Similarly, if it started on the other side Charles was almost sure to stop it. Seldom did a question go by either of them.

But he was rather relieved to escape the campus on weekends. The weight of history and tradition could sit heavily on one's shoulders. Besides, certain of the college rules inspired uneasiness if not rebellion.

"All profane language and intemperance, the playing of cards and every form of gambling, and the frequenting of taverns for the purpose of drinking are strictly forbidden. Any medical student who shall violate this or the preceding regulation or shall be concerned with a college student in an irregularity and discord, shall be liable to be expelled."

Not that Fred was tempted to offend. Thanks to Mother, even the prohibition of profanity was inbred. But still more inherent was his yen for freedom. Once on the road to Freeport his step livened, his lungs swelled. Yes, and as the weeks and months passed, his pulses quickened in

greater and greater anticipation. For the act of stopping at
a certain farmhouse about two miles from home became
first occasional, then frequent, finally confirmed habit. The
object of his attention was unmistakable. He could not be
calling on the Ring brothers, for it was not at their house he
stopped. Since the age of twelve Sarah had been living on
the next farm with her grandparents. The interruptions of
his weekly trek, brief at first, became longer and longer,
often extending through supper and into the evening. Obviously Fred Pritham was courting Sarah Ring.

It was not a sudden or spectacular romance. In fact
some, unused to the restraint and realism of the "down-
east" syndrome, would not have called it romance at all.
He took her cruising, sailing, fishing, picnicking, drove or
walked her home from literary club and singing school,
escorted her to church socials. Sometimes they sailed over
to Harpswell to visit her uncle. There was little sentimen-
tality in their relationship, though no lack of sentiment.
The depth of their feeling for each other was seldom expressed in words. In fact, Sadie could not remember afterward that he had ever proposed. But there was no absence
of communication. A pattern of understanding developed
which was to persist for a lifetime.

It was during these years that Fred satisfied another long-
cherished desire. He became a musician. Time and again
when neighbors had gathered at the Holbrooks' for evenings of singing he had envied the Holbrook boys their skill
on the violin. Now, daringly, in 1902 he determined to
join the Freeport Harriseeket Band. He picked the E flat
alto horn because the band needed an alto and because
that instrument was the easiest to blow. He took no lessons.
All he needed was the horn, the will to learn, and a good
lip. He certainly had the latter. When he sat on the doorstep practicing in the evening, people over in Yarmouth
said they could hear him. And if the wind was right the

sound could be heard in Chebeague seven miles away.

Rehearsals were held in a Freeport room lighted by a big hanging lamp with a circular wick six inches in diameter. Mr. Rice, the director, was not satisfied with the sound coming from the alto section. "Blow," he told the man next to Fred one evening. "Blow as hard as you can." There came a feeble little toot. Mr. Rice turned to Fred. "Let's hear *you* blow." The blast blew the lamp out. Fortunately it had gas enough to ignite itself and go on burning. Mr. Rice grimaced and clapped his hands over his ears. Fred was never asked to blow hard again.

He was sufficiently proficient to play with the band that Fourth of July at the dedication of Casco Castle, a huge hotel-tower complex built by the electric railroad company. He played with the band until after he graduated from college. The money he earned helped pay his expenses.

Since 1900 the Maine Medical School had given the last two years of its course in Portland. Its headquarters was a building on Chadwick Street, close to the Maine General Hospital, in which all the teachers were medical or surgical officers. Each week during his third and fourth years Fred went to Portland on the train, rooming first on Congress Street, later in a house next to the hospital. Both school and hospital were easily accessible from any point in the city by electric cars, the Congress Street line (red) giving free transfers to the Spring Street line (blue) which ran just one block from the school. The course, which began the last week in October, continued for eight months.

Now at last he could see some of the long months of grinding study being put to practical use. Subjects for the third year included internal medicine, surgery, materia medica, therapeutics, and obstetrics. Lectures were supplemented by clinics and bedside teaching. Fred's most absorbing interest was surgery, under the tutelage of the brilliant Dr. Stephen Holmes Weeks. He had an opportunity to witness operations at the hospital almost every day. Clinics were held every Saturday from ten to twelve with visiting surgeons. Students were required to apply bandages and dressings and perform operations on the cadavers under the supervision of instructors.

The insistence on strict sanitation was still scarcely ten years old. It had taken fifty years for a stubborn medical profession to accept the proven doctrines of Semmelweiss relating infection to uncleanness. Only in the nineties had the irrefutable evidence of Lister and Pasteur persuaded surgeons to discard bloodcrusted operating gowns, wash their hands, and sterilize their instruments. Now in the Maine General Hospital such ideas were just taking hold. Dr. Weeks was a stickler for sanitation, sometimes to the impatience of his more careless assistants. When he picked up a scalpel one day so dull that it would scarcely scar the skin, he held it up with sharp derision.

"Dr. Weeks," the intern protested, "our disinfecting system is so rigid that it takes the edge right off the knives!" The doctor snorted.

The course in obstetrics ended in frustration. Fred had had little actual experience and had seen no unusual cases. He wished he could afford to buy a course at Harvard to serve on the Out-patient Department of the Boston Lying-In Hospital, as many of his classmates were doing. Then when his classmate Nat Barker was unable to undertake the course when his time arrived, Fred secured the opportunity. He took the ten-day course at the Harrison Avenue branch, then continued for his three weeks of service.

He was incredibly lucky. The branch was very busy at the time, and he had the good fortune to draw all the unusual cases during the period and attended only one normal. For five days and nights he traveled continually

from one patient to another making the first visits, while
the men higher up in the course who followed him in
after visits enjoyed none of the thrilling experiences, only
the humdrum routines. It was the rule that, on encountering an unusual case, the student must call in to headquarters; then an intern would come out with his big
satchel to do the more difficult job. Fred had to ask for him
daily since most of his cases were abnormal. One night he
called the intern about one o'clock.

"I had to hire a cab," said the disgruntled intern on arrival. "That's altogether too much extra expense."

"O.K. If you're not satisfied with the deal when we're
through," Fred threw back promptly, "say so, and I'll
gladly refund your fare."

After it was over the intern was full of apologies. He
would gladly pay double the fare to see another such case.
When Fred came to write it up, he found it was so rare as
to be one in about ten thousand.

A day or two later, a Sunday, he called the intern again
to attend another *placenta previa* that was bleeding freely.
The intern was in church and did not want to leave.
"Watch it and call me again," he suggested.

Fred refused. His place was with the sick woman, not
running around telephoning. O.K. Then what did he plan
to do? Well, if the case didn't progress to suit him, he
would boil forceps and apply them. The intern was horrified. It was against the rules for a student to carry forceps,
much less use them.

"You mean you've been carrying them?" he demanded.

Not only forceps, Fred returned coolly, but all the other
tools the intern had. There was a brief silence, followed
by hems and haws. Very well, the intern told him finally.
If he thought it necessary, go ahead and use them. Fred
turned from the telephone in satisfaction. Silly business,
anyway, applying all the Harvard rules to a Maine medic

here for only three weeks! Some of the other rules were still more absurd, like the one forbidding the taking of food in a patient's house. He would have missed some fine meals of dark bread, sweet butter, and schnapps by adhering strictly to regulations. Many of the houses had no fuel or cooking utensil in sight, not even a washbasin, making it strenuous work mixing two or three basins of bichloride of mercury solution as the rules called for, as well as boiling instruments. Naturally there was no food there. But some houses were luxurious with plush furniture, drapes, and plenty of good food. After standing on one's feet continuously for seventy-five to a hundred hours, it would have been stupid not to eat good clean food when it was offered. One of his families even invited him to a dinner and christening, and he accepted.

Even on his sixth day, the first one off duty, rest was interrupted. He was shaving when a call came to go to a house on C Street. He could see a car going to South Boston from the depot on Atlantic Avenue. Leaving his upper lip still unshaved, he grabbed his satchel and ran. The conductor was standing on the rear of the car with his hand on the rope. Fred caught his eye just in time and swung aboard. In the house in C Street he found two Irish women, one in a bed, the other sitting in a chair. As he entered, the recumbent woman, a formidable creature weighing some two hundred pounds, erupted in language which made Dad's Grand Banks vocabulary sound like baby talk. The infant had already arrived. Its whole body was black as ink. Fred seized it by its legs, swung it in the air. About a quart of amniotic fluid burst out of its mouth. He left a normal-looking baby and a mother spouting blessings instead of curses. Back in his room he picked up his razor again, then, stroking his bristling upper lip with sudden favorable interest, laid it down. A mustache seemed decreed by fate. Hadn't it saved a baby's life?

He took his duties so seriously that some of the other students, more inclined to mischief, decided to play a joke on him. When it came his turn to go out on a call, he found a notice tacked on the bulletin board: "Dr. Pritham. Go to attend Lillian Russell at the Hotel Touraine." He went.

The three weeks were more valuable than a year in the classroom. His certificate, issued on November 26, 1904, certified that "Frederick John Pritham took a graduate course in this School in Clinical Obstetrics given by Dr. Howard T. Swain, October 12–22, 1904; that he served as an Externe House Officer of the Boston Lying-In Hospital for three weeks, doing good work, and that he attended and made very good reports of ten complete cases. Charles M. Green, Sec. of the Faculty of Medicine, Medical School of Harvard University." One of these cases served as substance for his thesis the following year, entitled "Labor Abnormalus, Fredericus Johannine Pritham." Only by the sheerest luck could he have gained such intimate knowledge of a case involving so many unusual features: partial *placenta previa,* anticipation hemorrhage, multiple pregnancy, premature labor, and the delivery in one case with unruptured bag and in the other with prolapsed hand. In the ten neatly hand-written pages preserved for posterity in the Bowdoin library there was evidence not only of professional competence but of unexpected poetic sentiment.

"The exact lesion of the foetal heart would not be verified by an autopsy," ran the final paragraph. "It may have been a patent *foramen ovale* or a previous ductero arteriosis. Its blood was not passing through its lungs as in the adult, so it was not oxidized, and the little one faded away like some tender flower whose blossoming too early is blighted by the ruthless frost."

He himself seemed to lead a charmed life that year. That summer of 1904 he again narrowly escaped death. He was haying alone with his father, driving the mowing machine with a six-foot cutter bar. Foolishly he crossed a ditch, and trying to keep the swath straight, went diagonally. To keep the cutter bar up he leaned far down on the lever and was thrown from his seat. Grimly he tried to hold on without striking the front of the cutter bar. He just managed to get behind the bar before falling head first into the ditch. The horses started feeding, letting the machine roll back, one of the wheels rolling straight over his face. The cogs smashed into his cheeks, loosening some of his teeth and knocking one completely out. What to do? There he was with the machine across his mouth, Dad down over the ridge out of sight, and would be for at least an hour. As the horses lurched ahead for more grass, the cutter bar had wedged solidly into the bank, holding the machine fast. Just one thing to do: lift the wheel high enough to drag his head from under it. He was strong, yes, all tough wiry five and a half feet of him, but—that strong? Enough to lift not only a big mowing machine but to spring the huge steel cutter bar—and from a lying-down position? He got both hands under the spokes of the wheel and lifted. His muscles bulged almost to bursting. Atlas with his world could not have strained harder. But at last he raised the thing about an inch and slipped his face from under. He rescued the missing tooth and pushed it back in. He wiped the blood from his face. He got back on the machine and kept on mowing until it was time to haul in another load of hay. He arrived home with the hayrack, bloody and battered but without permanent damage. Even the lost tooth grew back in, and the loosened ones tightened. Sixty-five years later he would still be chewing on them.

. 6 .

THE FOURTH YEAR, also at Portland, continued the studies of the third, with the addition of medical jurisprudence, public hygiene, and courses covering a number of diseases: of women and children, of the mind, the skin, the genitourinary system, the eye, ear, nose, throat, joints. As the year drew to a close Fred shared the dilemma of choice with his seventeen fellow graduates. What now? Where dispense this vast knowledge for the benefit of mankind? Some of the men had influential friends to secure them internships in hospitals. Not so Fred. Freeport? No, it had plenty of doctors. Some other town nearby, perhaps? But there was that strange bit of advice given by one of his professors.

"If I were you, Pritham, I would get away from the city and go just as far into the wilderness as possible."

He did not resent the inference that he still looked and acted like the farm boy he was. And he would probably have been gratified had he realized that the advice bore another implication: that already he bore the marks of a nonconformist.

With his classmates Fred attended that spring the meeting of the Maine Medical Association in Portland. A detail man at one of the commercial exhibits asked him his plans and, on finding that he had none, advised him to go to the main hall and ask for a Dr. Hunt of Greenville, who was looking for an assistant.

Greenville! Instantly Fred's interest quickened. The name aroused a rushing succession of pictures: a huge lake, mountains, lusty red-jacketed lumbermen, boats, forests, and—yes, deer and ducks! He hastened to the main hall. Dr. Hiram Hunt was not hard to find. He had been president of the Maine Medical Association the previous year. A stout dark man in his mid-forties with huge hands, black eyebrows, and snapping eyes, he towered over the short slight youth like Goliath over David. Uncowed, Fred introduced himself and stated his business.

"Pritham, eh? And you think you'd like to come to Greenville?"

"I'm interested, sir."

"It's a tough country, boy, and you're—" The keen eyes, scoring the short slight figure, were more eloquent than the lips—"pretty much of a greenhorn. Think you could take it?"

"I think so, sir."

"All right. Give me the names of some doctors who know you, and come talk to me again tomorrow."

Fred mentioned Dr. Gray and Dr. Gerrish. He was probably the only one in the class who would have dared to use the stern professor as a reference. The interview the next day was satisfactory. Fred agreed to go to Greenville but asked that his arrival be delayed until the first of August. He wanted to take the state board exams and help his father with the haying.

That May he had a severe attack of appendicitis. Dr. Weeks, his professor of surgery, recommended an operation, but Fred argued him out of it. It would have meant losing his diploma for that year, necessitating another full year's course. After a few days in bed in his room, he returned to classes, took his examinations on schedule, and graduated with the class.

It was a wet summer, and there were tons of hay to cut. Night after night they would take the hay into the barn wet, take it out, hopefully, to dry in the morning. By the twentieth of July there were still twenty-five acres to cut, and he was glad when Dr. Hunt asked him to postpone his coming to Greenville until the first of September. On

one of the most inauspicious-looking evenings he had a
hunch.

"Dad, I'm going to put the horses on and mow tonight."

His father eyed the heavy fog and shook his head. "It
don't look too good."

"Don't worry. At nine o'clock tomorrow you'll be glad."

Fred started mowing, the horses barely visible in the
pale orb of fog and lantern light. Toward midnight his
father came out to look. "Got down quite a pile of it, ain't
you!" Fred mowed until one in the morning. He was up
again at four. A little after eight, sure enough, he saw the
fog lifting. The hay he had cut dried well and was all in
the barn the next day.

He was working in the field in August when a message
came from Dr. Gray asking him to assist in an operation.
Walking hurriedly to the specified house about a mile
away he found the patient, an aged fisherman with a
gangrenous foot, already stretched on the dining table,
with Dr. Hyde and Dr. Gray all ready to amputate near
the knee joint. He scrubbed in the kitchen, its walls lined
with sober—or was it hopeful?—relatives. They had barely
started the operation when the patient stopped breathing.
Dr. Gray immediately attempted resuscitation while Dr.
Hyde administered a hypodermic prepared for just such
an emergency. It had no effect.

"He needs a stimulant," muttered Hyde, "and quick."
He spied a bottle of 4-Star Hennessey on a shelf. "What
say? Would that help?"

"Yes," assured Fred. "We used it on a mother at the
Boston Lying-In."

Hyde opened the bottle and tried to suck his syringe
full. But it was his first all-glass syringe, and haste made
him clumsy. The plunger pulled free, and both barrel and
needle sank to the bottom. He stood helplessly, long bony
arms spread wide like a caricature of Father Time.

"Reach into my pocket and get my metal syringe," snapped Gray. Hyde did so, then rushed to the kitchen for hot water to dissolve a tablet. Through the open door Fred caught a glimpse of faces. Anxious? No, definitely hopeful. They're dividing up the old man's property already, he thought grimly.

"Finish operating," ordered Gray, thrusting an instrument into his hand, "while I try to get him breathing."

Fred's hand closed about the tool. Only for an instant did he hesitate. While Hyde plunged the hypodermic and Gray kept swinging the patient's arms to revive him, the young doctor performed his first major operation. So intent was he on the job that he scarcely heard the triumphant "Good! He's breathing!" When the leg was bandaged he took the pan of instruments to the kitchen to wash them. "It's over," he told the anxious inquiring faces.

There was obvious rejoicing. He must have mistaken their emotions. "Well," someone observed, "so poor Uncle George has gone at last."

"Not at all," Fred retorted cheerfully. "He's all right. Probably live another ten years." He took a wicked pleasure in their visibly falling faces.

Not even the passing of his state board exams at Augusta had given him quite this sense of fulfillment. At last he was a full-fledged doctor. The episode was a fitting finale in the dress rehearsal for the long-life drama ahead.

CHAPTER TWO

On with the Play!

. 1 .

Wнем Doc Pritham arrived on the stage, the human drama was well into its second act.

First came the Red Paint people of the Stone Age, leaving no more distinctive mark than the red ochre mingled with the bones of their dead. Then after a million or so sunsets came the Dawn People, the Abenaki, disturbing the ancient pattern almost as little as did their gliding canoes, giving names, like Adam, to the creatures of their primeval Eden. The big lake shaped like a moose's head they called *Mspame,* large water, the highest mountain to the east *Kta-Adin,* a great grand lofty mountain. Other lakes and streams became *Chesuncook,* place where many streams enter in; *Caucomgomoc,* gull lake; *Pen-*

47

obscot, rocky river; *Piscataquis,* branch of a river; *Umbazooksus,* meadow stream; *Ripogenus,* river; *Allagash,* hemlock bark.

It was one of the braves, a legend goes, who gave his name to the stark headland crouching at Mspame's narrowest part. Here came all the tribes of the east, braving white angry torrents and wind-tossed lakes, because the great mass of igneous rock, rising eight hundred feet straight up from the water, was unique in all the country, providing the best flint for arrowheads, spearheads, scrapers, and grist stones. Here also came Chief Kinneho with his tribe. On the mountain he posted a guard, who signaled that canoes were coming from the north. Enemies? Swiftly the chief climbed the sheer cliff edge. Yes, they were enemies, the dreaded Mohawks. Descending to the camp, he ordered the women and children, "Go south!" The squaws took canoes and fled, hugging the western shore. They went up a stream and into a pond and camped, then climbed the high mountain with twin crests and kindled a fire to let the chief know they were safe. Kinneho with his small band of braves went to war and routed the Mohawks, then lighted a signal fire on the headland, that the women and children might know and return. The stark headland became Mount Kineo. The twin-crested height became Squaw Mountain, the bay through which the canoes glided Squaw Bay, the stream Squaw Brook, the pond Squaw Pond. Ages passed, and the first act merged into the second.

Came the white men. But not with soundless moccasins and softly gliding canoes. With cleaving axes and lumbering oxen and belching engines. With shining blades which sent chips flying big as platters and the giant pines crashing with a swish and a roar, to be dragged and floated down to Bath and Portland for shipmasts. With yells of "Timber!" and "Let the blasted daylight in!" Later, after the great

white pines were gone, with crosscuts and bucksaws, cant
dogs and peavies, ripping swaths through the forests,
choking the rivers, feeding endless fodder into the sawmills
which were the spawners of civilization.

They were a unique breed, those early Maine lumberers.
"Bangor tigers," they liked to call themselves, and the
name followed their migrations from the Penobscot to the
Mississippi, on to the Snake and the Columbia, leaving at
least ten other "Bangors" in their wake. Red-shirted, red-
blooded, two-fisted, they ripped through the forests with
the same lusty bravado as they roistered through the
saloons in Bangor's Haymarket Square, flirting with death
as boldly as with the bawdy wenches in Fan Jones's celebrated house on Harlow Street, its huge sky-blue chimney,
repainted twice each year, a landmark for women-hungry
loggers and sailors.

For years Bangor had been the lumber capital of the
world. "A star on the edge of night," Thoreau had seen it
in 1846, "still hewing at the forest of which it is built."
At its zenith, back around 1870, the city had shipped 250
million board feet of long lumber a year. Three thousand
ships had cast anchor in the river, so tight-packed that a
man could walk across their decks from Bangor to Brewer.
But now, with the gradual supersedence of pulpwood over
long lumber, the glory of the "Queen City" was waning.
Fred was not sorry he had to bypass it, changing from the
Maine Central to the Bangor and Aroostook at Newport.
He was far more interested in what Thoreau had called
"the howling wilderness that feeds it."

Yes, the human drama was well into its second act when
Doc Pritham arrived in Greenville on August 31, 1905.
But for him and thousands of others the play was just be-
ginning.

He rode the mile from the Junction to the Village on
Woodie Bartley's stage, getting almost as thorough an in-

troduction to the town as to his small and friendly driver.
Dust rose from the horse's hoofs and the hack's clattering
wheels, and through it and the gathering dusk the landmarks Woodie pointed out with his whip were almost in-
distinguishable. Information poured as through a sluice
gate.

"Moosehead Inn, John Gibson runs that, he's cuttin'
spruce right now from Little Squaw Mountain Township . . . Crafts' house on right, Rebecca she's got money
. . . Henry Carleton's there, he's the barber, wife runs hat
'n' sewin' store, next is Walter Gerrish's, he's the best carpenter around, built half the houses here at the Junction,
clinched every nail he drove on the other side, so it'd stay
built . . . Methodist church on left, Charlie Capen's opposite . . ."

The steady flow ebbed as they left the thickly settled
Junction, became intermittent spurts. "School on right,
fifth grade up on first floor, high school upstairs . . . Center
Cove there, lake juts into town at three places, West Cove
where your train come in, this one here, and East Cove at
the Village . . . Doc Hunt's office ahind that cedar hedge,
he's been here a long time, since the eighties, got here before the railroad, come by stage from Blanchard . . . Now
we're gettin' to the Village."

Again the sluice gates opened. "Tinknockers, Frank
Sawyer workshops, Shaw Block there on the left. Been
Shaws in Greenville since the 1840s, when Milton started
buyin' up forest at twenty-five cents an acre. Worth three
to five dollars now, sons big lumbermen and millionaires
. . . Bernards', Carletons', Morrisses', Harris the druggist,
Brown's Store . . . That there's Harry Sanders' store, buy
'most anything there from a lollypop to a huntin' outfit. I
hear tell in the old days they used to package tobacky
under two names, Johnny Horner and Lazy Tom. When
the lumberjacks got tired o' one, they'd pull out t'other.

Got away with it for years. Then one day a driver sitt'n' on the deacon seat took out his can of Lazy Tom and took a whiff. 'Y'know,' he says, 'I got a notion you're an own brother to our friend Johnny Horner!' "

Fred chuckled. Already he was beginning to feel at home. Woodie took him to Clark Allen's, the boarding place he had recommended. Fred liked it, comfortable but not luxurious, and settled immediately for a room. Later that evening he walked back up the road to Dr. Hunt's. He had forgotten how big and impressive the doctor was. They would make oddly matched partners, the one tall, paunchy, huge-handed, jolly but a bit intimidating in his black-browed dignity; the other short, thin as a reed, tight-muscled and slender-fingered, his five feet six and hundred and twenty-five pounds a meager and unimpressive complement. Like a mountain and a hill, or a big voice and a little echo. Big Squaw and Little Squaw, Fred would dub them when he became used to the country's topography. But Little Squaw was no mean mountain in itself. And Fred Pritham was in no danger of being anybody's echo.

Dr. Hunt did not approve of his boarding house and said so. Surely he could find some more—er—respectable place. More suited to the dignity of the profession, his manner implied. Fred said nothing, merely listened while his new superior definitively detailed his duties.

He liked his boarding place and had no intention of changing it. He liked Clark Allen, who was an expert teamster, at present driving many spans of horses hauling equipment for an electric-light plant being built at Wilson Stream. He liked Lilla Allen, Clark's wife, and Mrs. Buckingham, the cook, and Mrs. Allen's father, old Uncle Tom, who was usually sitting in the corner by the stove. He liked the dozen or so other boarders, some lumberers, other mill and farm laborers working for the Shaw company. They were a jolly lot, full of badgering and practical jokes. Young Lancaster, who clerked for Davis and Marston, often came in late at night from their camps at Brassua and Machamp, to find hundreds of feet of cordage and two or three teamsters' bells strung about his bed, and his efforts to dig his way in would waken the whole household. Fred enjoyed the pranks.

And he liked Greenville. Used to the flat country around Freeport, he found the mountains exhilarating, the clear air zestful, and, with a fifty-mile-long lake at his doorstep, he scarcely missed his beloved bay. It was a frontier town, to be sure, at the end of a rough dirt road unpassable in winter, what the loggers called "two hundred miles from nowhere," yet amazingly cosmopolitan. The daily trains on the Canadian Pacific and the Bangor and Aroostook brought not only lumbermen but vacationers and sports of all kinds, to be met at the West Cove by the luxurious, flag-bedecked steamers of the Coburn Company—the *Moosehead,* the *Reindeer,* the *Marguerite, the Louisa,* the *Rebecca* (purchased in 1903 from Rebecca Crafts), or— most luxurious of all—the *Katahdin,* queen of the fleet, captained by Charles Robinson, resplendent in his blue uniform with brass buttons. Tons of freight went up the lake daily, plus scowloads of supplies for the lumber camps. The hotels at the Junction—the Mount View House, the Moosehead Inn, the "Push and Pull"—were usually overrun with guests, and half the homes took boarders. The town had grown lustily since 1824, when Nathaniel Haskell and Oliver Young had built the first house over on East Ridge above Wilson Pond; since 1844, when the Village had consisted of one hotel, one store, two dwelling houses, two blacksmiths' shops, and a school. Frontier town, yes, but neither rough nor ramshackle. Its houses were square, austere, and solid, some of them, like the Crafts' and the Shaws' and the Sanders', imposing mansions, as sturdily built for eternity as their three mausoleums in the cemetery.

Fred liked everything about his job—except the job itself. He was supposed to arrive at the office at eight in the morning and stay until eight at night, attending any patients who called, many of them injured woodsmen who came into the hotels with cuts, boils, or other ailments. "Cussed monotonous," he appraised it. He broke the tedium by getting up early, as usual, eating a light breakfast, then walking three or four miles exploring the country. At night he would run to the top of the hill on East Road to get his breath and stretch his muscles.

September was a beautiful month. A good rain came soon after his arrival, somewhat relieving the fire danger. The fear of fire, he discovered, was harrowing in this area which depended so largely on the forest for its livelihood. In the devastating fires of 1903 more than 267,000 acres of Maine woodland had been burned. This very year, 1905, the first fire lookout station in the state had been established on Squaw Mountain by the Shaw Lumber Company. William Hilton, its lookout man, kept a complete report of his observations from June 10 to September 12. There had been no trail up the three-thousand-foot mountain. What a chore to get the telephone and shelter equipment up the slope! Whenever his morning and evening jaunts took him up the surrounding hills, Fred was conscious of Big Squaw dominating the stage. A man living in its dominion could hardly remain unchanged. He might be dwarfed into increasing littleness, or then again even a small man might grow to giant size.

As October approached the air frosted and livened. Everybody began talking of "open season." Guides put away fishing equipment and cleaned rifles. Red hunting jackets vied with red lumberers' mackinaws on the passengers unloaded from trains to boats at the Junction. Of course Fred caught the fever.

"Take my 32–40 and go look for a deer early tomorrow morning," suggested one of the boarders on the last day of September. "Rumor's got it that out at the old Gerrish place deer come into the orchard every night."

The whole household was eager to assist. He couldn't miss the "old Gerrish place." It was at the end of the road. If he got up at four, he would have four hours for the trip. Rose Churchill, who doubled as waitress and nurse, offered to call him when she heard Mr. Allen get up to start the fire. Suspecting no chicanery, Fred fell asleep, to be roused in what seemed an incredibly short time. Getting up at two or three so many times to go down the bay had conditioned him to a good idea of how long he had slept. Too drowsy to think clearly, he pulled on his clothes, took Lonz's rifle, and went outdoors. A glance at the moon jolted him awake. It sure hadn't moved far! It must be about ten o'clock. He could almost see the jokers lying in wait for his return with a pail of water at the head of the stairs.

O.K., he would fool them. Setting off at a good pace, he soon arrived at the Gerrish place, crawled into the barn, and dug himself a hole in the haymow. Waking at dawn, he set out to find the orchard, succeeding so clumsily that he frightened away the deer feeding in it. If he had only waited until it was light! With ducks he would have known better. Oh, well—he would learn. After trying to track them through the woods until he dared not delay longer, he hurried back to town, to be met with excitement and tears. The guilty jokers, deeply repentant, had believed him lost in the woods and were about to send out a searching party. He took pleasure in retaliating a few nights later by slipping into Rose's room and pouring an ounce of new sharp Epsom Salts down her side of the bed. The jar of the house when her heels struck the floor was sweet music.

"If a man could just have a week this time o' year," Dad had said on that day long ago, "to get way up around Moosehead Lake and hunt deer!"

In mid-October his wish was granted. Fred obtained a week's leave from the office. His father came to Greenville. They hired a guide, one of the men boarding at Allens', bought supplies, took the steamboat for Lily Bay, debarking at Beaver Creek, where they transferred into the guide's canoe and headed for Harrington's Camp on the southwest side of Prong Pond. Just as they turned into the pond, there behind a ledge on a little beach they saw three beautiful deer drinking. The guide pushed the canoe up to the ledge, and all grabbed their rifles. Not one shot hit its mark! Fred and his father had alibis. Charles Pritham was using Dr. Hunt's gun, the front sight of which slid back and forth across the barrel with every motion. Fred was using one Dad had brought from Freeport, with its sights set for a mile to shoot seals in Casco Bay. He could see the bullets cutting off branches in the trees over the deer, though he was pointing into the water beneath. The guide had no excuse except buck fever. But he had a good eye and kept them supplied with partridge all that week. Though they could hear deer all about, they caught not so much as a glimpse of a white tail. The woods were dry and noisy, but when threatened rain presaged better hunting, Dad insisted on a return to civilization. Ironic— to have faced storms off the Grand Banks without flinching, then retreat in panic from a little rain in the Maine woods! Ironic, too, and a bit pathetic—that in all the times he was to fulfill his dream of hunting near Moosehead, he would never once get his deer!

Return to the confining office brought on another virulent attack of appendicitis, accompanied by severe chills. Fred said nothing and kept on working, taking no food and treating himself three times a day with an enema of salt solution. Once the doctor discovered him lying on the office couch and reprimanded him. Fred only buttoned his lips tighter. At the end of three days of pain and hunger his temper as well as his reedy body was wearing thin. When on the fourth morning Dr. Hunt scolded him because he had not gone out to visit one of his patients a half-mile distant, the hot core of anger and self-pity exploded. True, he had volunteered to help with the case, but the patient had refused his aid, insisting on the attention of Dr. Hunt. Instead of bothering with explanations, Fred let loose all his pent-up emotion.

"Ha! That's the first time any man ever told me he wasn't satisfied with my day's work! And, by jinks, it won't happen again in a hurry!"

Seizing his satchel, he emptied one container after another of the tablets they held and turned them back into the office bottles. Dr. Hunt watched him, black brows beetling and eyes snapping sparks. But when he spoke he sounded almost amused.

"Well, you young whippersnapper, and where do you think you're going? To Jackman, maybe? I hear there's a good opening there for a bright young doctor. Not a lazy one, however. If you go there, you'll either root hog or die!"

Fred continued to pour pills into bottles. "First thing I'm going to do," he spat, "is get this appendix out before it kills me."

Dr. Hunt snorted. "Who told you you had appendicitis?"

"Dr. S. H. Weeks of Portland," Fred shot back. There! He guessed that would tell him. They both knew that Dr. Weeks was the best man in the state.

Now that Dr. Hunt understood the situation the rift might have been bridged, for the big doctor was both fair and sympathetic. But once he had set his hand to the plow, Fred was not one to look back. Nor was he cut out to be any man's assistant. Perhaps both knew that the dissolution of partnership was inevitable. They parted in anger mollified by a bit of sheepishness, Dr. Hunt because of his misjudgment, Fred because of the stubbornness which had made him suffer in silence.

. 2 .

FRED RETURNED to his boarding house, to quiet and a warm bed. Improvement was rapid. The next day he and the jolly young nurse, Rose Churchill, were treating a cook whom Lancaster had brought down from his lumber camp on Brassua Lake.

"For heaven's sake cure him," pleaded Lancaster. "The cook's the most important member of the crew, not excepting the boss. And this man's a good one."

Fred could find nothing wrong with the man, who insisted he was sick and refused to eat. "He's homesick," he diagnosed privately to Lancaster, who nodded wisely and dispatched a letter. Fred sent for a bottle of bitter tonic at the drug store and ordered the nurse to bring the patient tempting trays of food. Each time he refused the viands a dose of bitters was faithfully administered. The third day he yielded and with tears running down his face cleaned up the tray. That night his wife arrived, with news that she had brought warm clothes and was prepared to stay all winter. Now he wept tears of joy. Recovery was complete.

Fred felt so much better that he made a sudden decision. He would not return home in complete defeat. He

would try to get a deer to take back with him. The next
day he departed with Lancaster, the cook, and his wife.
Obligingly the train dropped them at the woods' road
close to the camp rather than at the section house a half
mile farther on. Fred's reception was almost as flatteringly
hearty as the cook's, for on one of the bunks a man lay
groaning, on his hand a flaming sore fast developing into
a carbuncle. At Fred's direction Lancaster called Charles
Davis at Greenville, who fetched his satchel from Allens'
and gave it to the trainman of the first freight west, who
passed it off to Lancaster as the train went by. It was in
Fred's hands inside of an hour, fast travel for twenty-five
miles in the wilderness! While Fred cut into the flesh and
removed the ugly mass of inflamed tissue, the lumberman
sat on the "deacon seat" as stoically motionless as the split
half of log under his solid buttocks. But his lips were not
motionless. He eloquently summoned the aid of the loggers' entire roster of saints, from "jeazly damned sufferin'
Moses" to "holy old mackinaw (blank)!" Inured to Grand
Banks expletives of equal if dissimilar pungency, Fred did
not bat an eye.

It was his first experience in a lumber camp. He marveled
at its simplicity, its crude efficiency, its complex organiza-
tion, which could spring full grown, almost overnight, in
the middle of stark wilderness. Lumbering itself had
changed mightily in the last fifty years—white pine to long
timber and now more and more to pulpwood, axe to bucksaw, cant dog to peavey, lone "timber barons" to big corpo-
rations—but the structure of the camp remained almost
the same. Buildings were of round logs one on top of
another and locked at the corners, one long tar-papered
roof covering the cook's portion, kitchen and dining room,
another the men's bunkhouse, the two connected by a passage called the "dingle." The hovels for the horses, the
shack for the saw filer with its numbered pegs under a roof

projection where each man hung his notched saw each
night for sharpening, the boss's and scaler's bunkhouses—
all were of the same round logs. The bunks, two tiers high,
were built along each side of the bunkhouse, floored with
small round poles and filled with straw. Along the lower
tier ran the deacon seat, the split half of a log, flat side up,
surface planed with a broadaxe and smooth as glass. In the
center was a big stove which even on these October evenings held a roaring fire.

Crawling into his bunk between two "spreads"—each
made of two woolen blankets with a thick layer of cotton
batting between—Fred spent the nights in cosy comfort.
In fact, he fitted into the woodsman's life as neatly as the
moss chinked into the cracks at the bunk's head. He felt
far more at home in red flannel shirt and mackinaw, wool
socks and moccasins or high boots, than in the conventional suit Dr. Hunt had considered appropriate for his
professional status. He enjoyed the meals eaten in unbroken silence at the long oilcloth-covered table of rived
pine. The food, thanks to the cook's renewed euphoria,
was adequate if one liked salt pork, salt cod, beans, pea
soup, johnnycake, molasses, and tea "strong enough to
float an ox." Fred did, all but the tea. Fortunately his
erstwhile patient was not in the category of the cook immortalized in the old woods ballad:

> *"And there on a morning about all you could see*
> *Was a dirty old cook and a lousy cookee."*

Perhaps it was Joe Joulay, known as "Joe Bully," who had
inspired the words, noted for being the dirtiest cook in
the woods; or the Penobscot cook who had stirred his beans
with a cant dog; or possibly the one who had kneaded
bread with his mittens on to keep his hands warm. Whatever their faults, the old cooks who had kept a tub of sour

dough behind their stoves could still bake biscuits that were snow white and four inches high!

Fred heard other legendary names as he sat quietly among the loggers crouched on the deacon's seat or sprawled on their bunks after supper: Sebattis Mitchell, "Big Sebat," who had first run the falls at Sowadnehunk, a "beeg t'ing!," piloting his bateau through the angry current among great rocks, shooting the perpendicular falls into the maelstrom of boiling foam and thrashing logs, whipping "Right!" "Left!" "In!" "Out!" to avoid the logs and great rocks and bringing it safely to shore; Larry O'Connor, who had died on the treacherous gorge of Ripogenus.

"Smartest man ever was on West Branch Drive." The tale was punctuated by sizzling volleys of tobacco juice shot unerringly at the hot stove fourteen feet away. "Exchange Street Irishman from Bangor. Always wore somethin' red on 'is bullet head, cap, kerchief, end of an old comforter. Wicked, swearin' old cuss. Had a log jam in that canyon where waters come thunderin', smashin', fall over seventy foot to the mile. Not a big jam, only hundred-fifty-, two-hundred-feet pine, but bad, big key log, devil of a jam. Out steps Larry, calked shoes, blue shirt, red handkerchief around head, cocky. Runs out on logs, skippin' an' swearin'. Put 'is scarf on *upper* side of log, couldn't hear it splittin'! Logs jumped 'n' thrashed. Men tumbled. Larry was quicker'n three cats, but not quick enough. Said he'd break the jam if he went to hell, and he did. Nothin' left of 'im, nothin' at all, but nex' spring they found a huming skull with one front tooth missin'. Stuck it in a tree fork. Now when you see somethin' red in woods, it's Larry's ghost walkin'. But if you see it, by Judas, run! Man who sees a ghost don't live the year out."

Holman Day, the lumbermen's poet laureate, had writ-

ten a poem about Larry, someone recalled, and quoted a
few lines.

> *"You could hear him when he started from the*
>   *Ripogenus Chutes,*
> *You could hear the cronching-cranching of his*
>   *swashing, spike-sole boots,*
> *You could even hear the colors in the flannel*
>   *shirt he wore,*
> *And the forest fairly shivered at the way*
>   *O'Connor swore."*

And then, of course, there was John Ross, who had been
one of the most famous river drivers on the Penobscot. Already Fred was familiar with his name, had heard small
boys around Greenville yelling at each other, "Say I'm
John Ross or I'll kill you!" For three decades, the sixties
to the eighties, he had been God on the West Branch. With
another lumberman from Bangor, Cyrus Hewes, he had
been immortalized in more than one lumberman's ballad.
Scarcely an evening went by without one such ditty being
roared to the rafters.

> *"Who makes the big trees fall kerthrash*
> *And hit the ground a hell of a smash?*
> *'Tis Johnny Ross and Cyrus Hewes (ditto,*
>   *ditto, ditto)!*
> *Who gives us pay for one big drunk*
> *When we hit Bangor, slam kerplunk!*
> *'Tis Johnny Ross and Cyrus Hewes (ditto,*
>   *ditto, ditto)!"*

The ballads were often long and tragic, like the one that
began:

> *"O the night that I was married O,*
> *I laid on marriage bed,*

Up rose John Ross and Cyrus Hewes
And stood by my bed head,
Saying, 'Arise, arise, young married man,
And go along with me;
To the lonesome hills of 'Suncook
And swamp them logs for me.' "

As he mingled with the loggers while treating his patient Fred knew that, as with any greenhorn, the men were taking his measure. He managed to inhale the reeking fumes of the frightful "Canada shag," made from home-grown tobacco imported by the "Canucks" (French Canadians) without coughing, and refrained from wrinkling his nose at the indescribable redolence of mackinaws, sweat shirts, and steaming red underwear strung from the rafters. He looked suitably amused but unperturbed by gruesome tales of wild animals—the hodag, the side-hill elk, the high-behind, the Maine guyanousa, the lethal tree-squeak —obviously resurrected for his benefit. He crawled into his bunk in the boss' office before the kerosene lamps were extinguished and was up long before dawn at the sound of the cookee's wailing reveille: "R-r-roll out! Da-a-aylight in the swamp!" Each cookee, it appeared, had his own peculiar lingo. This one observed considerably more decorum than the one noted for "Get up, get up, get up! Dyin' old (blank), ain't you goin' to get up?"

Fred would hunt up to the top of the hills from this camp, then hunt down the other side to the Macamp, where he would stay that night and hunt back the next day. Both camps furnished an education in lumbering and lumberers which was to serve him well for half a century. Before the week was out he got his deer, a nice fat doe. All he had to do was shoot and dress it. The foreman dragged it to the road, and the horses hauled it to camp. Lancaster phoned Jackman and had it billed. When the train came the baggageman was standing in the open door of the baggage car with a slip of yellow paper in his hand.

A week later Fred was in the hospital in Portland. Whom did he want for a surgeon, he was asked. He was not fussy. Whoever was on the staff was good enough. But concerning one detail he was decidedly fussy. He had no intention of going through the usual rigmarole of being purged, then waiting another day for the operation. He asked permission to leave the hospital and went to see Dr. Tyson, the designated surgeon. "I would like the operation tomorrow," he announced firmly.

The doctor considered. Was he in good shape? In good or better shape than anyone he had ever operated on. Calling the hospital, the doctor announced that he would operate the next morning. Oh, no! There was violent objection. The patient had not had his purge. Strenuous argument followed. Dr. Tyson was as obdurate as his patient. Who was doing this operation, anyway? All right. It would be at eleven tomorrow morning.

The patient had other unorthodox ideas. The third day after the operation he was up, scorning the nurse's ministrations with respect to his bodily functions. As he walked through the ward, he could feel adhesions letting go. Good! If anything came loose, let it happen right here in the hospital. Passing two beds, he heard one patient say aggrievedly to the other, "Look at that man walking off. Here we've been here ten days and are all blown up like poisoned puppies, and *we* can't walk to the bathroom!" He recovered promptly and was free of gas pains. The experiment taught him a lesson. Forty years before early ambulation was the accepted technique in post-surgery, he would be telling his patients to get out of bed whenever they could catch the nurse with her back turned. A lot of them would have been walking around a week before the nurses discovered it.

Now that the little matter of an appendix was settled,

he could turn his attention to more important problems.
Two of them. With whom and where was he going to
spend the rest of his life? The first required no agony of
decision. He had made up his mind long ago that Miss
Sarah Ring should in due time become Mrs. Fred John
Pritham. Now, with a minimum display of sentiment, he
converted what had been a mutual but tacit understanding into words. Would she—? Miss Ring would. She con-
sented to become Mrs. Pritham as soon as the doctor's practice should become sufficiently profitable to warrant the
increased responsibility.

Now for the other momentous decision. He had scarcely
distinguished himself in his professional career to date.
In fact he had returned home from his first skirmish not
in triumph but in acknowledged retreat. A deer, while a
welcome by-product, was hardly a professional trophy. No
wonder his parents regarded him with disappointment
and some concern! But, though he secretly suspected that
he could have severed the relationship with more diplo-
macy and finesse, he had no regrets. He was a loner, not a
collaborator, and certainly nobody's underling. He would
rather be a lone farm horse pulling a plow than one of a
pair of Morgans drawing a fine carriage.

But—where? Jackman, as Hunt had suggested? Some
other Maine town in need of a doctor? There must be
plenty of them. But whenever he tried to picture one of
them, all he could see was what Thoreau had called a half
century ago "a suitably wild-looking sheet of water, sprinkled with small, low islands, which were covered with
shaggy spruce and other wild wood, seen over the infant
port of Greenville, with mountains on each side and far
in the north, and a steamer's smokepipe rising above a
roof." The flat country around Freeport had lost its charm.
Even the beloved bay could not compete with the wild, untrammeled lure of mountains, unnumbered lakes, and
forests. And where else would he be likely to find ducks,

the same kinds as here in Freeport—scalp, chivelry, black, occasionally a mallard, and, best eating of all, the little hairy-headed hooded merganser?

He made inquiries about other locations, but always his choice was the same. And why not? The town needed two doctors, heaven knew! As well two independent of each other as in partnership. He returned to Greenville in mid-January, 1906, and opened his office at the Junction, a mile from the Village. It was the beginning of a practice which was to last at least sixty-five years.

· 3 ·

LIKE MANY OTHER Greenville residents, Johnny Brochu would never forget his introduction to the new doctor. "Doc," as he was soon designated by popular consensus, had been called up to the hotel at Kineo to visit a patient. As he was about to leave, he saw half-a-dozen carpenters sitting around in the lobby. Johnny, who was exactly Doc's age, was one of them. So was a workman suffering from a painful toothache. Would the doctor remove it for him? Accustomed by now to emergencies at all times and places, Doc was agreeable. He promptly opened his satchel and dug out a forceps. At the abrupt approach of the gaping pincers, the patient quailed. "I—I'll probably bite you," he quavered.

Without a word Doc dropped the forceps back in his bag, picked it up, and headed for the door.

"Wait!" hollered the sufferer in alarm. "Come back here!"

Meekly and with jaws spread wide, he submitted to the mercifully swift surgery. Johnny would chuckle over the speed of the new doctor's unexpected reaction for the next half century.

Doc's new boarding house, with the George Potters on

Maple Street, was as congenial as his first. Mrs. Potter was a sister of Mrs. Allen, stout and jolly. George, a house painter and interior decorator, was an ardent hunter. His accurate knowledge of the whereabouts of the warden kept the household dining on trout and venison both in and out of season. Doc slept with the son, Blaine. There was one other boarder, Pearl, who worked at Crafts' store, over which Doc had his office.

It was a pleasant room in the southeast corner, with a couch, desk, and chairs loaned him by Mr. Crafts, and plenty of heat and sunshine. Hollingsworth and Whitney, the big lumber company which had an office across the hall without sunshine, was not so lucky. Mr. George, who occupied it, complained of freezing and was constantly telephoning down to Annie Johnson, in the Crafts office, for more steam heat. She would make fun of him. Doc grinned as he passed the dark, chilly room on the way to his cosily warm nook. He had little time to enjoy it, however. Though he was in it by seven each morning, most of the day was spent out on calls.

There was no dearth of work. His office was at the hub of a wheel, its spokes radiating in a network of dirt roads, railroad tracks, and, at this season, solid ice. The jangling telephone on his wall might send him rushing out on any one of them. Trains on the Canadian Pacific, connecting New Brunswick with Montreal by way of Maine, and those on the Bangor and Aroostook line running from the south into Greenville, rattled the glass in his office window. The three Junction hotels were within a stone's throw: the Mount View House run by Henry Bartley on the hill beyond the B and A, the "Push and Pull" (of lesser repute) to the rear just beyond the overpass, and the Moosehead Inn run by John Gibson up the road a piece opposite the Crafts' imposing residence. Doc was often called by their proprietors to give first aid to injured or drunken lumbermen. The West Cove, even with the Coburn fleet drydocked for winter, was entrance to a busy thoroughfare, for horse-drawn stages ran up and down the lake all winter carrying mail and passengers. There were trails brushed fifty yards apart from the Junction to Lily Bay, to Kineo and the head of the lake. To combat the gales and flying snow the drivers all carried marine compasses in their pungs to steer by when unable to see the next brush.

But this winter there had been a long spell of fair weather, and the lake had frozen clean and hard without the abominable wrinkles which, with their stretches of open water, were so dangerous to cross. The two owners of automobiles in town, Dr. Hunt and the Shaws, soon put the horsemen to shame, and the two families often motored to Lily Bay and Kineo on the glare ice to dinner parties— a real triumph for the horseless carriages, which were often outstripped by horses on the mile stretch between the Village and Junction.

Dr. Hunt had apparently forgotten their brief altercation. Another doctor in town was welcome, whether partner or competitor, the latter preferable if the medic in question was a bit too self-willed. There was more than enough work for both. And Hunt was thinking of even farther and longer holidays than a trip down the Allegash. After twenty years in northern Maine, Florida would feel good in winter.

But the fair weather passed, and by late February, when Doc got his first call to Rockwood, deep snow covered lake and countryside. Rockwood was a tiny settlement about halfway up the lake at the narrows, opposite Kineo. Though the Maine Central Railroad was in the process of laying a branch line into the settlement, there was as yet no road or railroad connection. Doc took the train to Askwith and was met by Harry Johnston, who had sent in the call. Harry was a full-time guide, honest-eyed, clean-

shaven, and Doc liked him on sight. As they drove down
Misery Stream in the pung, Harry pointed out a crude
marker nailed to a tree.

"See that, Doc? It's a grave. Right there a woodsman was
murdered. Somebody wanted the few dollars the poor
bloke might have in his pocket."

Doc was duly shocked. He had heard of other lumbermen memorials scattered along riverbanks—battered boots
nailed to a tree marking one of the countless lives lost
among pounding logs and thundering torrents—but somehow this was more tragic. One thing to die valiantly, victim
of heroic foes or even of one's own immense bravado,
quite another to be meanly sacrificed for a few pennies!
But he was to see more of such memorials to human greed
in coming years.

It was a pleasant drive of about six miles, pung runners
squeaking and crunching on the snow, mountains towering on the right, presently the broad expanse of Brassua
Lake on the left, the tangled dri-ki strewn like bleached
bones along its edges. The afterglow of a brilliant sunset
washed the hills with most beautiful and unusual tints of
amethyst.

"Those colors!" exclaimed Doc. "Almost purple. What
do they mean?"

"You'll find out by morning," returned Harry dryly.

His house, on the west side of the river abreast of the
rapids, was a log cabin, crude, but tight, snug, warm. The
one room downstairs contained a pot-bellied stove, a cookstove, a rough table, a deacon's seat, its wood furnishings
as hand-hewn from the forest as the log walls and bare
spruce floor. The patient lay moaning on a bunk at one
end of the dim, lamplit room. Johnston held the lamp
while Doc made his examination. Diagnosis was easy, a
large and painful peritonsillar abscess. He called for boiling water and sterilized his knife. But then came problems.

It was impossible to pry the patient's teeth apart enough to slip the blade flatway between them. But luckily there was an upper tooth missing on the abscess side. He realized too late that he should have brought his head mirror. He looked around the sparsely furnished room.

"Do you happen to have a hand mirror?" he asked.

The members of the family, gathered curiously around, looked blank. Then one of the children remembered that they had picked up the fragments of a broken mirror the summer before. They began searching through their toys and treasures. Presently they returned with a triangular piece perhaps an inch and a half across. Holding this in one hand while Harry held the lamp, turning the wick so high it began smoking the chimney, Doc was able to reflect the light through the gap in the teeth and see the "point" of the abscess. With a swift motion of the slender blade he lanced it. Relief followed immediately. By morning the erstwhile sufferer was able to empty the bean pot for breakfast.

Driving back to Askwith, Doc soon discovered what the "purple sunset" meant. The thermometer had plummeted to thirty below zero. Passing along the open riverbank with the mist driving straight into their faces and freezing wherever it struck, Doc was sure it had hit nearer fifty. The horse crunching through the crust, coat frost-rimmed, icicles seeping like stalactites from his nostrils, walked all the six miles or more to the station. But discomfort was more than offset by the chance to get better acquainted with Harry. Their friendship would last a lifetime.

A few days later the jangling telephone summoned him again to Brassua. Don Harden, a classmate at Bowdoin who had taken a berth as assistant to Dr. Hayes on the Canadian Pacific, had a case on which he needed help and more medical equipment than he had with him. The company assessed all its employees from Brownville to Megantic, fifty cents each month for a single man, a dollar for one married, to pay for medical aid. The patient was the wife of a section hand and had suffered a severe miscarriage. Arriving at the cabin, Doc found Harden vigorously but vainly trying to rouse the husband, sprawled on the kitchen lounge, from a drunken stupor.

"No use," he snapped. "We'll just have to operate without his help. And she's lost so much blood we'd better hurry."

The drenched bed was in no condition to be used as an operating table. Don went out in the yard and dug an old mortar bin from under the snow, swept it clean, and brought it in. They lifted the woman onto it, Don marveling at the ease with which his shorter and slighter colleague raised his share of the burden. While Don administered the anesthetic Fred performed the necessary curettage. Then they put clean sheets on the bed and laid her back. After filling the stoves with wood Don was all for stretching out on the cold floor for a few hours' sleep before the train came. But Doc had a better idea.

"Davis' and Marston's camp where I hunted is only about a mile from here. It's about time for the feeders to be up. Why not go and crawl into their nice warm bunks?"

Don was enthusiastic. The mile was soon covered. Don climbed into the cook's berth beside the hot stove and was asleep in a minute, but Doc wasn't so lucky. George Malone from Greenville was among the crew and wanted to hear all the town news. He even passed up breakfast to continue talking, then went directly to the hovel, hitched his team, and worked until noon before eating. When he left, it was time to wake Don. They ate, went to the section house and refilled the stoves, then a few minutes later flagged the train.

It was while boarding with the Potters that Doc first experienced what he called a "hunch." One Sunday he de-

cided to walk over to Wilson Stream to see what changes
had taken place since October. When he was halfway
across Sid Young's pasture, he thought suddenly, "I'm
wanted back at the office." Looking at his watch, he hastily returned home. Sure enough. Blaine met him with the
report that a call had come for him. "I can tell you exactly
when the man came," said Doc. He was right. Both Blaine
and his father had noted the time of the call. When he told
them almost to the minute, they stared at him in amazement, almost with suspicion. What was he, some goldanged
psycho or something? He was as much at a loss to explain
the phenomenon as they, either then or at numerous other
times during years to come. But he accepted the faculty
for what it was worth, untroubled by its apparent mystery.

"Why not?" he shrugged after the repetition of just such
a hunch years later. "If a TV can stick something up in
the air and pick something up in Bangor, why ain't it possible for people's minds to do the same thing?"

Spring came even later than usual that year. There was
good sledding until May. But it sent out advance signals.
Ice began cracking like pistol shots. The road to the Village and its side streets, head-deep in snow compacted all
winter by a horse-driven roller, slowly softened, so that
horses often sank to their bellies and had to be pulled out
by other horses. The Coburn steamers were freshly painted
and overhauled. Men who had worked at odd jobs for
months dusted off their guides' licenses. Sanders' store
blossomed with shining new fishing equipment.

And when spring did come finally, it was with a burst
and a rush. With a suddenness that made one blink the
ice "went out" in Moosehead. One moment it was there,
the next it was gone. The town sprang to life like the
palace of the awakened Sleeping Beauty. City sportsmen
loaded with smart fishing tackle were disgorged from
trains, to be swallowed by the gay-bannered steamers and

hustled off to sporting camps. Lumbermen poured into the three hotels, peeled off several layers of red underwear, took their first baths in months, and availed themselves of all the inspiriting recreation the town afforded. Doc found his duties multiplied as the bottle proved as conducive to accidents as the axe and peavey. But while the season brought respite to choppers, sawyers, sled tenders, swampers, teamsters, for the rivermen the hardest and most treacherous business was just beginning.

Doc saw his first river drive from his office window. John Gibson, proprietor of the Moosehead Inn, who had been cutting spruce from Little Squaw Mountain Township, was now driving it down Bog Brook to Moosehead, where it would be floated into the boom, hitched fast to a steamer, and towed away either to local mills or to the East Outlet. A far cry from the headworks of the old days, the huge raft of hewn logs with a capstan manned by twelve to fifteen men who, tramping round and round, winding the straining warp inch by inch, would draw the great boom of logs from the upper end of a pond to one of the outlets, moving perhaps a mile or two a day!

Doc watched the drive with a fascination not untinged with horror. The quiet little stream, fed by the melting snows, had turned into a vicious boiling torrent, tumbling the great spruce logs, rearing them on end, twisting and tangling them into piled-up snarls. He marveled at the agility and skill of the drivers as they leaped from one slithering, slippery round to another, sparring with peaveys and pike poles as easily as he had once speared eels, unloosing the key log from a small jam as unerringly as a skillful player at jackstraws. And if little Bog Brook was treacherous, what about the angry boil below the falls of Sowadnehunk or the churning fury of Ripogenus Gorge! No wonder that the "Bangor Tigers" had carried their legendary fame across a continent! It was said that some of them could do a handstand on their peavey stuck into a floating log, or even a somersault! Clad in his jersey trousers, little black-felt hat, red shirt, and calked boots, the riverman might well be a cross between a panther and a mountain goat.

But Doc had other things to think of than river drives and, to him, more exciting. He was being married in June. And the first of May he bought himself a house, square, sturdy, practical, on the main street just beyond the Methodist Church. The minister, Mr. Moore, who was then occupying it, was not too pleased to move upstairs with his five children, but Fred insisted, wanting to make some improvements before Sadie's arrival. There were six inches of water in the cellar, plus six setting hens from which the cleric hoped to raise himself a flock.

Doc tackled the office first, choosing the room on the left of the hall. After pulling twenty 40-penny spikes out of the walls, he applied what he had bought at one of the local stores for calcimine. Finding it to be only whitewash, he swept it off with a broom, put it back in the box, and set it on the lawn for the store's delivery cart to pick up, then bought some good calcimine from Sanders'. He made a table out of the box in which his medical supplies had been shipped from Portland, and Lilla Clark gave him a piece of oilcloth to cover it. The same cover on the same table would occupy the same spot sixty-five years later. Another table and a strip of carpeting long enough for the stairs came from a house seized for rent, where the family had owed him money. Another patient who had no means of paying let him have a bed. Other furniture—he trusted —would be contributed from surplus housewares in the bride's and groom's families.

To Fred's disappointment his brother would not be present at the wedding, for Harry was in California working with the Rob Hunt Laboratory. Yes, and making a name for himself! He had always been a cool actor in a crisis. In April at the time of the great earthquake, when he found that the company building was doomed in the fire, he had the forethought to salvage the balances used for chemical analyses and transport them safely to his home in Oakland. In the wake of the holocaust the company held a meeting. When Harry entered the room, he heard the executives talking. "If we only had the balances," someone was saying, "we could start again. But we can't afford the ten thousand dollars to get new ones. We're finished." Calmly Harry pulled the balances out of his pocket and became a hero.

That year 1906 saw another triumph for Harry, the crowning of his ten years' devotion by marriage to his beloved. The family approved his choice, for Stella was strong and gifted, a good piano and organ player as well as a hard worker in the Shaw shoe factory, where she had been employed putting in laces. . . .

But they were still secretly unhappy, though resigned, over Fred's selection. To add to her liabilities, Sadie had been sick that spring with appendicitis. She was slender to the point of emaciation, weighing only ninety-six pounds. She had suffered, it seemed, from every ailment possible: psoriasis, nose bleeds, periodic indispositions. "She don't winter well," her grandfather had once said jokingly, "waren't really worth keeping." That reedy, anemic little spindle-shanks a fit doctor's wife? A pity they could not have looked a few decades into the future!

"Nobody could be that small," grumbled the dress-maker, trying to fit the crepe de Chine wedding dress to her sixteen-inch waist. And she insisted on making it eighteen.

The wedding was on June 20 in Sadie's Grandmother's house, where she had lived since she was thirteen. Though her grandfather had died, her grandmother was in prideful and loving attendance. It was the other way with Doc, whose grandfather was still living. They had a daisy wedding, Sadie's young sisters having tastefully decorated the parlor with wild flowers. Sadie's sister Laura was her attendant; her brother Charles was best man, and his wife Myra made the bride's cake. The wedding march was played on Sadie's organ by Fred's cousin, Agnes Whitten. They stood under a bell of daisies for the ceremony, chains of daisies were hung in great festoons, and everywhere there were vases, jardinieres, pitchers, and bowls filled with daisies.

Their wedding picture showed a slender graceful figure with slightly angular but attractive features, hair loosely waving upward from a central part, white gown gathered into a high ruching at the neck, full in waist and sleeves but tapering to tight narrow lines at waist and in the long cuffs; skirt wide and full and sweeping the floor; beside her, seated stiffly in an ornately carved chair, a small, grimly sober male, hair meticulously and sleekly parted, eyes fixed immutably ahead, mustached lips unsmiling, long slender fingers carefully arranged as in death, glistening boots firmly planted on the floor, neat white bow tie and well-pressed best suit, models of the 1906 proper bridegroom's attire. Since he would seldom be seen in such conventional garb during the next six decades, it was well that he was thus preserved for posterity.

· 4 ·

NOT UNTIL YEARS LATER did Doc know how homesick and lonely his young bride was during those first hours, days, weeks, months.

They arrived in Greenville in one of the worst thunder showers she had ever seen. It splintered, crashed, raged, slashed about the train, making the remote north country seem even more strange and wild. Dr. Hunt met them at the station with his car and drove them to their new home.

"If the rain lets up, I'll come back and get you," he said cheerfully. "If it doesn't, I guess you'll have to starve."

He came back, and they had an excellent dinner. But on their return the new home seemed even more bleak and empty. Fortunately there were the bed and the two chairs and the table, plus the little black stove in the kitchen, the bare essentials.

"There's a lot to be done," Doc told his bride.

It was a remarkable understatement. Almost every room needed refinishing. The sink had no good drainage. The sills were rotten. The house had been built with the intention of coating its wooden frame with bricks, so that when the wind blew it was little better than a chicken coop. The sturdiest features on the premises were the two huge rectangular stone slabs by which the bride mounted to the front door of her new home. Harry Bowser had helped saw them out of solid slate when the house had been built fifteen years before. They were good for at least a century.

Sadie hadn't expected much, and the liabilities—even the family of seven upstairs, using the kitchen pump, keeping chickens in the cellar and a cow in the church shed —did not disturb her—or the fact that the furniture, donated jointly by their two families, was ten days in arriving, since the freight car had got on the wrong branch and gone to Aroostook. It was her nature to take what came and make the best of it. But she was inexpressibly lonely. Having grown up in the country knowing all the neighbors, never having been away from home except for short visits, she felt as if she had come to the ends of the earth. Her new acquaintances were kind. Mrs. Potter and her sister, Mrs. Allen, with whom Doc had boarded, could not do enough for her. She went on walks and berrying ex-

peditions with Mrs. Capino, a member of one of the fine
Indian families in the community. The women in the
Methodist Church next door welcomed her cordially. But
it would be years before she felt really at home.

Doc tried to make her life as easy as possible. He got up
at four each morning and prepared his own breakfast, a
habit which was to persist for a lifetime. Not more than a
half-dozen times in the next sixty-five years would Sadie
cook his breakfast. All through the busy summer he tried
to find time to take her fishing. September had almost
gone, with the end of the fishing season, and still they had
not gone. He tried to persuade the minister, who was a
sportsman, to go with them.

"No use," scoffed the cleric. "There aren't any fish in
the big lake, and there's no time to go to the distant
ponds."

Doc consulted one of the guides about the necessary
equipment. He named a vast number of articles, and Doc
despaired of getting them all in time. He noticed that Phil
Capino, an Indian guide and trapper, was getting equipment together. "I've been wanting to take Sadie," he told
Phil. When he related all the equipment he had been told
was necessary, the Indian hooted. "Tommyrot! You don't
need hardly none of that stuff! Bring her over at two this
afternoon. I'll show you how to get fish without them fancy
fixin's."

He did. They fished until four. Then, as it was nearly
dark and beginning to rain, they came home and put the
catch, all seven- or eight-pound togue, in the kitchen sink.
When the minister set his pail under the pump to get
water, he was dumbfounded to see it racing off toward the
foot of the sink. He replaced it and started pumping, and
away the pail went again. He was peering at it in amazement when Sadie reached up and turned on the light. His
eyes popped.

"*Where* did you get those fish?"

"In the lake," replied Sadie composedly.

"Then I must go and get me some!"

"You'll have to go tomorrow," said Sadie.

"But—tomorrow is the Sabbath!"

"And Monday," reminded Sadie, her eyes twinkling, "is the first of October."

She split one of the fish, stuffed and baked it, and invited the minister's family to join them at dinner. Though all ate generously, there was a good bit left over.

When the minister and his brood left for a more lucrative position in the West late that fall, Doc and Sadie were able to occupy the whole house, and the place began to feel more like home. The office profited by his departure. For seventy-five cents Doc bought a folding cot which had been surplus baggage, and set it up for an examinations couch. Sixty-five years later it would still be there and in use. A sensible gadget he found it, because it was down close to the floor. Children would gladly jump up on it when he wanted to feel their tummies or look at a sore toe. Worlds ahead of those miserable iron contraptions! (He bought one of those later, and one of his less sober patients, sliding down on it so that his feet hung over, upended the thing four different times. He saw a good chance to get rid of the blamed thing when the hospital was built. The directors gladly accepted the gift and turned it in for a later model.) With the addition of a medicine cabinet built by Wendell Hubbard, who doubled as cabinet maker and undertaker, plus two straight unpainted armchairs of the Windsor variety ("cussed uncomfortable!") his office furnishings were now complete, to remain virtually unchanged for three generations.

Major improvements were under way which would take years to finish. Much had to be done that fall to make the house comfortable for winter. Drainage was laid from the sink to a dry well. The twenty-five-foot double chimney was sitting on a birch stump. Doc had to cut the chimney off nine times and jack it up before he finally dug deep enough to hit a ledge and got it to remain stable. There was only a small area dug out for a cellar. Later he would put a basement under the whole house with cement floor and walls, doing all the work himself and mixing the concrete right there in the cellar, providing all the gravel by staving up the slate ledge and mixing it six to one with twenty-two barrels of Portland cement. However, it would be thirty years before the draughty walls were made tight with insulation.

But most household jobs, including tending a garden and sawing enough wood for all the stoves, must be done between four and seven in the morning, his scheduled time for being in the office. His world was rapidly expanding, and he was constantly in search of new media to reach it. One of the best ways, he soon discovered, was a "jigger," the three-wheeled railroad handcar which could be worked by one person alone, or, if two went along, they sat on a board placed across the seat, and both worked their passage. Then there was the four-wheeled handcar, a small platform on which several men could stand and work the propelling mechanism.

One night in July, a month after Doc's marriage, an accident at Moosehead brought Pat Conley, the section foreman, to the Junction on one of these handcars. Could Doc return with him pronto? Doc could, and five men, pumping together, made the return eleven-mile trip to the East Outlet in just thirty-six minutes, a record which was never exceeded. And this included the time they had to stop at the rock cuts and listen for the oncoming train, which was so close that they had time only to get the handcar into the shed ahead of it, none to stop for their hats which had blown off. It was Doc's first experience on a handcar, but by no means his last. In fact, he was back on a three-wheeled "jigger" the next day visiting the accident victim, this time pumping alone.

"Ha! There's the crown of my felt hat!" he noted, spying it on the head of one of the extra gang of Italians repairing the Moosehead siding. And there on another head was the rim, obviously severed from the crown by engine wheels. When he came back the men were eating dinner by a little fire beside the track. Gleefully they had piled a stack of their stovewood on the rails, hoping to derail the greenhorn. But they laughed too soon. Doc managed to stay on the jigger and hold his weight to the inside so that the handcar only struck and scattered the wood. The recipient of a stick in the face or belly quickly stopped his laughing.

He had to visit the patient once or twice a day, traveling by handcar each time with the railroad's permission. Pumping along a day or two later he knew he was running a fifty-fifty chance of meeting the down freight. Seeing the section crew at work in the bend of track just south of the ledge cut, he stopped and asked their advice. Would he have time to get through the cut before the freight came? All agreed that he had plenty of time. But when he got halfway across the fill, there was the engine popping out of the cut! His swift jamming of the brakes threw the jigger off the track. The shock broke his satchel from its fastenings, and it rolled between the rails. Almost with one motion he set the jigger out on the shoulder, reached back, grabbed his satchel, and as he straightened up he tipped the little wheel of the jigger into the air. The engine cylinders came so close to the wheel that it vibrated like a fiddle string. Not until the train had roared past did he fully appreciate his achievement. He was sitting only two poles distant from the cut, and the train had been moving at thirty miles an hour!

"Pretty lucky," was his later comment, "to have saved

both satchel and jigger!" Of little consequence, apparently, that he had saved his own skin!

Railroads and public steamboats, plus occasional motorboats, canoes, pungs, lumbering wangans, stages, and—most utilized—sturdy legs, were all good methods of transportation, but with limitations. All but the legs were dependent on others. Doc soon felt the need for more personal conveyance. Early that first December the need seemed happily answered. He was in Dr. Hunt's office one morning when Jack Gerrish, the baggage master, called to tell the doctor that his horse was at the station. Hunt promptly disclaimed ownership, knowing his horse was in his barn.

"But there's a horse here in a freight car," insisted Gerrish, "shipped from Dover by a Mr. Sanborn, and plainly labeled for 'the doctor.'"

Speculation yielded only one solution. The dealer had known Fred had no horse and, thinking he might want one, had furnished a candidate. Fred was agreeable. He wondered suddenly how he had gotten along without a horse this long. Certainly he would try it out. He secured a stall at Alex Lemieux's at the top of the hill and took the animal there for overnight. Ed Moore, the blacksmith, heard of the arrival and suggested that they drive in to Coll McEachern's lumber camps at the head of Upper Wilson Lake and hunt. This would give a chance to see what the horse was like.

They soon saw. Leaving about four the next morning, they drove across the solidly frozen ice of the ponds. Although there was a plainly marked trail, the animal would rear its head and charge across the ice in any direction, paying no attention to the road. The hunting was more rewarding. Doc got his second deer of the season, the first one in November on a trip with Cecil Lancaster to Spencer Bay. Fortunately it was a small one, for he had shot it three or four miles from the nearest road and carried it curled around his shoulders all the afternoon, arriving at camp after dark, where a party was starting out to rescue the "lost" hunter.

The horse was returned to Dover, but the search for a more worthy successor was already under way. During the next few months Doc built a stable and bought a horse from Waldo Spencer, an animal bearing a marked resemblance to an old moose. It was not an ideal purchase, but far better than traveling shanks' mare. Until its untimely end a few years later Old Moose drew him faithfully through dust, mud, ice, snow, heat, cold, fog, rain, and, happily, some sunshine.

Fred had been well tutored in the stern code of a doctor's duty by both Dr. Gray and his medical school professors. He accepted it for exactly that, a duty to be performed, without unnecessary emotion or spiritual dedication, certainly without fanfare. It was just a man's job to do, the best he knew how. He even planned, when the occasion arose, to perform a task which neither the Hippocratic Oath nor any other code of medical behavior expected of a doctor: to deliver his own child.

The event took place, like most others of its time, in the family bedroom. Sadie's mother was there to act as nurse. It was an agonizing day. One of Doc's patients, a victim of locomotor ataxia, was having one of his crises. A brakeman on the B and A passenger and a very rugged man, he had been handling one of the fighting drunk woodsmen with his usual efficiency when one of the troublemakers bit him and caused infection. Doc went over on the hill ten times to attend him. Sadie was suffering with prolonged delivery, and only stern duty forced him to leave her. About six o'clock, after hours of ineffectual labor, when he considered her capable of dilation, he called Dr. Hunt to help him. Finally Fred administered ether, while his colleague used the forceps.

"First time I ever saw a perineum tear before the head came down to make any pressure," Hunt commented. When Master Carroll finally made his appearance on November 22, 1907, after thirty-six hours of labor, it was with an agonizing rending of flesh.

Though by this time Fred had delivered many children, the act of birth had heretofore been a mere exercise of skill to be viewed with clinical detachment. Its complications had been matters of professional curiosity and challenge. Now suddenly he was an intensely involved participant, racked by vicarious pain and emotion. Natural, of course, to feel unusual sympathy and worry and relief because this was his own wife and child, but he found the sense of involvement disturbing because of its possible wider implications. Suppose he came to feel emotionally involved in every case of childbirth, as if he were a sort of partner in the whole divine plan of creation! An upsetting thought. A doctor was just another man with his job to do, like a farmer or a carpenter or a blacksmith—wasn't he?

It was only a few days later that a messenger arrived from Levi Lancaster's camps at Rum Pond asking him to come and attend some sick lumbermen.

"You're to get yourself a saddle and ride into the camp," the man told him.

Doc protested. It would be much easier and quicker, he felt, to leave his horse at Wilson Stream and walk the remaining distance. But the message to ride was insistent and, since he did not know the condition of the roads, he reluctantly agreed. Borrowing a saddle from Don Davis, he went to the end of the road with his buggy, saddled his horse, forded the stream, and made his way to Morkill, where the tote road began. It was just as he expected, a sea of mud winding through the woods crusted with ice nearly an inch thick. At each step the poor horse broke through and sank nearly to his belly in mud.

Doc fumed. Sadie was still in very poor condition, and

he would be needed badly at home in a short time to pass
the catheter. He had also left a young patient who had
been playing with some left-over Fourth of July explosives
and lost part of his thumb and some finger tips. The boy
needed immediate attention. The slowness of the six-mile
trip was galling. Harassed by the certainty that he could
not possibly be back in time, plus the agony of watching
his poor horse struggle through the morass in constant
danger of cutting his legs badly on the icy crust, he was in
a fury of disgust and frustration. It took him nearly three
hours to cover the six miles, when he could easily have
walked straight across to the camp from the dam in forty-
five minutes! And when Lancaster met him in the yard,
he emphatically told him so.

Though Lancaster never again attempted to define Doc's
medium of transport, it was not the last time he misjudged
his self-reliance. When Doc was called to the camps on another occasion, he went to Walden's place on Wilson Pond,
procured a skiff, rowed himself to the Rum Pond Carry,
and walked through the woods to the camp.

"I'd better send someone back with you to show you the
way to your boat," said Lancaster when the medical visit
was completed.

"Nonsense! Found my way here, didn't I?"

But a snowstorm was in the offing, night would soon be
coming on, and Lancaster insisted. He detailed the cookee
to show him the way. Doc was carrying his rifle, hoping
to see a deer, so he moved cautiously ahead, directing the
cookee to follow. When he arrived at the landing, his
escort was nowhere to be seen. It was a wonderful time to
hunt. The big-bellied snow clouds over Rum Mountain
were already sloughing off a few flakes. Before dusk the
ground might be soft and well covered. But he had no time
to spare. Regretfully he rowed back across the pond and
walked home. Sometime after dark the camp called him.
"You all right? You got home safe?"

"Sure. Why?"

"The cookee's not back yet."

Doc snorted. He should have been able to walk to camp from the pond in half an hour. *He* had in less. And there had been plenty of daylight left. Lancaster sent out forty or fifty of his crew with what lanterns they could muster and they began searching. About two o'clock they found their cookee curled up on a big boulder less than a quarter mile from the place Doc had left him. Maybe a good cookee, but what a woodsman! And Lancaster had selected him as a guide!

Before Doc had been in Greenville a year, he had been forced to revise his evaluation of a doctor's duty, gleaned from Dr. Gray and others, by a few pertinent phrases.

It's a doctor's business to go where he's called, come hell —yes, or fire, rain, snow, mud, fog, wind, ice—as well as high water!

CHAPTER THREE

It's a Doctor's Business—

. 1 .

ONE OF DOC's early casualties as a Greenville physician was his beautiful handle-bar moustache. It was a patient who had occasioned its birth; it was another who effected its demise. One season there was a huge epidemic of boils among the lumbermen. Somehow the mustache became host to the minute organisms of infection. It went the way of other frivolities of appearance, such as neckties, dress shirts, formal suits, polished boots—all victims of expediency.

Patients with such ailments often came to him out of the camps. Many times he was called to treat them in one of the three hotels within a few rods of his house. He was always glad when the call came from the Mount View House, of which Henry Bartley was proprietor.

86

Henry was the most efficient hotel man in the area. Not only did he operate a clean, well-heated, comfortable house, but he was in rigid control of everything in it, including the perennial cigar that migrated magically from one side of his mouth to the other. His memory of faces, names, and destinations of his hundreds of patrons was phenomenal. He could tell in a second whom any one of them was working for and where he might be found at any given time. He kept order, by persuasion if possible, by other methods if necessary. Take the time when he was standing behind the counter making some entries and a man walking in front of him commenced to make foul remarks about the hotel and its proprietor. Without looking up, Henry swung him a backhanded cuff that snapped his lower jaw as though it were loose matches. Calmly Henry put him in a wagon and carted him up to the sanatorium run by Dr. Hatch, paying all bills until he recovered.

More than once Doc blessed this genius for control. On one occasion he had several typhoid patients in the hotel who badly needed rest and quiet. Doc explained to Henry that the noise downstairs was harmful to his patients. Immediately Henry explained the situation to the roomful of woodsmen waiting to take the boat up the lake, and they hushed at once—all but one. The exception began to shout, hopped out of his chair, proceeded to dance about and pound his feet on the floor. Henry stepped from behind the counter, grabbed him by the shoulders, and set him down on the chair, the floor in fact, for the chair legs flew into splinters, and the house was jarred to the eaves when the chair seat hit bottom. Getting up, the man meekly dragged himself outdoors. The hotel was remarkably quiet until the men recovered.

On another occasion Doc had been called by Henry to pull some teeth for a patron. The patient insisted on ether, but Doc had no sooner given him a teaspoonful than he tossed bedding, clothes, anything he could lay his hands on. Doc knew he would be next. He went quickly downstairs.

"That man doesn't want his teeth out," he told Henry. "He wants to wreck things."

Henry rolled his cigar into the other corner of his mouth and took the stairs two at a time. He towered over the man's bed. "Do you want those teeth out, or don't you?" he demanded. The man allowed that he did. "O.K. Then you're going to have 'em out!" He turned to Doc. "Give him the ether and pull 'em," he ordered. As soon as the patient got a few more whiffs, he again became belligerent, but this time he faced a different situation. Few men could toss Henry. He jumped on the bed, took a wrist in each hand, put a knee on each thigh, and spread the man's arms wide above his head. His victim could not even squirm. He took his ether, and the teeth were removed. Henry rolled his cigar back to its original corner, laughed, and went downstairs.

His saloon was as well regulated as the rest of his hotel. More than once he gave free shelter to drunks who had been thrown out of less respectable haunts and had no place to go. If two men became quarrelsome, he would pick one up in each hand, knock their heads together, and throw them into the "dead room" at one side to cool off. When two lumberjacks fought, it was by no means unusual for one to walk with his spiked boots on the other's face or break his skull with an axe or cant dog. Doc was often called in, both to mend such damages and to restore the inebriates to sanity.

"I say, Doc," Henry once asked him curiously after he had successfully piloted a derelict through an especially bad case of the "horrors," "you've attended a lot of these boozehounds. How come you never lost one?"

"Why should I?" retorted Doc. "No reason to. They're all strong and able men."

"Maybe," said Henry dryly. "But other doctors that I know of have lost plenty of 'em. And I could name 'em."

He did not need to. Before Doc's arrival he had sent many inebriates to the sanatorium, the institution a few miles up the lake in the shadow of Squaw Mountain. He well knew there was no love lost between its physicians and the Greenville doctors.

Though there was friendly rivalry between Bartley's Mount View House and John Gibson's Moosehead Inn, both were decent places to attend patients. Not so the old "Push and Pull" just beyond the CP railroad tracks. There was a scarcity of bedding, and wind blew freely through its cracks. George Archibald found that out one night. It was late fall, and he was coming in on one of the steamers returning with its empty scow in tow after taking supplies up the lake. The captain ran into the "mink-hole" to tie up for the night.

"Watch out for the scow," he told Archibald. "Don't let it hit the boat."

It was dark astern. Archibald stuck out his foot to feel the scow, and did! It jammed his foot between its iron projecting edge and the iron-covered guardrail of the boat, bursting it lengthwise from heel to toe so that the muscles were squeezed through the skin. He was carried to the "Push and Pull," and Doc was called to do the repair job. The patient passed a painful and chilling night. When he asked for more coverings, the proprietor assured him there was not another spread in the house. Though his friends filled some empty whiskey bottles with hot water and stowed them in his bed, his toes were chilled. The next morning he amused himself by trying to spear the rats through the spaces between the laths where the wall plaster was nearly all peeled off. Fortunately in the afternoon he was able to cross the B and A tracks to Grammy Bowser's, whose house was headquarters for many of the lumbermen. There he remained comfortable and warm until he recovered.

One spring Doc had five typhoid patients on the top floor of this hotel, plus a pulmonary tubercular case in a bed near by. He hired a man named Stinneford to nurse them. With no extra sheets to work with the doctor and nurse were as frustrated as the patients were uncomfortable. The rough dirty spreads chafed the skin off knees, elbows, and hips. Finally Doc bought some new sheeting by the web, so that fresh squares could be placed under the patients, changed frequently, and burned. The men lay in a stupor for weeks, incontinent, unable to help themselves. Oh, for a decent hospital! But the crisis passed, and all recovered. Then to disinfect! Stinneford had done a good job throughout, keeping the floors wet with formalin. Now as a final precaution Doc put in five pails of a mixture of formalin and permanganate, adding a small amount of sulphuric acid to warm it up, stepped out and locked the door, leaving the vaporizing substances to finish the work. Removing the key, he turned to procure a piece of wet paper to seal the keyhole. The attendant took this opportunity to peek through the keyhole to see how the fog was rising. At that moment the acid did its work, and the whole mixture fairly exploded, driving the gas forcibly through the keyhole and into the open mouth of the peeper. He nearly strangled to death. Doc dragged him downstairs and to an open window where, after much gasping, he finally succeeded in drawing a full breath.

"Curiosity isn't always a blessing," Doc told him dryly.

There were times when the railroads furnished almost as many patients as the lumber camps. In addition to the Canadian Pacific and the Bangor and Aroostook lines meeting at the Junction, there was now a Maine Central branch built in 1906 to Kineo. Its junction with the CP was at Somerset, which rapidly grew in size and importance. It was a rough frontier settlement, with a good bit of rowdiness and drunkenness. Henry Bartley built another hotel there, the Somerset House, which followed its proprietor's tradition of order at whatever cost. Doc was frequently called to Somerset to patch the ravages of violent incidents, as when Billy Shesgreen received a charge of shot in the stomach when inspired by stimulants to stave in the hotel door with an axe.

Many of the hotel's personnel would come to Greenville on the Canadian Pacific "Mixed" in the afternoon, shop, go to a show or dance, then return on the late "Express" which stopped each night at Moosehead to leave the mail. This left them a five-mile walk to Somerset, a mere "little jaunt" to such hardy souls. One of these was the hotel cook, called "Big Clara" because of her excessive weight. It happened that one extremely dark night the engineer pulled past the station, and, instead of descending to the level platform as she expected, Clara stepped on the roadbed shoulder and pitched head over heels down the embankment, striking heavily on her ankle. Rushing her to the section house, they found she had driven the astragalus clear through the skin of the ankle joint. While one of the railroad men pulled on her foot, Clara covered the protruding bone with her handkerchief and managed to push it back into the joint. Doc treated the wound the next day. In spite of the liabilities—the cinders and gravel into which the bone had been driven, the five-mile ride after midnight on a handcar—between his skill and Clara's buxom courage and resilience, the leg healed well and quickly.

He had a far more difficult job in a home not far from the hotel. One of the Maine Central trainmen had built a cabin in the swamp within the triangle formed by the

two rail lines and the spur. Both he and his wife contracted pneumonia at the same time. There was no help
available except from the railroad men who, as they passed
to and from work, replenished the fires. Doc was appalled
every time he entered the cabin, which for a time was
once or twice daily. The place was so damp that icicles
formed on the rafters, some of them a foot long. He felt
like a tourist in the Mammoth Cave gazing up at stalactites. The two patients recovered, though how they did so
was a wonder. Certainly it was not wholly his skill in a day
still thirty years removed from the advent of sulfa drugs
and penicillin!

He was rapidly discovering through experience what
remedies proved most effective. Treatment for pneumonia
varied with every case. If the heart was weak, he would
give digitalis. Most of his pneumonia patients received a
certain amount of strychnine. Some were given hyoscya-
mus. If they had difficulty getting up the sputum, ammonium chloride would be indicated. For very high fever,
he administered hellebore and Veratrum viride. The old
onion and mustard poultices used on him in childhood
usually did some good. The Indians and other old-timers
in the area used poultices made of the wild onions found
abundantly all through the woods. Grammy Johnson
would gather yarrow and make poultices of it, apparently
with some success. But, while Doc never scoffed at such
ancient medicines, he did not use them. And he was apparently a bit skeptical of some of the drugs he did pre-
scribe.

"You might try this," he occasionally told a patient.
"Won't do you any harm, and maybe it will do you good."
And the chances were it would.

He had his own pet remedies. His treatment of croup
was unusual and very successful. For internal medicine
he gave Abbott's calcidrine. And on the outside of the

chest he rubbed guiasorb, procured from the Columbus Pharmacal Company in Ohio. Why other doctors didn't use it was a mystery. You could rub it on the chest and in fifteen minutes detect the guiab in the urine. It was good for rheumatism also, penetrated the muscles. Decades later, when he was ninety, people would still be coming to him for this remedy.

He used a lot of Abbot's granules, too, for many kinds of sickness. Abbott was the first to isolate alkaloids and coat them up in little pills. They contained the active principle of many healing plants.

He also had his pet peeves. One was iodine.

"If I had my way," he often said, "when the men get off the train here at the Junction, every pack would be searched for the stuff. Why? They take raw iodine and pour it into a wound. It rots. I have more trouble with the stuff."

He considered it almost as great an anathema as sugar doughnuts. "Pisen!" he characterized the latter when served them on Ladies' Night at the Masonic Lodge.

But the cases he treated at Somerset and its environs were not all as depressing as the pneumonia episode. It was on the other side of the CP tracks that he attended a case smacking of the ludicrous. A woman had slipped and fallen backward down the stairs, striking her head on a corner of a stair step and peeling off a piece of scalp at least three by four inches. It bled copiously. Neighbors flocked in to render both assistance and advice until Doc could arrive by the next train. The flap of skin was replaced and the area dusted heavily with flour, one of the favorite woods' remedies for all kinds of wounds. No good. The bleeding continued. Then one friend, blessed with a happy impulse, tipped a jug of molasses over the wound, giving it a generous application in order to thicken the flour. This measure also was ineffective. Then an old woodsman, standing quietly by, fathered the happiest inspiration of all.

"I know how to stop the (blank) thing!" he crowed.

Opening the stove door, he shoveled a liberal measure of hot ashes from the ashpan and added it to the other applications. As Doc commented dryly when he arrived on the up train, this really "cooked the goose." It had stopped the bleeding, yes. Attempting to cleanse and treat the wound, he found a thick layer of molasses candy, reinforced with hair and dried flour paste, all liberally coated with clotted blood. And unless he could finish the job in the hour between trains, a fifteen-mile hike in prospect! But he had always been able to step lively. Somehow he managed to dig away the accumulations, free, clean, and repair the wound in time to return to Greenville on schedule. The fifteen-mile hike would not have fazed him, but there were patients waiting for him back home.

During his early years as a physician Doc saw all of the growth of Somerset and most of its recession. He was a chief actor, though operating from the wings, when its first calamity struck. One cold night in midwinter he received a rush call to go to Rockwood. Hastily gathering his satchels, he ran to the station just in time to catch the train to Somerset. On the way up he discovered that he had no rope to tie the satchels together in order to toss one over on his back and let the other hang in front. Without the freedom of his hands, to clap them together or burrow them into his pockets, it would be a cold five-mile hike indeed from Somerset to Rockwood. He decided to stop at the Somerset House and borrow a rope. The clerk was asleep at the counter. "Wa-wazzat?" He roused and blinked. "A—a rope?" Sure, he would be glad to lend a rope and procured a small one from under the counter. Doc left him wide awake and started on his sub-zero hike.

About a mile from Somerset he looked back and saw a

strange light in the sky. A fire somewhere, he thought. But his call was urgent, and he went on. The sky was still lurid during his return trip. Sure now that it portended disaster, he hurried, covering the five miles almost at a run. Arrived at Somerset, he found the hotel a smoldering ruin. Soon after he left, the clerk had opened the cellar door planning to replenish the furnace with fuel. He had been greeted by a burst of flame. Shouting, he had rushed up the stairs and roused the inmates. Most of them had been forced to jump out the windows in their night clothes. Since the building was lined with Southern pine, it had exploded into flame like gunpowder. Mr. Poland, the stationmaster, who had just been married, had lost all his wedding gifts. But such small tragedies, even the loss of the hotel, were minor disasters compared with the deaths which had almost resulted. And Doc was credited with a heroic role in preventing this greater holocaust. Had he not wakened the clerk when he did, the fire might well have worked up the partitions without being discovered and many of the occupants perished.

There were other ways for a doctor to save lives, it seemed, than by dosing or cutting people open or trying to piece them together!

. 2 .

THE CHILD SCOOTCHED on the kitchen floor and peered with awed fascination into the gaping black satchel. Big enough certainly to hold a baby! Was it in this bag that the doctor had brought her big brother, Walford Henry Budden, on that snowy, blowy Saturday night in March, 1906, the very first baby, her parents boasted, that he had brought to anybody in Greenville? She had heard her father tell about it, how he had given Doc his supper be-

cause Mother had been in bed, and afterward Doc had
read *The Call of the Wild* while he waited. Only, if he
had the baby here in the bag, why did he have to wait?
Why couldn't he have just taken it out? Was it asleep,
maybe, and he didn't want to wake it up? Now Brother
was sick, and Doc had come again. To take him away, as
he had brought him? At least he couldn't get him back in
the bag!

She stared entranced at the spreading racks, all climbing up like steps and all filled with little bottles of pills
in the loveliest rainbow colors. She reached out a grimy
finger and touched one of them, pink, like the candy beads
on a birthday cake.

"Well, well, what's this? Going to have some help, am
I, dosing my patient?"

"Erma!" It was Mother's voice, shocked, rebuking. "You
know you've been taught not to meddle. What will the
doctor think?"

Squelched but curious, she raised her head to find out.
To her surprise the gray eyes not far above her own were
twinkling. The doctor took one of the bottles, removed
two beautiful pink pills, and held them out.

"What are they for?" she asked suspiciously.

The eyes twinkled even more brightly. "For your dirty
hands."

She giggled, took them, and popped one into her mouth.
It tasted sweet, like candy.

The doctor turned briskly to her mother. "The boy
will be fine. Just a stomach upset. Nothing to worry about."

The child sighed happily. Everything would be all right
now that the doctor was here. She followed him and the
black bag to the door like an adoring puppy.

But juvenile interest in his medical appurtenances was
one thing. Meddling was quite another. On another occasion a little boy employed fingers as well as eyes in his

investigations. Though his mother admonished him to leave the bag alone, he still persisted.

"Do you have anything in that bag for a naughty boy?" she asked in desperation.

"No," snapped Doc. "But I could find something pretty quick in the woodshed."

Little Erma Budden was not the only child in town who found a sense of security and well being in the presence of the little doctor. In spite of his abrupt manner he had a way with children. Another who became his staunch devotee was young Ella Gerrish.

One day Doc followed her to the door and patted the small bony shoulder. "Good girl! You didn't cry. Some of these kids just whoop and holler all over the place."

Lips tight together, Ella nodded. Cry over the extraction of a baby tooth? Hastily she took off for home to do just that. But she returned. For some reason the Pritham house, with its human combination which in later years she was to dub affectionately "the odd couple," held a peculiar fascination for the child, the growing girl, the adolescent. Perhaps it was the attraction of baby Carroll or the dry unsmiling wit of Doc or the gentle humor and quiet confidence of Sadie which drew her, or just the delightful informality of the house itself; but Ella Gerrish came to spend almost as much time in the Pritham home as in her own. Later, as an adult, she was to marvel at their complete courtesy and forbearance, for, though she must at times have been a nuisance, there was never any indication that she was not welcome. She was never treated as "company," but with all the naturalness of a member of the family. Indeed, for Sadie she must have filled the need, in some measure, of the daughter she would never have.

Slowly and quietly Sadie made her adjustment to the new life: the draughty house, the uncertain routine of a doctor's life, the unholy rowdiness of the frontier lum-

bering town. The latter was perhaps the most difficult.
With Doc out on cases many nights, often all night, she
would lie tense and wide awake, listening to sounds of
drunken carousing in the streets outside. In winter when
the small Carroll would toddle gleefully to the window at
the jangling of bells signaling the daily arrival of the Lily
Bay stage, she would run as if in the vain hope of shelter-
ing him from the sight of a sled full of rough lumberers
always likely to erupt in explosive arguments and flash-
ing knives. Some of Doc's office patients—burly men with
black eyes and slashed cheeks, boys with painful welts derived from rock-packed snowballs—set her nerves quivering. See her innocent Carroll reared amid such dangers
and temptations?

But, Janus-like, the town's face was as pious as it was
rowdy. In the small Methodist Church next door, of whose
"Willing Workers" she soon became an active member,
and in the neighborhood groups which welcomed her, she
found kindred spirits as staunchly chaste and upright as
the square, austere houses they inhabited. There were
the Walter Gerrishes, parents of Ella. Walter, a pillar of
the church as sturdy as the stout walls of the houses he
built, could write poems and spin yarns with the same
skill that he could wield a hammer, and with the same
clean rectitude. There were the Carters, who lived next
door, parents of a promising boy, Manfred. Effie Carter,
wife of the taxidermist, soon became a bosom friend of
Sadie's. There were Mrs. Allen, Mrs. Potter, Mary Mc-
Clure, Mrs. Buck. But of all her new friends none was
kinder or more compatible than Mrs. Newall Miles, one
of the Indian family of Capinos, who took her strawber-
rying, picnicking, exploring, and rendered all kinds of
hospitable services. Sadie neighbored with them all in
the little free time she could wrest from the demands of
house, office, and new baby.

Not all of her adjustment was to the world outside. There were quirks and vagaries of her husband's personality which would have strained the adaptability of the most amenable of women. Not the easiest process, adjusting oneself to the habits of a man who retired with the twilight (when possible) and rose with or prior to the sun; who liked his food served without salt and neither sweet nor sour, cold nor hot; who spurned tea and coffee (happily also liquor and tobacco); who could make johnnycake, gingerbread, and biscuits as well as or better than his bride; who seldom displayed by expression what he was thinking and, though possessed of a vast sense of humor, almost never laughed aloud! To say nothing of professional liabilities; that the telephone was constantly ringing, that the house was a public clearing place for petty ills and major tragedies, and that one's husband was often a hundred miles away in the wilderness when one wanted and needed him most! But, being the sort of person who "took what came," she accepted both assets and liabilities, resigned herself to the fact that she must either go to most places alone or not at all, and developed a pragmatic philosophy which would serve her well for the next seven decades.

"I don't plan," she expressed it once cheerfully. "I just live."

Adjustment included involvement in Doc's favorite medium of recreation. Her initiation into the art of gunning was not propitious. Soon after their marriage he took her down the railroad tracks to a gravel pit where he set up a target for her. She was not proficient as a marksman. Suddenly as she swung the heavy gun around, it went off accidentally, hitting a spot not far from where Doc was standing. Without a word Sadie dropped the gun and started home. Sometime later Doc came in carrying both guns. He likewise made no comment. Only years later did Sadie give vent to her emotion: "Why, I might have shot my husband's legs off!" But she grimly persisted until in time she became an adequate, if not skillful, hunter. She knew she had better! It was one of the few forms of recreation they would have a chance to pursue together.

For somehow, in spite of his grueling work load, Doc managed hunting trips. He built himself a float and hunted ducks. On long walking treks to visit patients he sometimes carried his gun along with the wicker basket filled with medicines, instruments, and sundries which he wore strapped to his back. And occasionally he found time for a two- or three-day hunting expedition. One of these was in October when his father was visiting him. Perley Redmond had built a double-ended motorboat powered with a three-cylinder Kennebec engine, and he and his father, Will, invited the Pritham men to go hunting in Doughnut Cove to try it out. Anchored in the Cove, they made up a long bed in the boat so that they slept, two headed forward and two aft, legs overlapping.

"I'll wake you in plenty of time," Dad promised. And he did, by scratching a match at least each hour to look at his watch. None of them slept more than a smidgin.

Doc was lucky that day—and unlucky. After an hour's hike he saw a small herd of deer running out of a little depression. He fired nine shots as fast as he could pump the lever. He knocked down two deer and saw hair fly off others, but before he could reload the two jumped up and ran off. Perley heard the shots and came on the run. After looking the gun over, he exclaimed disgustedly, "That box of shells you got yesterday were duds! Look. There's the marks of bullets on trees, with hair on 'em. You were hittin' all right. But those shells don't have power to kill anything!"

Seas were high on the way home, and Doc arrived just in time to attend a confinement. With lack of sleep and rough travel, he was overpowered with drowsiness. Not even in the five sleepless days in Boston had he found it so difficult to keep awake. But somehow he saw the new life safely into the world and snatched a few hours rest. That afternoon he bought a fresh box of shells, fired one of the old ones to prove their decomposition, and disgustedly tossed them into the little pond by the dugout. Then he went up one of Gibson's old lumbering roads and shot a nice deer before dark. But bad shells were not his only gripe. He and Perley continued to lose many deer with their old 38–55-calibre rifles. In 1912 they sold them and bought 33s. Then they found deer where they had shot them.

A much more important purchase that same year was a motorboat. How he had gotten along without one of his own for almost seven years was hard to figure. Certainly by now dependence on others for lake transportation had become intolerable. His new purchase was the initial passenger launch built to run on the New Meadows River in lower Casco Bay. He had it freighted to Greenville on a flatcar and dropped a mooring for it in the West Cove. He also bought a small rowboat from a Harpswell man, a skiff which proved to be a mean thing to handle, always swinging off sideways and, when turned, ramming into the motorboat. Tiring of it, he built a gunning float at St. Germain's shop where he had access to a power saw to shape the planking, setting up a keel and moulds exactly as he had seen Gus Holbrook do. It made a satisfactory tender for the motorboat and was good for hunting ducks and fishing, but too heavy to carry into ponds. For the latter use he subsequently built several lighter floats, under sixty pounds in weight. On occasion he turned one of these bottom up on his head at the dam of Spencer Pond and carried it to the lake two miles away without stopping or removing it.

The motorboat, too, needed improvements. Almost

immediately he had the old four-cylinder motor changed from a make-and-break to a jump-spark. There were sight-feed glasses to feed oil to each cylinder and a gravity drip of sixteen tubes to the crankcase bearings. A full-time job for one man to see that they were all dripping properly! She was called *The Rose,* not the most appropriate of names for a craft which was to travel hundreds of miles through fogs, squalls, mountainous seas, and grinding cakes of ice.

Doc was soon using *The Rose* not only for medical excursions but for taxiing sportsmen, taking friends and family on hunting and fishing trips, transporting such heterogeneous merchandise as deer and lumber and potatoes. One fall the Redmonds had a makeshift hunting camp on Black Sand Island a bit northeast of Moose. Will had planted potatoes on Moose Island and as he dug them, Doc would take a boatful of lumber for the camp and bring a load of potatoes back to Greenville. Dad had come up to help dig and sack them, incidentally to try his luck again at hunting. But as usual luck was against him. Though he and Will tented at the camp and deer came into the potato field each night to help harvest the crop, he went home with no game. The next year it was the same. Again Will and Perley took him to the camp on Black Sand, staying all night and starting at daylight to hunt Deer Island. Doc had planned to join them at noon for hunting on Sugar if he could get away, but Dr. Hunt was taking a patient to Boston, and he had to be back home before three. Still a fair-weather hunter, Dad decided to come back with him since it looked rainy. There was an hour left to hunt. Doc landed at the sand beach at the foot of Deer Island and, leaving the end of the Island for Dad to hunt, went across toward the west side. Presently rain began to pour down. Since he was in his shirt sleeves, he ran for the boat. Suddenly just ahead he saw a small deer eating beechnuts under a tree. Swinging his rifle into line, he shot and killed it, quickly tossed it to his shoulders and, curling it around his neck, kept on running. When he reached the steep bank above the boat, he could hear Dad muttering to himself.

"Why in thunder don't that boy come! Might know no one could get a deer in such a rain!"

Ducking his head, Doc pitched the deer down through the trees so that it landed within a few feet of the boat. Immediately Dad changed his tune, became chipper as a cricket. Doc let him steer while he dressed the deer on the way home.

Perhaps it was this interest in hunting which instilled in him an unusual empathy with sportsmen, at times almost exceeding the bounds of legality. Once, for instance, he received a call on Sunday to attend a man at Lily Bay. It was before he owned his own boat, so he got Sam Cole, who lived by the lake, to take him. Arriving at the camp, he found that a young man had accidentally shot himself that morning near Mountain Pond. While fishing on Saturday, it developed, the youth had noticed some beautiful black ducks in the pond. The next day he had taken his gun along, although he was fully aware that Sunday was closed season for hunting. Nearing the pond, he had loaded his gun, then soon after had slipped and fallen. The jar fired the gun and the load lodged in his legs. The business of digging out the shot was long and, for the patient, excruciatingly painful.

A few days later Dave Brown, the warden, came into Doc's office.

"I say, Doc, do young people about twenty ever get a shock?"

Doc was suspicious. The question suggested a sequence of ideas. Wardens—hunters—law-breaking. He pulled down a textbook from his bookcase and proceeded to cite several quotations showing how many became paralyzed at that age. "Why?" he inquired innocently. The warden, it seemed, had seen a young man on a stretcher being put on board the Maine Central train at Rockwood that noon who, he was told, had suffered a shock. "Last Sunday," he added thoughtfully.

Doc's features revealed only an impersonal interest. He made no comment, and the warden, satisfied, left. Good! Doc nodded to himself. No wonder the boy had suffered a nervous shock. Who wouldn't with a charge of shot barging into his leg? And he'd already suffered enough having the stuff dug out without paying the penalty for hunting on Sunday!

But his protective sympathy extended to others than hunters who got themselves in trouble. One day before the telephone service was put on the railroads he came into the Junction on a freight and noticed that the yard was full of trains. As he swung himself down a worried trainman came running up to him. The agent, he said excitedly, was so drunk that he could not read the wire. "And his father's the conductor on the train that's just coming in. You know him, Doc. He's a stickler for all the rules. He'd be sure to have him fired if he found him drunk, even if he is his own son. Can't we do something, Doc—quick?"

Doc did know the young agent, a bright fellow and usually dependable. And he knew the father, a good man but with a conscience that leaned over backward. "Run to the water tank," he snapped, "and bring me a dipper of water."

Digging into his bag, he drew out a bottle of ammonium chloride and poured some into the dipper. The train was in. "Hurry!" urged the young man's friends. It was a short-order treatment, all right. They had no longer than the few minutes it would take the conductor to walk the length of the train. Doc poured the liquid down the dizzy boy's throat. When his father arrived, the young agent was reading the wire and the trains were already beginning to clear the yard. Doc closed his bag and hustled home, leaving the boy's peers to deliver the necessary lecture. He was reasonably sure the misdemeanor would not be repeated.

· 3 ·

DOC BOUGHT ANOTHER HORSE from Ed Moore, brother of the recent preacher. She was a beautiful little sorrel with just one defect. When a colt she had suffered an attack of pneumonia and been badly blistered with a cantharides poultice, which had left an area on her back devoid of hair and covered with very thin skin. Riding in saddle soon made the area sore, and she resented it. But when there was little snow, especially on the Lily Bay tote road, horseback riding was much easier than dragging a pung over the rocks. He bought a McClellan saddle, with a little pommel, comfortable and light, which made his weight as easy for her as possible. She was not only faithful but remarkably intelligent. One wintry day in drawing the pung to Kineo over the ice, she broke through on what seemed to be a good safe crossing place on a wrinkle. Before Doc could jump out to help her, she had climbed out, shaking and dripping. She had learned her lesson well and after that was more cautious.

And Doc certainly blessed the caution on one trip in April! It was when the dam was being built at Ripogenus. In blasting ice with dynamite one of the Italian workmen got caught with too short a fuse. In the explosion he received a broken lower jaw and many cuts about the face. Doc drove to Lily Bay, changed horses and went on to

Kokadjo to get the patient and bring him back to Greenville. Driving back, he found that the man had had nothing to eat since his accident. Arriving at the boarding house at Lily Bay about eight in the evening, Doc decided to stop and try to get his patient some milk. He stabled the horse he had hired and went into the house. Sure enough, there were two pails of milk on the kitchen table, but there was no fire in the cookstove and seemed to be none in the building. Curious to learn why the downstairs was deserted, he went upstairs. There, pacing the hall with a double-barreled shotgun, was the proprietor, a new man from Eustis, while his chore boy, similarly armed, was stationed at the rear stairway.

"What's the matter?" demanded Doc, nonplussed.

"Those r-river d-drivers!" stuttered the terrified proprietor. He shivered at the sound of an ear-splitting yell. "H-hear them? There's s-seventy-five of 'em! I dassen't leave my wife alone a minute!"

Doc was both amused and disgusted. Of course the drivers were having the time of their lives upstairs, laughing their heads off at the frightened imbecile. Doc tried to assure him that he was in the safest place on earth, but to no avail. He was not going to relax a minute "until them drivers left." But of course they could have the milk. Take the whole of it. Doc took a big dipperful to the injured man, who managed to get it down while Doc hitched his own horse to the pung.

They drove down on the sandbar above the wharf, and the horse bravely waded in until the breastplate was under water, then reared up and jumped on the ice, dragging the pung after her. There was rotten ice at the Thoroughfare, but they managed to pass it safely. Down at Burntjacket wrinkle there was a flooded strip about sixty feet wide along the fold of ice. By this time it was pitch-dark. The horse waded in almost to the seam, then backed up and followed alongside the opening for sixty or seventy yards, then went in again and crossed. She seemed to sense when the ice weakened beneath her. Doc had not touched the reins since leaving Lily Bay. Threaded through the hole in the dash and buckled there, they had lain slack all the time.

The little sorrel followed the trail along the ice to the point of Burntjacket where there was a large rock offshore about which the ice always melted early. The road passed outside of it, but the horse left the road and went on the shore side of the hole, picking her way so close to it that open water gaped black in the circle of lantern light just beyond the runners. The injured man was frightened almost out of his wits and, though unable to talk with his broken jaw, expressed volumes of expletives merely by swinging his arms. Doc did not touch the reins. They arrived in Greenville safely. When the toters went up the next morning, they found fifty feet of open water in the road which the little horse had bypassed at midnight!

· 4 ·

"I wish I could ride horseback," young Ella Gerrish once remarked wistfully.

Sometime later, on a rather rainy day, Doc rode into the Gerrish yard, threw the reins over the horse's head, and came up to the door. "Here's the horse," he told Ella. "You said you'd like to take a ride." While she stood staring, he turned and went down the steps, then turned again. "If she should put her head down to eat grass beside the road, let go of the reins, or she may pull you right over her head."

Ella had never been on a horse. She knew only that you faced the ears. She put on a poncho, climbed timorously on the sleek back, doggedly clutched the reins, and, petrified, started up through the main street. Sure enough! At the foot of the hill the horse saw a nice green patch of grass and, regardless of her frantic remonstrances, put her head down and began feeding. Fortunately Ella let go of the reins in time. Just when she thought she was marooned there forever, a man she knew came down the hill. "Do you have a self-starter?" she asked with apparent coolness. Retrieving the reins, he put them back in her hands and headed her up the road. Still petrified, she managed to reach the top of the hill without further side trips. Already she had had more than enough. But—give Doc a chance to chuckle over her cowardice ("Back pretty quick, ain't you? Thought you wanted to ride horseback!"). She steered the horse into the driveway of a friend, descended gingerly, and went into the house for a call, spending enough time to give the impression of having taken a long ride. Mounting again, she managed to get back down the hill and turned into the doctor's driveway. I'll just tell him I've brought the horse back, she decided, and he can put her where she belongs. But the animal was as strong-minded as her master. She was accustomed to going straight into the barn, and into the barn she went. The door was low. Ella ducked just in time to keep her head intact. It was the last time she expressed an idle wish in the doctor's hearing.

But such evidence of a certain brusque callousness by no means diminished her youthful hero worship. Indeed, she felt a jealous proprietorship in the Pritham household and a personal affront at the slightest suspicion of criticism. For instance, one evening she went with her parents to an official Board meeting at the church. Doc was church treasurer, a post to which he was appointed in 1913 and which he was to occupy for at least fifty-seven years. Among the items in his report was a payment for retired preachers. With poker-faced sobriety Doc read off the amount he had dispatched for "dilapidated ministers." The pastor, Cyprian Bryant, burst into a roar of laughter in which most of the assembly, with slightly more Yankee restraint, joined. Ella, believing they were making fun of her doctor, remained highly indignant until later when she heard the minister himself making the pun with great relish.

She was not the only child in town with a keen loyalty to the little doctor. Perhaps it was his unimpressiveness in size which gave confidence to his younger patients, together with that low couch on which it was easy for a young child to jump. Or perhaps the sight of him lustily blowing his horn in one of the two bands, first at the Village, then in the new one formed in 1910 at the Junction, jauntily marching in parades on Memorial Day and the Fourth of July, made him seem like one of themselves, not much bigger and certainly no less lively and adventurous. But it was not until the smallpox scare in 1911 that Doc discovered to his surprise just how popular he had become with the younger set.

Smallpox, like typhoid, was always an imminent peril. Infection in the lumber camps, where men were crowded together from far and near, many having crossed the border from Canada where there were outbreaks of the disease nearly all the year, could quickly swell to epidemic proportions. And this year many cases were being reported throughout the state. Constantly on the watch for signs, Doc diagnosed the illness of a trainman named Taylor as smallpox.

"But it can't be, Doc. Why, not many years ago I nursed a crowd of men who had it, terrible, thirty-six of 'em died, and I never come down with it. And all I did was go into this house in Wytopitlock after a pail of water two weeks ago when my train was stopped on a siding there. I tell you, Doc, I'm immune!"

"Can't help it, you've got it," snapped Doc. "And I have to quarantine you."

Cheerfully the man agreed, and Doc sent to Augusta for

vaccine. Alarmed, the town fathers ordered wholesale vaccination. The doctors were to have the vaccine furnished to them and be paid fifty cents per person for performing the job. As usual, supplies were slow in coming, and by the time they arrived Taylor's son had come down with the disease. "Well," the man admitted, "guess I must have had it."

When the vaccine finally arrived, Dr. Hunt characteristically assumed direction of the campaign for immunization. "It's your duty to go at once to the stricken family and vaccinate them," he told Doc, "since they're your patients. Meanwhile we'll get things started here."

And get all the credit, as well as the preponderance of half dollars, thought Doc with grim amusement as he departed to do his "duty." Meanwhile, as he expected, the senior doctor, with young Dr. Bryant, a physician then in town, went posthaste to the big school building, which contained the largest assembly of prospective victims, and started vaccinating. However, when the first room of pupils were ordered to roll up their sleeves, one small boy, John Owens, raised his hand.

"Aren't we allowed to choose our own doctor?" he inquired. Yes, Dr. Hunt admitted, they did have such a privilege. "Then I'm going to have Doc Pritham vaccinate me."

Returning home from his humble mission, Doc found his yard full of enthusiastic children all waiting to be vaccinated. When the epidemic was over, he had vaccinated over twice as many as the other two doctors together.

One balmy October day in the following year Doc received a telegram from the Canadian Pacific Railway reporting that a man had come out from Del Wood's camp on Brassua and stopped at their Tarratine section house, then boarded a train for Megantic, where he had been diagnosed as having smallpox. Happily the "Mixed" was at that moment in the station. Grabbing vaccine and disinfectants, Doc ran to the station and caught the train for Tarratine, where he vaccinated all exposed persons, then went down to the lake, disinfected the camp, and vaccinated the crew. He returned on the late afternoon freight and sent a report both to the railroad and to the state health department. The latter, while complimenting him for the quick service rendered, regretted that, since the trip had not been sanctioned by the department, he could not be recompensed for the job. This was the law. Doc was disgusted. What would they have liked him to do? Wire Augusta and wait a day so he could be paid for doing a too-late job and run the risk of a major epidemic? The fact that the department shortly corrected the injustice by appointing him a sort of deputy, so that in case of a similar emergency he could act at once and receive ten dollars a day for his time, did little to temper his disgust. Not that he cared a hoot about the money. It was just another instance of infernal delay caused by unnecessary rules and regulations. Your patients could die while you were trying, Houdini-like, to get your hands free of red tape!

But that year of 1912 yielded far more satisfaction than frustration. Teddy Roosevelt with his new party was not the only one to go "Progressive." For one thing Doc bought his first car and built a little garage for it. Summers were hard on a horse. It was hot and dusty. Flies tormented the poor animal. When idle, she was likely to drag the hitch weight and graze on someone's lawn to the detriment of public relations. Now she could be put out to pasture on Moose Island all summer and return in the fall fat as a butter ball.

The new acquisition was a second-hand Duryea bought by mail from a man in Pennsylvania. One of the high-wheeler horseless buggies, it was astonishingly simple in mechanism, with a two-cylinder engine, air-cooled, no radiator, no piping, no gear shift. The engine had a telescopic shaft. On each side of it was a roller, perhaps six inches across, that meshed into a three-foot ring on the wheels, which were about five feet in diameter. When you shoved the engine ahead, the flanges on the axle would come up and make contact with the wheel. Also, on the outside of the shaft was a little flanged wheel. When you telescoped the shaft and shoved the engine ahead and this little flange made contact, that little bit of wheel on a three-foot ring gave you tremendous power. In fact, salesmen of these cars would demonstrate their power by running them up and over the highest pile of logs they could find. And its power was equally impressive on its kickback. One day when Doc was cranking it in front of the "Push and Pull," it backfired and threw the crank completely over the four-story building. A boy came running around the hotel from the farther side, carrying it. While its hard rubber tires, jouncing over the rocks and ruts of tote roads, rattled teeth as well as cylinders, the car got places with expedition and economy. Doc could run it all summer for five dollars' worth of gas. Because of its popping pistons the boys in town dubbed it the "peanut roaster."

. 5 .

BUT THE NEW CAR was a minor blessing compared with another of the year's developments. Hollingsworth and Whitney, one of the big lumber companies, had erected a Y.M.C.A. building on the lake front at West Cove, close to the CP railroad station. It was opened in December of 1912 and was a genuine addition to the life of the town. There was a bowling alley in the basement, a hall for entertainments, lectures, movies on the first floor. The second floor contained rooms for the boarding lumbermen.

But there was also a third floor. Doctors Hunt and Pritham
had an inspiration: Why not use it for a hospital? With
the cooperation of the lumber company, who realized
its value for their employees, it was done. Dr. Hunt super-
intended the assembling of equipment. When finished
rather crudely, it contained one four-bed ward, six single
rooms, an operating room, and an etherizing room.

The development spelled PROGRESS, in capitals. No
more freezing of patients in the draughty barracks of the
"Push and Pull." No more shipping of appendectomies
to Bangor with risks of ruptures. A head nurse, Bess
Galusha, was soon installed, and several young women,
most of them local girls, were permitted to assist and receive rudimentary training in nursing. The need was soon
justified. Patients came pouring in from the camps with
great cuts, broken limbs, severe illnesses, to say nothing
of the need of a bath, usually remedied under sufferance.
"(Blankety-blank), why should I take a bath now? I never
have before!" If the lumberjack changed his fleece-
lined underwear occasionally, he was a sissy. A bath in
winter was as rare as a breakfast without beans and molasses.

Though the small operating room in the east end was
hardly the latest in equipment and design, it furnished all
the necessities for anything but the most specialized of
operations, even boasted a skylight which, besides letting
in light, often served Dr. Hunt as a convenient target
while putting a cast on some woodsman's broken leg.
Watching the enormous hands rid themselves of surplus
plaster of Paris, landing it unerringly on the panes of
glass with a great slat and flourish, Doc was nostalgically
reminded of old Gus Holbrook and his festoons of eel-
skins in the rafters. Needless to say, the senior doctor's
colleague enjoyed this diversion more than the nurses who
had to climb a tall stepladder to clean up behind him.

The operating room was there, the equipment. But Doc had never performed a major operation in his life. The first appendectomy occurred in 1913, soon after the hospital was opened. The patient was Nellie McDonald. Dr. Walter Hunt was summoned from Bangor to act as surgeon, and Dr. Hiram Hunt gave the ether. Doc assisted. He watched every step of the process with an eagle eye. A short time later a man came in at night in desperate need of immediate relief. It was a man named Williams from Alec Lemieux's crew in a camp about a mile down river from the East Outlet. Fortunately Sam Bigney, a clerk, arrived at the camp that evening and, seeing the man's serious condition, told him to get his coat on. He was taking him to Greenville.

No sending to Bangor for a surgeon this time! And certainly no sending the man there! The job had to be done at once. So of course Doc did it. It was a pus case, and drainage was necessary. The patient made a good recovery, and, remembering his own experience, Doc got him up in an unconventionally short time.

"Weren't you scared?" someone queried later. "Your first major operation?"

The reply was typical. "No. Why? I just went in, saw what needed to be done, and did it."

It was only the beginning. Of necessity Doc soon developed a skill equal to almost any emergency. He had to. Since Dr. Hunt from that time on spent many winters in Florida, Doc was often the only doctor in the whole Moosehead area. Fortunately, in addition to medical knowledge commensurate with that of most other doctors of his day, he possessed boldness, imagination, a vast amount of common sense, and keen ingenuity.

There was the time, for instance, when he removed four inches of a descending colon and was faced with making an end-to-end repair. Since the colon was attached firmly to the side walls, bringing both ends together would stretch it to its limit. How use the least possible lap-over of the cuffs in sewing? Taking two needles, he would pick up a little piece on each side, then cross the threads to opposite sides, tying half a knot with each crossover. The knot prevented any slide of the flesh on the stitch to cause a leaking, and the one layer, instead of the usual two, sealed the opening effectively. Happily there was not the slightest leakage, the incision was closed without drainage, and the patient recovered promptly.

Without any specialized training Doc learned the complicated techniques of X ray. With the nearest radiology department in Bangor, seventy-five miles away, the need was exigent. In 1914 the hotel people at Kineo raised a fund by donation and bought the hospital a little suitcase filled with x-ray equipment. Doc set it up and used it, mastering its mechanism very much as he had conquered the complexities of that first disk harrow. It was quite a trick, he found, to make it respond properly. He had to get the globe a nice green color, which was achieved by discharging the spark onto the antenna. For at least ten years he was the sole x-ray technician in the hospital, taking, developing, and reading all the pictures. Those which he was unable to read to his satisfaction he sent to Bangor.

Like Dr. Hunt with his plaster festoons, Doc exhibited eccentricities in his hospital work, but none necessitated a cleaning-up process. If anything he was too scrupulously neat. When he put a cast on, there was nothing left for the nurses to clean up. He did it all himself. If he spread papers around, he would gather them up, not expect the nurses to do it. If there were dressings to do, he would often come in about six in the morning, take the tray, perform the necessary work, and clean up afterward. He enjoyed working with the young student nurses and had infinite patience with them—provided they did exactly what they were supposed to. In fact, he preferred students to one head nurse who worked with him later and who possessed an independence equal to his own. When she assisted him with dressings and persisted in grabbing the medications and going ahead with the work, there was a verbal if not physical tussle.

Doc—or "F. J.," as Bess Galusha got the doctors and nurses in the habit of calling him—was as independent in surgery as at the bedside. He abhorred the rubber gloves available at the period, heavy and cumbersome. Instead, after scrubbing he would use a hand lotion somewhat resembling shellac. It never slipped off, never tore. Dandy, he maintained. You could keep your hands covered all the time you were working, and when you got through just take 20-Mule Team borax, rub your hands together with some water, and you were through with it. He often carried it in his pack for emergency operations in the wilds. He never wore a mask, but he saw to it that there were no germs flying about in his vicinity. He never sneezed. He kept his mouth shut. If anyone tried to start a conversation, he would be ignored. But he always kept his cap on. If he forgot, the nurses would remind him and put it on for him. Very often, in these days before adjustable tables, he stood on a stool to operate. And his motions were so swift that only the most efficient of nurses could keep pace with him.

"His operations were wonderful to see," marveled Henrietta Bigney, one of the early students in the Y.M.C.A. Hospital who, having graduated as R.N. from a school in Philadelphia, had wide experience elsewhere. "I never knew anybody who could keep a sterile field and use as few tools as Doc. He would perform a whole operation with only two or three sponges. His appendectomies were something to behold. He would make such a small incision on a boy that, later, when he went into the service, he would have to write back to verify that he had really had an appendectomy, there was so little scar."

Henrietta, a niece of Dr. Hunt, had occasion to observe Doc at work amid other environs than the neat and sterile operating room. One night when she was at home in the winter visiting her family, he called her on the telephone. As usual, he was as economical of words as of tools and sponges.

"Meet me at the Junction at midnight. Emergency. We're going to Brassua."

She went. They rode on the midnight train to Somerset and started the trek up the Maine Central railroad tracks to Rockwood. Fortunately it was bright moonlight, but, unfortunately, bitter cold. Doc let Henrietta set the pace. It was an eerie, glittering night. The woods were full of slinking shadows. Earth was frozen solid. Even the stars looked brittle. It would have been hard walking even in daylight. The railroad ties, too close for a single step, too far apart to cover two at once, were compacted hubbles of ice and snow. She soon realized that she had started off too briskly, but refused to lower her pace. She was young and healthy, used to the outdoors. Grimly she set one foot ahead of the other, stumbling occasionally, breathing hard, wondering how Doc could keep his wind sufficiently to spin a duck-hunting yarn about her ears. When she saw a mile signpost looming ghostlike beside the track, she felt infinite relief.

"There!" she threw back gaily. "We're doing all right. Only another mile to Rockwood!"

"Hardly. Hate to disappoint you. We're a mile from Somerset, not Rockwood."

Henrietta choked. "H-how far—"

"We've come one mile. About five more to go."

After that Doc moved ahead and set the pace, with an easy rhythmic lope that somehow made the going less difficult. Shoulders thrust slightly forward, reed knapsack strapped across his back, he looked a little like a gnome conjured out of the moonlight. His feet seemed to sense just where to step, on the ties, between them, on again, and she adjusted her own to their rhythm. "We're ninety-nine miles from home, we're ninety-nine miles from home . . ." Soundlessly she accented the words of the old ditty as she moved one foot ahead of the other. Only they didn't "walk a mile and then rest awhile." They kept on and on.

Another milestone . . . and another. They must be half-way there.

"Are you hungry?" asked Doc in the midst of another hunting story.

"Oh—yes!" Wonderful, she thought. We're going to stop somewhere for a lunch. Perhaps there was a camp near by. Her throat felt as if she had swallowed a mouthful of thistles. Something hot—and wet—!

He handed her back a cold biscuit. She took it, held it, regarded it with profound distaste. A handful of gravel would have been as easy to swallow. She lifted her hand to throw it away.

"Don't do that! If you don't want it, give it back. I may need it before I get home."

They went on. Her cheeks stung, her eyes ran. Her legs felt like lifeless stilts. Her arms and hands grew numb, even with the latter doubled inside her mittens. "Swing 'em," ordered Doc, startling her with his intuition. "Swing 'em hard!" Every breath was painful, rasping through her throat, constricting her lungs, absorbing the coldness into every fiber of her body. But somehow, step after crunching step, the miles were covered.

They arrived in Rockwood, where a truck was waiting. It drove them six or eight miles, as far as the tote road was passable for a truck, to one of the lumber camps. Though it was only about four in the morning, to Henrietta's surprise everybody was up. The daughters of the Frenchman who owned the camp were already cooking breakfast. The warmth, the smells of coffee, frying pork, hot beans, and corn bread were as soporific as they were tantalizing. After a quick breakfast Henrietta would gladly have curled up on the floor behind the stove and slept.

But the journey was not over. She was bundled into a huge fur coat and deposited in a pung. For some reason Doc rode in another, behind her. They started for another camp, their destination, perhaps ten miles further on. The coat felt stiff as a board, but it was warm and she could easily have slept; in fact, did, only to be sharply roused every time the pung ran over a little thank-you-ma'am, which was often. Then the horse would walk away from the thills, and the haywire fastening them together would snap. They reached their destination about six in the morning.

"Go right up to the office," directed Doc. "The patient's there. I'll be along soon."

Someone pointed out a path and a building, and she groped her way to it. It was even darker here than on the track, for the moon had set. She pushed open a door and was embarrassed to find herself stumbling into a dimly lit room crowded with people. A priest was there, intoning a mass, which her awkward entrance interrupted. But with Doc's arrival she became instantly the trained nurse. She went with him to the bunk where the patient was lying, watched attentively while he examined.

"Can't be moved," he pronounced tersely. "Appendix might rupture. Can't be prepped, either. You get the ether ready while I get the stuff boiled up."

He went to the cook's camp and presently returned carrying two pie plates, one over the other, in which he had boiled his instruments. Henrietta knew the procedure, for she had heard of other such emergency operations in just such camps. One of the pie plates would hold his instruments, the other his sterile goods, a meager supply of the latter, no more than a couple of small sheets. Instruments also were at a minimum, fewer even than he used in the hospital. The little leather kit which he used for wilderness cases like these was not much bigger than a manicure case. It contained pinch forceps, needle holder, catheter, scissors, artery clamp, and six knives. There was a flap for needles and suture materials. Sterile pads were individually wrapped. There was an additional forceps for removing teeth.

Henrietta was appalled. How on earth could he operate under such conditions! No table! The narrow space between a bottom and a top bunk! Almost no light! But obediently she administered anesthetic, watched while Doc hung a lantern at the head of the bunk, meticulously scrubbed with steaming water and strong soap in a tin washbasin, and, using his head mirror as a reflector, performed the operation. It was indeed an emergency. Had the patient been moved, even to a table, the appendix would surely have ruptured. It was as neat and sterile an operation as could have been performed back at the hospital. Henrietta remained to care for the patient for several days, and he made a quick and complete recovery.

Doc left for Greenville directly after the operation to attend some other urgent cases. How did he get there, she wondered. Walk?

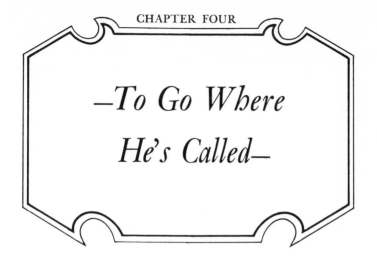

CHAPTER FOUR

—To Go Where He's Called—

. 1 .

IT WAS DOUBTLESS a groundless rumor which attributed to Doc the old gag that the Greenville population increase was the fault of the CP railroad, whose two and four A.M. trains with their piercing whistles roused inhabitants from sleep. But certainly the preponderance of successful births could be credited to his skillful techniques of delivery. For thirty-five consecutive years he registered the most births at the town clerk's office of any doctor in town, though only about sixteen hundred in all, for Greenville was a small town.

One Sunday morning a frantic call came in to attend a confinement at Rockwood. An elderly doctor from Massachusetts, who was hunting in the vicinity, had been per-

suaded to come in during the night and attend the patient
in labor. But he had brought no tools with him, and by
nine o'clock, when the telephone station opened, the situation was desperate. When Doc arrived at noon not even
the most pessimistic professor could have labeled a forceps
job an "untimely" or "meddlesome" interference. The
patient was completely exhausted.

"Good!" thought Doc. "This man has had years of experience, and these difficult cases are his specialty. I can
learn a lot by watching him."

But the visitor refused to do the job. "You go ahead.
I'll give the ether."

Fortunately Doc had a strong arm, well developed from
cranking the old boat motor all over the lake. He needed
it. He put all the strain he dared on the forceps, bending
the handles at least an inch and a half out of line when he
pulled down on the middle portion for axis-traction, without breaking them at the fenestra. The baby, a fat twelve-
pounder, had been dead for days, so long that the skin was
peeling.

After the successful delivery the visiting doctor took the
forceps and, getting a purchase by hooking it into the
stove, tried to bend it. He was unable to budge it by the
fraction of an inch.

"Seems to be the ordinary standard make," he remarked,
passing it back.

"Yes," said Doc. "Bought it from George Frye in Portland in 1904."

The visitor smiled ruefully. "Lucky for the patient I
didn't try to use it! Of all the hundreds of forceps I've
seen used, I never before saw one bent like so much whale-
bone!"

But more often the problem of successful delivery was
not so much getting the job done properly as getting there
to do it. The travel demanded of the doctor was sometimes
far more difficult than the travail of the patient.

The winters, in fact the whole years, in the early teens were unusually cold. Even in late June, nights were sometimes so frigid that ice froze on the shores of the lake. In winter temperatures often plummeted to minus forty, with gales of hurricane force. The snow blown by such winds would pack so hard that the horse's hoofs would leave barely a mark, and the roads were traveled just as the winds made them until a thaw came in the spring, when a rutting machine would be used to plow them down, so that it would be easier to stay on them. Many times in driving along the road in late April one would notice fence posts beginning to pop in sight, and one would dread the warmer days when the horses would flounder and slump to their bellies.

One of these very cold nights in winter a call came to attend a confinement at Rockwood and to bring along a nurse. Mary Cotier, head nurse at the Y hospital, agreed to go. The snow was so deep that the horse could only walk. Must be handy to fifty below, thought Doc when they were off Sandbar. And since it would be thirty-six below on land the next morning, this was not a bad guess. Accustomed to facing such weather, he had little trouble, but poor Mary found it intolerable. Wrapping herself in the spare buffalo robe, she crouched on the floor with her back against the dashboard. They were seven hours driving to the patient's house on the river, and when they arrived, the horse was dripping sweat. There was no barn available, but an elderly man volunteered to take the team back a half mile and stable it for the night. Reluctantly Doc relinquished the responsibility, for he was needed at the house. He delivered the baby, rested a few hours, left Mary to stay with the patient for a few days, and went to pick up his horse.

Judas priest! He exploded in anger and consternation. The old man had put the warm animal in a big empty barn where it was cold as out of doors, and there were icicles six inches long hanging on her belly. She was shivering so violently that she shook the stall. And right beside the barn there was another building containing cattle and sheep, where she could have been kept warm! Never again would he let her out of his sight without knowing where she would spend the night, no, not if the patient had to wait! He hastily hitched her to the pung, putting the harness outside the blanket, and drove her ten miles to Deer Island. Here he put her in a barn beside the cows and fed her a breakfast of warm bran mush because she always suffered from swelling gums after a hard trip. Once, after driving from Kokadjo to Grant Farm and home again, over forty miles, it was a week before her mouth resumed its normal condition.

He was far more thoughtful of his horse than of himself on such trips, and as considerate of other horses as of his own—yes, even of such ornery beasts as "Old Switch Tail." She was a peculiar animal that would go about a mile, stop, and violently switch her tail. If you slapped her with the reins or touched her with the whip, your ride was ended. You would walk back and get another horse.

One day Doc had to change horses at Lily Bay on a trip to Upper Soper Brook. Henry Bartley happened to be there, directing the hauling of supplies into one of the camps. Knowing Doc's way with horses, he ordered the hostler to give him "Old Switch Tail," the fastest horse in the barn—if one could handle him. Doc could. When the impasse occurred, he just sat still and waited . . . and waited. Finally the animal gazed back at him reproachfully, took a long look up the road, and struck off into a swinging trot much like a moose running. There was no letup, either up hill or down, even when they came to the steep inclines of Sias Hill. She took him straight to the Grant Farm barn door, sixteen miles of steady trot.

Far from being a farm in the ordinary sense of the word,

Grant Farm was a thriving community, a center for logging operations, and hub of a telephone network whose hundreds of miles of wire connected more than a hundred phones, all in use during a busy winter. In 1841 it had been a long log cabin built by Thomas Grant, an explorer for "pumpkin pine," but in 1853 it had boasted a barn which Thoreau described as "the biggest ox-nest in the woods, fifty feet by a hundred." In its heyday over a hundred horses were often kept there during lumbering operations. Since 1901 it had been the property of the Great Northern Paper Company, which had enlarged its big boarding house and added numerous other buildings. Situated on a bold flank of hillside at the foot of Ragged Lake, it commanded a wide panorama of Maine wilderness.

Doc stopped only long enough to refresh his soul with the splendor of snow-capped Katahdin, see that "Old Switch Tail" was comfortably stalled, and find another team. Someone had forgotten to order a horse for him, and none was left for hire. However, a span belonging to Mr. Flowers was there, and though Flowers had driven them to camps on Gero Island and back that morning—fifty-five miles—Doc took them and started out. He drove them into Number 4 Camp, told the hostler there to give them food and a good rest, then walked the four or five miles into Number 5, his destination. Returning, he found them well rested and, in Yankee lingo, "rarin' to go." He hitched them up and started back, letting the reins lie slack. The horses kept looking back at him, then they would look at each other, trot a little, then repeat the process. Finding they received no orders, they finally looked straight ahead and struck into a long swinging trot. Click, clack, click, clack . . . up hill and down, they never changed pace. As they went up the little ramp to the barn at Grant Farm, the hostler looked out the door.

"How do ye do it?" he marveled. "Them horses look as if they'd only been out for a half-hour's workout. Ears up, eyes bright, heads high. Pranced up smart, yet they've been a hundred and twenty-five miles today. I ask ye, *how?*"

"Easy," replied Doc, hitching up "Old Switch Tail." "Just treat 'em decent. Anybody could do it."

But, as he well knew, everybody didn't. There was another doctor who had hired a horse at Grant Farm and driven it to Gero Island and back, sixty miles, without even a drink of water, yes, and made it carry two people instead of one. But it was the last time he would hire a horse from the Great Northern, and probably the last time he would attend a case in the area, for he was reported to have said to the patient: "I can't do a thing for you. One hundred and ten dollars, please."

One April day Doc was called to Frenchtown for a confinement. He was to go in from Lily Bay, breaking his own trail through the woods and burnt land for eight miles to the farm which was back of Number 4 Mountain on the west shore of First Roach Pond. The trip could best be made in the saddle, so he borrowed a woods horse from a neighbor and started. This time he almost lost patience. He could stand a balky animal better than a plodder. Even on the good tote road this creature dawdled, and when it came to wading in the snow and mud, making their own trail, he barely moved. However, Doc reached the farm in plenty of time. Now delivery proceeded at almost as slow a pace as the horse. In late afternoon a high wind rose and blew down the telephone lines. But before they were completely isolated from the world a call came through that two of the drivers on Misery had been blown up and were being taken to the Y.M.C.A. Hospital. Then all went dead.

Doc paced the floor. He was the only doctor available

to attend these men, and here he was, like Sheridan at the battle of Winchester, over "twenty miles away!" What was a doctor's first duty, to bring life into the world, or keep life from going out of it? Fortunately he had no choice. This woman was his patient. By nine o'clock that evening she had completed dilation and was as tired of waiting as he was. He boiled up forceps, finished the business satisfactorily, and was through at ten. The old horse was saddled.

"At least have a cup of hot tea before you go," urged the farm family. "It will keep you awake."

It did. It also made him perspire so freely that, with the high wind and slow travel, he was soon shivering with cold. The footing was so poor that he could not get off and walk. By the time they had ploughed through the eight miles to the tote road he was nearly frozen. But here, happily, he could get off and run to keep warm. It was six in the morning when he crossed the little brook above the veneer mill. Stopping at the house just long enough for a bit of breakfast, he rushed to the hospital.

He was needed there, all right! Some of the drivers, it developed, had amused themselves by lighting grass fires and sitting near them as they ate lunch. A box of over sixty detonators had ignited. Thousands of pieces of brass had been blown into, some of them through, these men. Doc dug at them until he was so fagged and sleepy he could not hold his eyes open; then returned home for a short nap before starting again. It took him several days to remove all the fragments. There was no danger of missing any, for even the tiniest bit of brass formed a greenish pus, making it easy to detect. He used an eye spud for the job, making it possible to remove every piece without enlarging the entrance hole.

It was in 1914 that Doc was faced with another confinement case, and the travel required was no farther than his own home. In the spring of that year Sadie was expecting her second child.

She had long since adjusted to the new life. After Carroll's birth her sister Hallie had come to live with her for a time, working in Carleton's store, trimming and selling hats. Though she had returned later to Freeport, her presence had made Greenville seem even more like home. Then, after their mother's death, Sadie's sister Viola had come to live with her at age eighteen, working as a cashier in Crafts' store, and almost immediately Perley Redmond had become her devoted suitor. Now, the following June, they were planning to be married.

"Wait until September," begged Sadie, "and we'll give you a real wedding."

But Viola had no wish for a "real" wedding. She wanted to be married in June, the month of brides, and to have a simple ceremony at the minister's. Then they would move in for a time with Perley's parents. Apparently she was not even anxious to have members of the family attend the wedding, for she chose June 10, perilously close to the date of Sadie's expected confinement.

But Sadie was there. Not with Doc, however. He was too busy with patients to take her. One of the neighbors who had a car drove her to the parsonage. She witnessed the ceremony with mingled emotions, surprise that her baby sister, twelve years her junior, had reached marriageable age, regret that she was losing her, relief that she was yielding her to the care of a mature, reliable friend of the family, well able to care for her through his varying skills as guide, boat repairman, expert mechanic. A few hours later, and Sadie would not have been there. For the following night, the 11th, her son, Howard, was born.

It was a normal and fairly easy birth. Doc delivered. Did he have any reluctance or qualms about attending his own wife? No. Why should he? True, it wasn't the usual thing. But if a doctor could run at the beck and call of all creation and then balk at serving his own family, what good was he?

. 2 .

IN 1912 a trip to Chesuncook Village was a small odyssey. There were no passable roads yet on the east side of Moosehead, only the old tote road to Lily Bay. Ten years later Doc could go by car to the foot of Chesuncook Lake, then sixteen miles up the lake by boat to the Village, for already the Great Northern was in the process of cutting a road through the wilderness, piecemeal, to Ripogenus. But now, when he received a call to attend at Chesuncook in June, he took the usual means of travel, steamboat to Northeast Carry and canoes down the Penobscot River.

At Rockwood he joined the rest of the passengers for dinner at the Rockwood Hotel while the boat loaded cargo from the Maine Central noon train. The meal was both meager and unpalatable. Perhaps the cook had overslept or his fire had refused to burn, but the roast veal came to their plates half cooked. Always blessed with a good appetite, Doc ate his whole portion, then proceeded with other unsatisfied passengers to the store, supplementing the insufficient fare with not-too-ripe bananas.

At the Carry he made the mile trek to the river, having secured a good guide and a canoe. The wilderness along the West Branch of the Penobscot had changed little since Thoreau had made the trip with his Indian guide Joe Attean almost sixty years before. There were the same gloomy deadwaters, the same low banks densely covered with black and white spruce, mountain ash, hemlock, fir tops like sharp spearheads; the same darting of kingfishers (*skuscumonsuck*, Joe had called them), chattering of chickadees (*kecunnilessu*), and rapping of woodpeckers. They passed Lobster Stream on the right, so called from the fresh-water lobsters found in it, and, three miles farther on, the meandering Moosehorn Stream. In spite of the many drifting logs, for the spring drive was on, they made good time, arriving at the Halfway House in a little over two hours.

After the vigorous paddling Doc was again ravenous, and a lunch seemed appropriate. Alas, the same cook might have followed him! It looked as if he had sliced the raw ham, poured some hot water over it, let it sit while he dished up the rest of the meal, poured the water off, and served it. But Doc ate it.

Now haste was imperative. The lower end of the river, they were told, would be plugged full of logs, and they would have to walk into the Village from Pine Stream, a long and muddy trek if they landed after dark. They paddled swiftly, past Ragmuff Stream and Little Ragmuff, up around the big bend by Rocky Brook, the river becoming more congested with every mile. The walk through the woods was indeed muddy, and it was soon pitch dark but they managed to reach the big lodging house before midnight. As usual, "Uncle Anse" Smith, the proprietor, was curled up on the floor behind the stove, fast asleep. But he sprang up, eyes sparkling, overjoyed to see them.

At that time he was about sixty, kindly, merry, vivacious, the activating spark of the tiny settlement at the head of Chesuncook Lake. Brought there from Old Town in 1856 at the age of four, he had spent most of his life there, much of it—nights, at least—behind that very stove. The "hotel" of which he was proprietor was low and spacious, eighty feet long, with large stone chimneys. It had been changed only by improvements since Thoreau had visited it in 1853, describing its log walls as "large and round, except on the upper and under sides, and as visible inside as out, successive bulging cheeks gradually lessening upwards and tuned to each other with the axe, like Pandean pipes." He also had found an Ansell Smith in charge. Like Grant Farm, it had numerous adjoining buildings: barns, ice house, blacksmith shop. For six decades it had lodged and fed lumberers, guides, hunters, fishermen, and an occasional maverick like Doc.

"You must eat," urged Uncle Anse, always the hospitable host. "Eat right now."

"No." Was it duty that made Doc's refusal so decisive or memories of the quivering veal and ham? He would see the patient first. Then they would eat. That would give them full stomachs for the trip up river against the current. No, they could not possibly stay for the night. He had patients waiting back home.

It was some time after midnight when they left, two A.M. by the time they had waded through the mile of half-frozen mud and reached the canoe. Though it was morning of the twenty-first of June, they found that the logs clogging the edge of the river were solidly frozen together! It took them from two until five o'clock to break their way out through. Doc sat in the stern and held the canoe up with a paddle while the guide, Charlie McLeod, stood in the bow breaking the logs apart with a cant dog and sinking the smaller ones, to make a path for the canoe to work through. Reaching open water finally, they used paddles when possible, but Charlie was often forced to use the setting pole.

Their feet were nearly frozen. The only remedy was to go ashore and run and kick the trees in an effort to thaw them. A half-dozen such side trips slowed their progress. Without them they might easily have equaled the round-trip record that Charlie then held and which would not be broken for the next thirty years. However, they reached the Carry just in time to walk across and catch the afternoon boat down the lake. A hundred-mile trip which may have brought health to the patient but misery to the doctor! For the lack of sleep, the cold, the raw food took their toll. He suffered gastronomic tortures for the next three days.

He was called to the Halfway House again the following year late in March to attend a man sick with pneumonia. No traveling by boat this time! He caught the noon train to Somerset, the Maine Central train to Rockwood, and crossed the narrows to Kineo, where he was able to hire a horse and pung for the journey up the lake. It was not a pleasant ride. The weather had been mild of late, and a thick layer of slush had formed on the ice, so that the horse waded to its knees all the way. Time and again the water came in over the floor boards and the robes were soon soaked, also the human extremities. A southeast wind and heavy clouds soon realized their potential, adding to the discomfort by dumping a layer of mixed snow and rain, which soon soaked what upper clothing had not been drenched by the lake water. The melting flakes kept both horse and driver submerged in an icy bath. The twenty-mile drag through slush was enough for this horse, so he swapped it for a fresh one at Northeast Carry.

This poor beast had an even worse job. The winter tote road along the river was soft with melting snow, and he slumped with every step, often belly deep. At the Moose-horn Deadwater eight miles or so down the river he fell and was unable to rise. Doc had to unharness him, pull him out, haul the pung to more solid snow in the woods, reharness him, and proceed for the rest of the thirteen miles on higher ground. By the time he reached Halfway House, around midnight, the horse was too tired to eat. But Doc stabled him and left him food and water.

The sick man's wife, who had been up for several nights caring for her husband, as well as doing all the farm chores, was so exhausted that she had fallen asleep. Doc found the patient lying on a bed steadily coughing, a washbasin half full of frothy, bloody sputum beside him. His respiration was 66, his pulse over 100, and he was carrying a temperature of 104. As usual on such cases treatment had to be on a hit-and-run basis. One visit was all the time he could possibly manage. And yet a wilderness doctor was expected to get results. After treating the patient, Doc carefully laid out medicines enough to last for at least a week and gave the wife explicit directions as to their use. The patient was not a good risk for pneumonia. He had been drinking heavily for the last three months. Yet, due to the patient and meticulous care of his wife even more than to the doctor's single visit, he would recover.

Doc was hungry. He had had only a small lunch before rushing to the train the previous noon. But there was not much food in sight. At two A.M., after consuming a half slice of bread, half a doughnut, and half a glass of milk, he reharnessed the horse and headed for home. The trip up river was much like that down except that the horse was more exhausted. The storm continued all night and most of the next day. Doc reached the Carry at about seven-thirty in the morning. The Kineo horse was rested and made good time down the lake, though walking all the way. No more than three brush markers were visible at once along the trail, it snowed so hard. But he arrived just in time to get a ride on the stage taking passengers across the lake to Kineo Station on the Rockwood shore. A bit later, and he would have had to walk. No time, however, to get lunch either at Kineo or at the station! Arriving at Somerset Junction, he noticed a train order that the west-bound CP train then in the station was meeting another train at Askwith, and he immediately jumped on board, hoping to save three hours' time over the "Mixed" that the other passengers were taking. Good! There was a splendid boarding house at Askwith. He would get lunch there while the trains were taking water. No such luck! When he jumped off the train a workman who tended the stable was on the platform, one eye shut tight with an abscess of the upper eyelid.

"Doc!" he greeted joyfully. "Come with me, please! I need help."

They went to the man's room and by the time the abscess was opened the train was pulling out of the station. Doc ran after it, violently waving. The crew recognized him and slowed a bit, giving him a chance to "jump" the train, a skill at which he was now as adept as a track man. Now, he thought, swinging himself aboard, home soon to dinner. But again, disappointment. At Somerset the stationman had forgotten to throw the semaphore. There was a tangle of trains delaying his freight so long both at Somerset and at Moosehead that it was one in the afternoon before he arrived in Greenville. Twenty-five hours with only a light dinner and the half lunch eaten at the Halfway House!

"If anyone wants some honest to goodness hardship," he was heard to comment, "there isn't much better way than to sit in an old pung with ice water weeping down over you all night, hungry and cold, and watch an old horse plod sixty-six miles just dragging his feet through slush all the way!" The delay caused by the faulty semaphore was the least of the trip's liabilities.

And what would he have done through these years of limited transportation without the railroads! He rode them as passenger, he jumped them, he dropped from them, he climbed their iron ladders, he sat in their engine rooms, he pumped their jiggers, he helped work their handcars. It was the Canadian Pacific that was most cooperative. On their lines a doctor and a priest had priority.

If he needed a train in the woods and didn't flag the first one that came along, he was called to account by the dispatcher. He was expected to flag the train and ask later. Sometimes they would give him a torpedo with which to flag, a gadget with a strap at each end which could be folded over, side to the rails. One blast would mean stop. Two meant beware, go slow, something weak ahead.

But often there was no need of flagging, or no opportunity. Then he had to jump. He would walk down to Moosehead Hill from Somerset or East Outlet, then take his stand on top of the hill. The engines were small and couldn't carry a big load, so they would top the hill at greatly reduced speed, even with the steam wide open. With his basket strapped to his back, leaving both arms free, it was easy to climb aboard. In fact, he was known to do it with the train going full speed. The train crews came to respect him not only for his medical skills but for his acrobatic feats.

Once a new brakeman called down from the cupola excitedly to the conductor. "Hey, I just saw someone climbing up over the side of a car. He came running toward us, like a goat, with something on his back!"

The conductor laughed. "So? That's just Doc Pritham carrying his medicine pack and, maybe, snowshoes. He's likely to come aboard anywhere. Just open the window and let him in."

The train had been going full speed. "How in thunder did he do it!" demanded the green hand.

"When you can do that," replied the conductor dryly, "you'll be a real train man."

Doc could not have managed such maneuvers without his special bag, a wicker basket made by Bernard which he could strap on his back. It was fitted with a cardboard tray which he filled with medicines; then on top of that he would throw in whatever he might need, perhaps a spare pair of stockings or mittens or a sweater, strap it on his back, and away he'd go. He carried it on all his trips which involved walking, snowshoeing, any type of journey which he made without a car or boat.

Sometimes the feat of train jumping was in reverse, off instead of on. Once Doc asked the train man to slow up and let him off at Indian Hill farm, above the Village, so he would not have to walk back to the Junction. The man forgot to give the order, and when they reached the spot the train was going forty miles an hour. Nothing daunted, Doc threw off his bag and jumped into a snowbank.

The Canadian Pacific railroad was equally lenient with his use of its jiggers, once they were alerted to his needs. Early in his practice there came an emergency call from Squaw Brook, a tiny settlement off the road. No way to get there by boat or car, no time to snowshoe. Since the little cluster of houses was on the railroad track, Doc ran up to the storage house on the edge of town, sprung the padlock with a stone, and took out the jigger. Lifting it onto the track, he pumped away toward Rockwood, pulling it off the track when he reached his destination. After dealing with the emergency, he returned the jigger. But the next day the man in charge of the equipment discovered the sprung lock and guessed what had happened. He shot off verbal fireworks, then wrote a hot letter of protest to the railroad superintendent. The reply was short and to the point: "Any time Dr. Pritham wants any of our equipment, he can have it."

Soon after, the railroad superintendent posted in top place on the order board: "All trains stop anywhere and anytime for Dr. Pritham." A reasonable attitude, after all, since it was often the railroad families living along the tracks who needed him!

A jigger played a major role in a trip he had to take around 1915.

It was April again, that aggravating month of between-ness, when everything teetered in precarious balance, winter-spring, cold-warmth, ice-open water, solidity-mud, northeaster-balmy breeze, pungs-cars, skates-boats; when the skies were blue and heady with promise and the earth beneath was an unmanageable mess. All winter the two-horse roads had been piling up with snow, rolled, the homemade plows deepening the furrows on each side. Those like Doc with single horses had used a "set-over" pung; that is, the thills were set out in front of one runner, so that the horse traveled in one rut, the pung in two. By March, with the snow melting and the plow often dislodging masses where there had been little travel, hence no solid base, the poor horse would sink clear to her belly. Then, worse yet, would come the slush and mud. And, unfortunately, it was a season when sickness was rife.

On April 10 a call came from Camp Ogontz, about thirteen miles above Kineo, to attend a sick woman. At the same time came a request to see another patient at the Brassua section. Doc decided to take the early freight to Brassua, then let the section crew pump him back or, better yet, loan him their jigger. This would enable him to reach Somerset Junction in time to catch the noon Maine Central to Rockwood. But the day before the Brassua jigger had been caught in a rock cut and demolished by a train. The section crew was off to the west. Nothing for it but to walk the six miles to Tarratine! Arriving there, he called Somerset. Happily, Eddie Conley, one of the section men at Moosehead, had just pumped into the station on his jigger and came to meet Doc as he walked toward Somerset. They rode back together. At Somerset Junction Eddie set his jigger over on the Maine Central track and pumped him as far as the West Outlet.

"Don't dare go any farther," he explained with a grin. "If I got caught by the section crew riding the Maine

Central track without a permit, I'd lose not only the jigger but my job."

No need to tell Doc that! Maine Central policy was quite different from the CP's, though the company had some difficulty in making local employees enforce it. The officials were constantly trying to catch the doctors riding their rails without a permit. They refused even to allow a doctor to ride their tracks to attend their own sick section crews.

Doc walked the remaining two miles into Rockwood. The lake looked unpromising, but he was in luck. Toters for the Kineo Hotel Company were putting runners under their canoes so they could either move on the ice or paddle across patches of open water. He could cross to Kineo with them. Kate Carleton, wife of Guy, the barber at Rockwood, put him up a lunch, and he borrowed Guy's setting pole, an iron-shod ten-foot rod used to drive a canoe over rapids. A long light pole would be a great aid in crossing rotten ice. Phil Capino, one of the best ice men of the lake region, was among those hauling supplies to Kineo.

"Don't take to the ice until you reach Deer Head Farm," he warned.

Arriving at Kineo, Doc took his advice and walked the seven miles along the bank of the lake to the farm, eating Kate's lunch as he went. At Deer Head Farm he found Mr. Brown, the proprietor, just coming from the barn with a pail of milk. A glassful, fresh and warm, tasted good. But he refused to stay at the farm until morning, when crossing would be safer. "Thanks. Couldn't. There's a woman sick over there. They're counting on me."

He went on the ice and headed for Ogontz diagonally across the lake some ten miles away. Almost every step was a gamble. There were hundreds of open places, hundreds of other patches where the ice needles stood on end like jackstraws and, when poked with the pole, promptly tumbled, leaving you standing by a gaping stretch of open water. Then you must turn back and make your way around it on the firmest ice you could find. The pole was invaluable. If you broke through, it would usually hit on ice solid enough to hold you up, and you could quickly climb out on it. Then, too, it was handy for reaching out ahead and striking a suspicious-looking place before you stepped on it. Thank heaven for a good eye, a steady nerve, and an early acquired knowledge of how to travel on rotten ice! Without them he could easily have drowned once darkness came on. And since he had started across the lake at seven in the evening, this was soon.

Halfway across he found himself on a loose cake that tipped up and sent him sliding toward its edge. Nothing he did seemed to help. Wherever he pushed the pole it went right through. Here's for a swim! he thought as the water mounted to his knees. But happily when it was about halfway up his thighs, his feet struck a rough place, and he was able to face about and work back uphill toward the level surface at mid-cake. Carefully he retraced his steps to firmer ice.

Eventually he reached the camp at Ogontz, where they had long since given him up. Willie Marsh, one of the party, had gone down the lake about three miles in the afternoon to see if he was in sight, but since Willie had broken through three times on a traveled winter road where the ice was thicker than in the middle of the lake, he had assumed Doc would stay at Deer Head Farm waiting for the morning freeze. Doc treated the sick woman and went to bed, a welcome antidote to twenty-seven miles of walking since eleven o'clock, most of it in a foot of ice water. Alex McDonald, the caretaker, had fried ham and eggs, oatmeal, and other hearty items ready when he woke him at four o'clock.

"I'll make the Maine Central freight," Doc told him, "and get a ride to Somerset."

Fifteen miles of walking before 6:45? It seemed impossible. But the air had cooled enough to stick the ice partially together. He could pick out the firmest spots ahead, run, and jump on them. He made excellent time across the lake.

At the farm both Mr. and Mrs. Brown came out in the yard to greet him, overjoyed at seeing him alive. Having watched him last night as long as they could see, all they could do after that was hope. They had another glass of warm milk for him (everybody within fifty miles knew better than to offer him coffee!) and some doughnuts. Going to Kineo, he was able this time to walk along the ice edge of North Bay instead of on the summer tote road, and made far better time. There was even time to talk for a few minutes with Jim Findley, the caretaker at Kineo, before he crossed to Rockwood, obtained his permit, and caught the train for Somerset. There he was lucky enough to find a CP train stopped for orders, so he jumped aboard and reached home quickly. Two hours and fifteen minutes from Camp Ogontz to Deer Head Farm, then to Kineo, carrying one's pack, might well have set a record. He couldn't refrain from boasting a bit about it.

As for other details of the trip, such as the fact that he had risked drowning, he did not think them worth mentioning. They were all in the day's work.

Those years of the teens, especially the winters when Doc was for months the only physician within many miles, were grueling in their demands. More than once he treated a patient literally on the run, like the man who stopped him one day as he was driving in the pung. It was bitterly cold, with the thermometer at zero or below. Doc hadn't a spare minute, since he was already late for a train going to Kineo.

"Please, Doc," the man pleaded. "I got to get rid of this here tooth. It's killing me."

"Jump in," snapped Doc. "Sit down here on the seat."

He dug a forceps from his bag. "Now—open. And keep your tongue off this contraption, or, I'm warning you, it'll freeze right to it!"

He reached into the wide aperture, grabbed the tooth, and yanked it out. Less than a minute later the patient was standing in the road, dazed but relieved, the offending member in his hand, looking after the racing pung.

· 3 ·

IT WAS EXCITING growing up in Greenville in that second decade of the nineteen hundreds. Surely no frontier town of the Wild West could have given a boy higher adventure! Weekly installments of *The Perils of Pauline* flickering in the Crafts Hall to the tune of a tinny piano or lantern slides in the Methodist vestry depicting the awful consequences of *Ten Nights in a Bar Room* were pale entertainment beside the delightful hullaballoo when the red-shirted, tough-fisted lumberers came roistering into town. And what western rodeo or roundup could compete with the thundering, death-flirting fury of a river drive? Even the masked holdup of a stagecoach couldn't have much of an edge on the excitement likely to erupt with the arrival of the Lily Bay Stage!

It was the big event of the day when this tote team came in on its daily winter trip, coming down on the ice through the road of evergreens, then following the plowed road from the Village to the Junction. Carroll would often join other boys and run to the top of the big hill, listen for the jingling bells, then when the horses had slowed up enough, jump on the sides and hang on. The open sled would be full of lumbermen, heroic and husky, already a little rowdy with the anticipation of freedom. You would hang on for dear life, snow stinging your face, runners leaping and trying to throw you off balance. If lucky, you could ride it clear to the station. Then there might be excitement indeed! The men would crawl from under the thick woods' blankets and stamp the blood back into their feet. There might be an argument, then a flash of knives. A blade might puncture a face, the snow spot with crimson. Big Henry Bartley, constable as well as hotel keeper, might be sent for. You would watch, fascinated, while he restored order, maybe lifting two huskies by the collars and knocking their heads together. Then, as likely as not, the combatants would be taken up to Dad's office for patching.

But the Lily Bay Stage was nothing beside some of the lumbering equipment that the Great Northern and other companies often drove through the streets, like the Lombard steam log haulers. Big as locomotives, dragging three or four sleds loaded high with long logs, they went smoking, belching, snorting. At night, acetylene headlights aflare, exhausts lighting their surroundings for hundreds of feet, they held all the allure of fabled dragons. With almost as much excitement as his small wide-eyed brother Howard, Carroll would rush to the window to press his nose against the frosty glass.

"If you think that's something," he would tell the wide eyes loftily, "you oughter see it out in the woods. Down the big hills she goes, whoosh, blowin' steam and smoke, shootin' sparks way up in the trees."

Before the decade was over the boys saw the arrival of the first gasoline trucks and diesels, the first ones chugging, stuttering, jerking, unequipped with mufflers, making noise loud enough to wake the dead.

There were peculiar hazards to being a boy in Greenville in those years. Between the young of the Village and those of the Junction smoldered a feud smacking of the Kentucky Mountains or the New York ghettos, except that the implements of warfare were not guns or knives.

Once the four grades in the little Junction school were completed and pupils attended the big school halfway between the two settlements, training in both self-defense and attack became necessary. From the older boys like Manfred Carter and Elwin Dean and Norman Capen, Carroll, at an early age, learned the techniques of protection against the East Cove gang. Good weapons were snowballs with stones in them, or, better yet, lumps of ice which had been imbedded in a horse's hoofs. Venture into the enemy territory on a Saturday was like the adventure of a spy in wartime. Casualties of boyhood skirmishes (not always between enemies) were often swabbed and stitched in Dad's office. One of these occurred when Manfred had a fight with Dana Templeton halfway over to school. Dana hit Manfred with an elastic. Manfred doubled up the size of Dana's lip, whereupon Dana dug Manfred's face with his fingernails. Dad sterilized the scratches.

The thrill of adventure accompanied some of the hazards. Halfway between East and West Coves was an old Indian's weathered house. Beside it were some crabapple trees. Stealing apples wouldn't have been half as much sport if it hadn't involved dodging rock salt discharged from a shotgun. There were few thrills greater than to see the window starting slowly up just before making a wild dash for cover in the woods.

Except one. The first time you climbed Squaw Mountain. You had to walk several miles before starting the three-thousand-foot climb. On the way up through the trees you could see spruce tops below and a little black trout pond shadowed by the mountains. Finally, after a scramble almost straight up over sheer rocks you reached the flat rock at the very top. Then you stared, holding your breath. For there was your world stretched out below. So huge, and yet so small! The few buildings that were readily visible looked like small toys. There was an endless sea of green treetops fading into blue and faint lavendar to pale mountains blending into the sky. You could see a sweep of forest reaching away off into Canada and halfway across the state to the south. Below was the lake, looking as if someone had carelessly tossed water out of a giant cup. Yes, it did look like a moose's head, with Deer and Sugar Island its eyes, and Spencer Bay and the part below Kineo its antlers! That tiny white speck with a trail of smoke was a three-decked steamer taking guests to the hotel. Except for the tiny town, as far as you could see there were no buildings, no people. You felt suddenly terribly small, and yet terribly big, because you were a part of it all.

There were other thrills for a boy in those years. Carroll, and later Howard, experienced them all. Going fishing after supper at Greenville Point and coming back proudly with two or three trout. Skating on ice so clear that you could see pebbles far below, shining in the winter sunlight. Making skate sails and skimming along for miles, trying not to hit a patch of snow that would send you sprawling. The comfort of a black sealskin cap on mornings when the thermometer registered forty-four below. The feel of snowshoes sinking deep into a new drift, sliding gleefully over a crust. Fishing through the ice in winter and eating in a fir bough shelter before an open fire. Walking barefoot along the streets in summer, with the soft dust ankle-deep. The tickling coolness on your tongue of a sliver of ice from the ice wagon. Swimming at the beach called the "Vim." Crawling between soapstone-warmed blankets after your Saturday night bath in the washtub in front of the kitchen stove.

True, it was an austere life, with few of the luxuries that came later. The town outhouses, cleaned out periodically by John Curtis with his team of oxen, were uncomfortably cold in winter. The potbellied stoves with their roaring fires burned your front to a crisp while your rear raised gooseflesh. But a boy's muscles swelled from the weight of armfuls of wood and of a wide wooden shovel throwing a ridge of snow higher than his head. And, though he had his prescribed chores, Carroll was luckier than many of the other boys. He did little with the garden or the huge woodpile beside the house. Dad liked to work at both too well. By the time the rest of the family got up, he had been sawing and splitting, hoeing and weeding, for at least three hours.

Carroll was exposed to tough frontier rowdiness at an early age. He went with his father into the lumber camps, watched the steamers unload their lusty human cargoes at Coburn's landing, hustled past the small jail just off the boardwalk between Junction and Village, marveling at the bravado of the occupant reputed to have kicked his way out. While Dad was upstairs in the hospital, he hung about the basement of the Y.M.C.A., young ears absorbing the lumbermen's profane jargon along with the clatter of the bowling balls. He envied older boys like Manfred Carter, who were paid a few pennies for setting up pins, and stared fascinated at old Johnny bent over a checkerboard.

"Once old Johnny was drunk," he repeated the gossip with relish. "And they nailed him up in a box, thought he was dead. Then he come to and thumped on it and they let him out. Golly jeez, s'pose he'd got buried!"

But the influences of degeneracy were firmly counterbalanced. The boys often went to sleep to the melodious exhortations of the Reverend Cyprian Bryant from his pulpit just across the street or to the stirring strains of "When the Roll Is Called up Yonder" and "Throw Out the Life Line." Pastor Bryant, with his wonderful wide grin, was leader of the Boy Scouts, and his wife, stout and jolly, conducted the Junior League on Sunday afternoons. Even when too young to join the scouts Carroll went along when Dad used his big motorboat to take the troop to tent at Harford's Point, towing a small boat behind with all the luggage, and he accompanied his father when he went to a scout meeting to talk on first aid. Dad could make a lecture as exciting as a hunting yarn. He told about going to Northeast Carry where Stubby Doyle had been stabbed in the neck, and when he described the spurting of the arteries clear to the ceiling as he walked across the dining room, you could actually see it. The boys looked so impressed that Carroll almost burst with filial pride.

Scouts, Junior League, Sunday school . . . all were doughty adversaries to the forces of evil, and the fact that Manfred Carter, an admired adolescent, was one of the teachers weighed heavily on the side of virtue. And when Manfred, after two years as a scaler in the lumber camps, decided to become a minister and departed for theological school, the scales were tipped even further. Add to these influences a gently persuasive mother and an almost puritanical, if not church-going father, and the degenerating forces were completely outbalanced.

Of all Carroll's boyhood experiences, perhaps the most exciting was the arrival of the Kentucky horse. It was 1917. Doc had long felt the need of a good saddle horse. He wrote to a ranch in Kentucky, and they sent him a catalogue. Each horse was carefully described, its pedigree given, labeled as fit or unfit for a woman to handle, the price ranging from a hundred to ten thousand dollars. He made his choice and sent his order, to the consternation and derision of his friends.

"You poor dupe!" "Crazy!" "Only a cussed fool would buy a horse sight unseen!"

Dad was not upset. He was buying a horse, he told them, from a ranch where they raised horses as a business, folks who cared about their reputation. Not like a horse trader who had just one horse to sell and had to cover up its faults. If they thought he was a fool, just wait and see.

Carroll waited also, torn between worry and anticipation. A horse from the blue-grass country! Already he was the envy of boys much older than his ten years. But what if the scoffers were right, the horse proved a dud, Dad a laughing stock! The fateful day came. The horse, shipped by express, arrived in a passenger train. Dad simply opened the crate, led her out, and walked her home.

Dud? Laughing stock? She was a beauty, exactly as represented. They named her Cleo. Dad was exultant. It was a joy to ride her in the saddle, for she had all five gaits. Her running walk took him over the rocks and corduroy to and from Lily Bay in half the time he had formerly taken. In the busiest times—and in 1917 they were soon to come —he could lie across her shoulders and sleep for miles at a time. Some different from the first horse sent up from Dover, that would amble aimlessly in all directions! If he put this horse on any track, be it a man, horse, dog, deer, or what not, and told her to follow it, she would do so wherever it led, over roads or ice, through fields or woods, regardless of wind or weather. He taught her to do almost everything but talk. The critics were soon her reluctant but staunch admirers. Carroll rose mightily in the estimation of his peers. It was a wrench for both of them to see the little sorrel go, but she went down to Uncle Charles' in Freeport, where they could see her often.

One Saturday Dad had to go to Folsom Farm for a confinement case.

"Bring Carroll along," Mrs. Sam Bigney urged when she called. "He can fish while you attend to your business." It was no secret that the boy was her favorite.

Carroll was jubilant. It was one of his first experiences with the new horse. Though she preferred the saddle to the pung, she set off easily on the snow-covered ice, following the brush to Burntjacket. From there they struck out across the lake toward Rockwood, joining another brush trail above Sandbar. Cleo apparently did not have to exert herself, for there was no wet hair even under her harness when they put her in a stall at Rockwood. There the Great Northern gave them another horse known as "Runaway." He lived up to his name, starting as usual at a gallop. Dad held him as well as he could until they reached the lake, then let him go. He ran across to Kineo and nearly to Deer Head Farm, all the time working up a lather.

"Fools," muttered Dad, "sticking hardware like that in a horse's mouth! No wonder the poor thing's half crazy! It's got a hinged bit, what we call a 'sawhorse,' and every pull on it hurts like sixty. Watch now."

Dad stopped pulling and let the reins go slack. He kept talking to the horse. For a while it kept on running. But after a time it looked back, as if questioning. Finally it gave up running and walked, completing the journey at a reasonable pace. In spite of the fact that it was soaking wet it had made exactly the same time Cleo had made from Greenville to Rockwood, seven miles to the hour.

Carroll had a good time fishing, and Mrs. Bigney promised him a fine baked fish dinner. But by mid-forenoon, when Dad had finished with his confinement case, there was a nasty souther making up, with heavy snow already coming down.

"Can't wait," he told the aggrieved hostess, whose dinner was already in the oven. "With a storm like that coming, mustn't take chances for just a mess of fish."

This time the horse ran only about a mile, then, assured that it wasn't to be hurt, settled down to a steady trot. They found sick persons at the boarding house in Rockwood, so, in spite of the thickening snow, there was delay. In Dad's book food—and almost anything else— could be passed up, but not patients. Carroll passed the time visiting in the house with Jim Sargent's boy. When he was called back to the stable, he found three anxious hostlers trying to explain to Dad that they had been hunting in vain to find his horse's bridle.

Dad laughed shortly. "Haven't got one. Carroll could have told you if he'd been here. Just hitch the horse in the thills, run the reins through the saddle dees, and snap them into the rings in the sides of the halter."

They looked dumfounded. "B—but you—you can't drive this horse with a rig like that, no bit!"

"No? Not only can, but do, and will for as long as I have her. Yes, and let me tell you something. Let me take your Runaway for a month, and I'll bring him back with just such a rig and guarantee to drive him anywhere without a bit."

Dad continued to sputter as they headed into the storm. "Crime to put such a barbarous piece of hardware into that poor sensitive mouth. Kindly, intelligent animal if handled right. I'd sure like to have it to train for a while!"

The storm had increased in violence. They were unable to see more than a few rods, and unfortunately the brush trail did not last long.

"Guess the best way," Dad decided, "is to follow over till we can see Sugar Island, then come down under its shelter and strike for the brush off Burntjacket."

Carroll began to be frightened. How could Dad possibly know what direction to take! He felt buried in a white cocoon, unable to see or breathe. It was cold, too. The wind nipped his nose, darted icy needles at his cheeks. The chill dampness penetrated moccasins, even several pairs of wool socks, and numbed his toes. But then Dad took the horse blanket and wrapped it around their shoulders like a shawl, forming a long projection, like a visor, out in front, so that they could sit huddled together, almost comfortably, as if in the shelter of a tent.

And slowly, assured by some dynamic security in the contact with his father, the boy felt all nervousness disappear.

Suddenly Cleo turned from the trail and struck off for herself along the lake. To Carroll's surprise Dad let her go, leaving the reins to hang slack from the dash.

"Seems to be heading right," he commented. "We'll tell better if we find her crossing the bar."

Sure enough, she went right over the middle of the sandbar and headed straight into the wind.

"First time I ever saw a horse do that of its own free will," chuckled Dad. "Usually you have to hold them to it constantly with tight reins. What do you bet if the next thing we see isn't the fish house off Capen's!"

It was. And Cleo headed for it, remembering that she had stopped here on the way up for a drink of water. Frank Willer was fishing in the house. Dad gave him the oatmeal box of apples which Mrs. Bigney had insisted on their taking, and Frank, delighted with the gift, reached behind him and dragged out a dandy big lake trout.

"I'd be deuced grateful if you'd take it. I've eaten so many I can't look another in the face." So Carroll might get his baked fish dinner, after all!

Leaving Capen's, Cleo traveled straight down the lake and made good time, even though the drifting snow was often over the sides of the pung. Never had Carroll been so glad to climb the back steps and enter the warm, dry kitchen.

The next day Dad attended a veteran teamster, Mike Cullen, who had started the previous day to drive a party on a trip into the woods. He had given up at Grant Farm and come home. "Worst storm I ever saw," he averred, blaming it for the illness which was to keep him in bed for two weeks. True, he had driven in the storm all day but almost all the time he had been sheltered in the woods.

"Must be some horse you've got," he marveled. "Facing

that storm for twenty miles and comin' in home without any guidance. Gee whillikers, what a trip!"

Carroll could vouch for that. But he sagely suspected that the credit for a safe trip did not belong solely to the horse.

CHAPTER FIVE

. . . Come Hell . . .

. 1 .

Sherman was, oh, so right! And the Stygian miasmas were not confined to the stinking trenches of Europe. They penetrated deep into the wilds of northern Maine.

Doc would have preferred to wage battle in the stinking trenches—in fact, attempted to without success. Dr. Hunt saw to that. He, with some other doctors, was on a committee to assess the availability of the doctors of Piscataquis County for military service. Each doctor was supposed to fill out a questionnaire. Dr. Hunt was sufficiently cognizant of Fred's personal data to fill in the questionnaire himself, and Fred never saw it. On its back the senior doctor wrote with decisive finality, "This man should not be allowed to go even if he volunteers. Hiram Hunt."

Doc proceeded with his application for enlistment, obtaining the signature of Millard Metcalf, a selectman; then, unsuspecting, he went to Dr. Hunt and asked him to sign. The eyes under the black brows snapped triumph. "Nothing doing, my boy. You won't be going until all the other doctors in this neck of the woods have gone. I've seen to that."

And the good doctor had been wise indeed. For the two years were to exact a toll of medical skill and physical strength far in excess of all Doc's preceding ten years of practice, and the fate of innumerable lives hung on the decision.

Though the 1917 smallpox epidemic was not spawned by the war, it reared its head simultaneously, a demon capable of creating its own small hell. It started in the Great Northern driving camp on Elm Stream. After the drive the men came down via Rockwood to separate at Somerset Junction. Had the doctor then resident at Rockwood stopped them, the epidemic might have been concentrated in one place, but unfortunately he did not believe in quarantining. One man came to Greenville so sick that Reverend Tom Jones, the Methodist minister, had to help him to the Y.M.C.A. Happily Doc was able to secure vaccine from Portland just in time to arrest the disease with the appearance of only one smallpox pimple over one eye.

Others were not so fortunate. At one time Doc had smallpox patients at Kingsley's Camp on Second Roach, some in a pest house on the top of Simpson Hill in Greenville, one in a tent at Grant Farm, and some at Soper Brook Number 2 Camp, about fifty miles to the northeast in the shadow of Soubunge Mountain. It took miles of travel to cover and hold quarantine on these patients. The epidemic started on May 9, and by the first of June all the area was involved. He was making two trips each week to Soper Brook and riding into Second Roach en route. Each trip he vaccinated an average of a hundred men. Maintaining a supply of virulent vaccine was no easy task in warm weather. Doc had it sent from Portland in a vacuum bottle, well iced; then held about one hundred tubes of it at Kokadjo in Irving Hamilton's refrigerator, so if it was a very hot morning, he could take his supply from there, then replenish the store on a cold rainy day. He used nineteen hundred tubes during this epidemic and had the satisfaction of reporting that not one vaccinated man contracted the disease.

The Soper Brook trips were the worst. There were two ways of getting there. You could go to Chesuncook Dam by horse over the tote road, which in the spring was deep with mud, overflowed in places, and at best was a mass of rocks for a horse to slip on and stretches of floating corduroy for it to wallow through. From Chesuncook there was a ten-mile hike to Brighton Dam, then another jaunt across country to Harrington Lake and the camp at Soper Brook. Once the lake was open, you could go to Lily Bay by steamer, probably catch a ride to Grant Farm and maybe to Chesuncook Dam. But there was a long hike either way. Before Doc arrived to vaccinate the camp crew, four of the men decided to outsmart him by departing across country for Millinocket.

"You damn fools," an old Frenchman scoffed as they were leaving. "You tink dat doctor mind you? He catch you b'fo' you get half to Mill'nocket. He go troo woods like deer!"

Doc had no need to emulate the deer. He got the names and home addresses of the escapees and telephoned the county attorney. When the men walked out of the woods at Millinocket the sheriff met them with the promise of twenty-one days' detention at county expense.

"Damn fools," reiterated the Frenchman, who was enjoying the assets of quarantine along with its liabilities.

"Stay here, dey find nice brook, catch demselves some trout. Dey get no fried trout vere dey goin'."

These men were not the only ones to evade vaccination. At Kingsley's four men stayed out on the headworks until two o'clock in the morning in a nasty southerly snow-storm in order to avoid it. All four contracted the disease, which meant a long quarantine for the whole camp and a longer one for them.

On one of Doc's trips a physician was sent by the officials in Augusta to assist with the vaccinations.

"Hope you're in good form and fit to travel?" broached Doc.

Of course, assured the visitor blithely. He expected to leave for a Colorado camp to join the army in a few days.

Going in Doc's boat to Lily Bay, they secured a ride to Kokadjo with the mail. As they ate lunch there, the visiting doctor produced a long sheet of blue paper to note his expense of the meal. "I say, where's your paper? Don't you have one?"

"No."

"No? Somebody slipped up. I'll see that one is sent you when I get back."

"Don't bother." Doc was emphatic. "Don't need one, and wouldn't use one if I had it."

"But—your bills won't be paid until you do!"

"That's O.K. by me. If they don't pay bills just as I make them, then I'll stop making any. I've no time to bother with fool red tape."

The visitor was expense-conscious. When Doc hired Hamilton's car to take them to Chesuncook Dam, he strenuously objected.

"So? Then how do you propose to get there?"

"Why—we could walk, couldn't we?"

Doc regarded him pityingly. "I reckon you'll have all the walking you want after we leave the car."

He did. He had begun to slow up even before they

reached Ripogenus. Here Doc was lucky in finding the river drivers in camp, and he easily collected the personnel to complete vaccinations. The visitor appreciated not only the rest but the dinner of delicious baked beans which the skilled cook set before them . . . until said cook started replenishing the dish in the center of the table. As he tipped the big iron kettle, out with the beans plopped a big fat lizard about six inches long, landing with a flop which generously splashed bean juice over the oilcloth.

"Holy (blankety-blank)!" ejaculated one woodsman with a profane awe that savored almost of devoutness. Even some of the lusty drivers, contemptuous of the foaming furies of Ripogenus Gorge, looked a bit sick and, with the visiting doctor, headed for the outside door. Not so, Doc. The beans had tasted good, and, as he expressed it later, no darn lizard would make him waste them. In fact, he helped himself to more.

By the time they reached Devlin's camp over beyond Sowbunge Mountain, some fifteen miles over rough tote road, the visitor had had his fill. During the last of the trek he was making little more than a mile an hour.

"Better get your vaccinating done before supper," Doc told him. "Hold the supper shack shut until we get them all. Let them eat, and half will go out in the woods until they get hungry again."

With his own present job he had no such worries. All he had to do was to announce that he was there to take the draft. Uncle Sam would attend to any who skipped out. The two tasks were finished, and they had supper, the visitor exhibiting unusual wariness.

"Sorry," the foreman apologized to Doc. "I'm afraid you'll have to sleep with the clerk at the wangan."

Doc was agreeable. There seemed to be three good bunks in the supply shed, all made up with clean blankets. However, the clerk was more informative. He slept on the counter, he confided, after two o'clock. He kept his bedding on a wire outdoors until then and sat up to read until it started to grow light. Then he made up his bed and slept until breakfast time. He had observed that certain intruders were more active during the darkest hours.

Doc had about as much fear of bedbugs as of a lizard that had climbed into a beanpot and got drowned. Eightthirty was his bedtime. He piled his muddy clothes in a chair and took the middle bunk.

"Come over here," he called after a few minutes. "Bring your lamp."

The log camp had been lined with sheathing paper for warmth. Doc was prepared for the sight that met their eyes, for he had heard the sounds of clawing. Not so the clerk. Mouth gaping, he stared in astonishment at the hundreds of bugs all struggling frantically to mount the paper to the upper bunk. They were climbing, clambering over each other, running two or three deep, forming little clusters which slipped and fell, then scattering to attempt another mad ascent.

"Well, I'll be—!"

"There they go," commented Doc with satisfaction. "Now maybe I can get some sleep."

He did, sleeping like a log until daylight. His clothes, too, remained unmolested. Blamed convenient, this immunity—or should one call it repulsion?—that he enjoyed from bedbugs. A pity it did not extend to mosquitoes and black flies, though with the years he did manage to build up a sort of immunity toward the latter. If one bit him, it would usually curl up and die before it had time to leave.

The trip with the visiting doctor continued, much to the discomfort of both medics. Doc was late getting into Number 2 Camp, where he had hoped to register the men at lunch on the mountain. Instead he met the cookee returning with his bucket, then had to find both the foreman and an interpreter, for most of the men were Russians, and hunt through an area of some four square miles to find the men at work. The visitor, traveling back to camp with the clerk, got lost, wandering down a winter road where pulp had been hauled to Harrington Lake. Though why anyone should leave a tote road deeply cut by wheel tracks to go down a road all grass grown, without any telephone wires, Doc couldn't understand. The delays upset his schedule by at least a day.

But at last they were ready to leave the camps. Doc tried to maintain a moderate speed of about three miles an hour, but the visitor's feet hurt him so badly that it was not possible. Arriving at Ripogenus Stream, they found that the wind had shifted, piling several thousand cords of pulpwood between their canoe and open water.

"You go free," urged Doc. "If I were alone, I'd have to shoulder the canoe and run alone." But the doctor refused. He wanted something to cling to if he sank, which he did almost every step, often sinking to his waist in the water and pawing for a stick of wood on which to climb. By the time they reached the boom logs and slipped the canoe into open water, he was glad enough to fall into it and lie on the bottom panting, while Doc paddled to the opposite shore. The next day he returned home from Kokadjo, declining to accompany Doc into Kingsley's camp. "You really should go," Doc could not resist prodding innocently, "just to see if I'm handling the job right. After all, you have to report to Augusta."

There followed other difficult trips, all fortunately without benefit of visitors. On one of these trips to the same camps the ten-mile trek through the woods to Brighton Dam was in a severe rain storm over flooded road, and he waded to his knees for miles, only to find that no horse had been reserved for him. Later, after seventeen more miles of mud and water, he found himself back on the wharf at Ripogenus Stream with night coming on, and "Sweedie," who should have come from the dam with his canoe to paddle him away, unapprised of his arrival. The telephone line from Brighton had inopportunely gone dead. He stood on the wharf and waved his hat vigorously, but no response came from the Dam. His small store of matches, all seven of them, were wet, but since they were the old-fashioned sulphur kind, he had hopes.

The wharf was loaded with cord wood for the tow boats to burn. Digging into the pile, Doc made a little cave, then picked bark off some sticks until he had a heap as big as a water pail inside the cave. The matches would not ignite. O.K., he had another idea. His clothes were soaked, but inside his mackinaw was an inner pocket under the armpit where he carried a hypodermic syringe in winter when jumping freights. Protected by his arm, the syringe was not likely to be mashed when he was slatted against the corners of cars, as often happened when he climbed on running trains. Removing the mackinaw, he took two or three of the wet matches and rubbed them gently against the dryest part of the pocket, back and forth, back and forth. Sure enough, they ignited. He poked them in under the mass of bark which, catching like gunpowder, soon gave him a fire. His clothes being too wet to ignite, he picked the fire up in his arms and took it to the middle of the wharf. As he kept feeding it and adding birch bark, the wind would snatch the burning pieces and carry them hundreds of yards up the lake. Two hours passed. Just as he was beginning to think he might be camping there for the night, there came Sweedie with his canoe, grumbling because he had been forced to come out so late at night. He grumbled even worse when Doc insisted on putting the fire out before leaving.

"Judas priest, what should we do!" demanded Doc.

"Leave the wharf flooring on fire and burn all the wood that the tow boats have to use this summer?"

He carried water in his hat until the fire was extinguished, then paddled with the disgruntled Sweedie to the Dam, where the clerks kindly made room for him, and he passed a comfortable night. Somehow a good night often had a way of following a twenty- to thirty-mile tramp in a storm. But the next morning the foreman whose duty had been to watch for him admitted that he had sat and looked at his fire two hours before rousing Sweedie, thinking it was someone on the wharf with a lantern.

"Didn't you think that lantern flickered quite a bit," Doc inquired dryly, "when the wind carried that birch bark up the lake a half mile all afire?"

But the sunny days when he took these trips were delightful. Along the Soper Brook Deadwater there might be fifty or more humming birds darting about like jeweled sparks. Another of the pleasant features was a beautiful Siberian wolfhound belonging to Hemingway, one of Sousa's trumpeters, who was camping on Harrington Lake. The dog would meet him on every trip just above the depot and walk with him for a mile or more toward Number 2. They were an oddly mated yet strangely congenial pair, the big loping thoroughbred and the little doctor moving with head thrust a little forward, almost at a run, both possessed of that peculiar animal grace of motion belonging only to those at home in the wilderness.

Came the time to disinfect the camps. No easy job to fumigate all the buildings and beddings for a crew of seventy-five or more men! Doc wrote to Augusta for advice. They sent him a little syringe about a foot long. He tried it out on one camp.

"Fool contraption!" he fumed. "A good smart Chinese laundryman could squirt more water through his teeth in an hour than one could pump through that in a day!"

He returned it and sent away for a man-sized pump. This new rig could be placed in a horse pail of solution and steadied by a foot treadle while one hand worked the handle and the other aimed the hose. It would throw a stream seventy-five feet and a spray twenty-five and empty a twelve-quart pail in a matter of minutes. Get the straw and spreads off the bunks, and he could stand in mid-camp and disinfect the whole place with a few swirls. The spreads—about a hundred to each camp—he piled one on top of the other, sprinkling each surface with formaldehyde.

On the day when he went in to disinfect the Kingsley camp at Second Roach he met the cook coming out in great haste. About a mile farther on he met the four recovered smallpox patients who had evaded vaccination. Contracting the disease, they had kept the whole camp quarantined and prolonged the summer's work by many weeks.

"Seen that (blankety-blank-blank) cook?" demanded one of the men darkly.

"Yeah. Passed him about a mile back."

"Come on," yelled another to his companion. "We'll catch the (blankety-blank-blank) yet!"

They rushed away, one of them shouting back, "You'll find some nice trout at the camp, also some good salt pork and potatoes!"

Doc pondered. He had overheard a telephone conversation a month before between Jim Kingsley and Jack Richards. Jim had been insistent on something he wanted in spite of Jack's evident protests. Doc recalled Jim's final words: "You get this man for me, and don't you send any other." He recalled, too, a tale Walter Gerrish had told about a cook that Kingsley had hired one winter. Walter had been tending horses at the camp. The food was so bad that all the crew had struck. They would leave unless the cook was replaced. But it was against woods rules of etiquette to discharge a cook. The men left, leaving Jim and Walter and the cook alone. "Well," said Jim, "Walter and I don't need a cook to tend the horses, so I guess you might as well go out tomorrow." The cook had left. The crew had returned with a new cook, and all had been well.

Now Doc saw light. This was the same cook. Jim had hired him as an ironic punishment for these men who had refused vaccination. The men were out for revenge.

Doc proceeded to the camp and his job of disinfecting. A number of hogs had been left behind when the crew left, and they were now ravenous. One old boar was especially belligerent and followed him saucily about. While carrying the water for spraying, Doc kept a pitchfork in hand for protection. After completing the job at the main camp, he entered the cook's quarters, and, deciding to spray inside, opened the cupboards. He found a large supply of biscuits, hard as rocks, and threw them to the hogs. The old boar got three. On his way to the little camp down-stream where the victims had stayed Doc saw him stretched beside a puddle of water, belligerence quelled, barely able to grunt. Even hogs found this cook's victuals hard to stomach. No wonder the four had sworn vengeance.

But, thanks to the thoughtfulness of his erstwhile patients, Doc had an excellent dinner of potatoes, salt pork, and splendid fresh trout, three of them about a foot long.

. 2 .

SUMMER BROUGHT A welcome hiatus in the smallpox emergency; also the culmination of the most progressive health development which the Moosehead country had witnessed in all of Doc's years of practice. The limitations of the little Y.M.C.A. Hospital had been apparent from its inception in 1912. By 1914 the need for a health center ministering to the whole community was being agitated. But it was Dr. Hunt and his niece, Henrietta Bigney, who had finally set the wheels in motion. The head of the big lumber company, Hollingsworth and Whitney, which had been instrumental in erecting the Y.M.C.A., fell sick. Henrietta, who had received her initial nurse's training at the Y Hospital, was sent to take care of him.

"Talk hospital," directed her uncle succinctly. "Talk it all the time. Talk it until the idea chokes him and comes out of his ears."

She did for two solid weeks. She stressed the health needs of the town and its vast environs, the inefficacy of a ten-bed makeshift contrivance up two long flights of stairs under the roof of a building designed for other purposes and barely sufficient to meet the demands of company employees, to say nothing of the population of an area as large as the state of Rhode Island. He listened. He had to. Not long afterward the secretary of the company invited Henrietta to have dinner with him.

"Come early," he told her, "I'll take you up and show you where the new hospital is going to be."

She caught her breath. "You—you mean there's really going to be—"

"Sure. Didn't you talk hospital for two weeks to my boss?"

This was in 1916. The site chosen was a large lot at the top of the hill, slightly nearer the Junction than the Village, but convenient to both. Mr. Charles A. Dean of Wellesley, Massachusetts, president of the company, had directed proceedings of the building, and construction had started immediately. Now, a year later, the new units were nearing completion. The war years, it seemed, could spawn by-products of heaven as well as hell.

On August 1 the new hospital was ready for occupancy.

On the 7th, the first Board of Managers organized and met: Doctors Hunt and Pritham, C. F. Woodard (manager of the Greenville Junction Coburn Company), P. W. Hall (manager of the Veneer Products Company, later Atlas Plywood), and Ernest L. Dean, office manager of Hollingsworth and Whitney. Hunt was elected chairman. Room rates were set at $2 a day for the wards, $3 for private rooms, $4 for special services. Miss Grace Batson was the first superintendent. The first baby born was Charles Dean Noyes, on August 10; the first baby girl, Erma Sawyer Harvey, on September 20.

Doc could scarcely believe their good fortune. A spacious twenty-two-bed hospital! A two-story nurses' home adjacent to it, with thirteen rooms and three baths! No more boosting or tugging helpless or inebriated patients up two long flights of stairs, operating in a brick-lined attic, shushing uproarious revelers when patients must be kept quiet. And now there could be a legitimate school of nursing with students in residence. Not that the old Y Hospital had given inferior training in this department. "We turned out some mighty fine nurses," Doc would recall long afterward with a bit of nostalgia.

He adjusted to the shining sterility of the new operating room with as fluent adaptability as to the exigencies of surgery in a log cabin, and with no variation of techniques. His favorite preparation for a morning of operations was an hour or two of vigorous wood-splitting. He still stood on a stool to operate if his shortness of stature rendered it feasible. He employed the same meticulous neatness and economy in surgical procedure, the same paucity of instruments.

"I know who operated on *you,*" commented a medical examiner of war recruits, tapping a barely perceptible appendectomy incision.

It was in November that the dormant demon again

reared its ugly head. A case in the new hospital was soon diagnosed as smallpox and the patient hustled away to the little shanty on top of the hill. Finding that he had come from Fred Park's camp at Beaver Cove, Doc rushed there in his boat, for, though it was near Thanksgiving, the lake was still open. Tying his boat behind a ledge in excellent shelter at the Creek and draining the engine as was customary at that season, he went into the camp. A man with an obvious case of smallpox would not accept the diagnosis, claiming that he had had the disease as a child. But, yes, he would agree to let the state health officer examine him. Doc had other sick patients to visit at George Libby's camp near Mountain Pond. With three or four inches of snow on the ground, more on the higher spots, it was eight in the evening when he returned to Park's camp after his hike over Prong Pond Mountain and back. It was cold with a nasty northwest wind blowing up.

"Better stay here tonight," urged Fred, who was foreman for Hollingsworth and Whitney. Reluctantly Doc agreed.

After breakfast his boat refused to start. The batteries were dead. Walking home, a mere six miles, he attended his hospital and town patients. He was alone again this winter, with Dr. Hunt nursing an increasing physical weakness in Florida. The following day, Monday, was so windy that few ventured on the Lake. The steamer did not attempt its trip to Lily Bay, and even the *Abenaki*, the H and W boat piloted by Charles Marshall, remained in dock. But on Tuesday Charles decided to risk a trip into Beaver Creek with beef, and Doc, worried about his boat with freeze-up so perilously close, went along, taking a new set of dry cells.

It was a rough trip. To keep in shelter as long as possible they went first to the "Tin Storehouse" in Squaw Bay, then had the sea astern for the run across to Beaver Creek. The toter was on the wharf waiting, but landing was impossible. Fortunately Harry Ray had accompanied them. It took all three to handle the unloading. Charlie maneuvered the boat alongside the wharf. When it surged upward on top of a wave, Doc and Harry would toss off a side of beef. The toter drove his hayhook into it and dragged it over the rim of ice to safety before it slid back into the water. After unloading, the *Abenaki* ran into shelter beside Doc's boat, where he hooked up the cells and, priming with ether, soon started the engine. Now, irony of ironies, Charles' motor refused to start. His batteries were dead! Doc had to loan him his new ones, and, since the *Abenaki* was the larger boat with two men aboard, Doc insisted that he keep them in case his engine stopped again.

"But—that leaves you without any means of restarting if yours stops!"

"I'll manage."

He made a 75-foot chain fast to the bitts and coiled it on deck where it could be snatched off with a boathook in case his engine stalled. He couldn't start it without the batteries but had to depend on the magneto and pray that he didn't get a fuel line plugged with dirt. But the other two were not satisfied. Night was coming on and the wind increasing. After passing the little island and beginning to run into the swells, they turned back, picked up the chain, and took him in tow. A foolish business! The 75-foot chain was too short for such a sea. When it pulled taut, it nearly threw Doc off his feet. It was a relief when it snapped in two, and the *Abenaki,* being the faster craft, went along, soon lost to sight behind walls of frozen spray. Visibility was so bad that they didn't even know when they lost him, though his side-lights were burning brightly. The boat was icing so fast that he had to open the side windows to see and use his compass to chart his course. But even so he fared better alone.

"I'll soon be off Caribou," he judged. "Then I can turn south and stop this head-on course into the seas."

Just then the boat pounded the top of an extra high roller, and there was an ominous crash in the bow. Fearing he had run into a drift log and breached the planking he watched the bilge, tensed for action. If she started to fill, he would beach in a cove near Caribou and jump off the bow with boathook in hand. But, no, the bilge kept dry. Much later he would discover the cause of the crash. The gasoline tank had fallen about a foot when the board across the carlines had broken in two from the jar of the wave. He kept on.

It was a wild night. Occasionally the moon broke through the clouds and outlined the top of Burntjacket. Below, it was all a mass of frozen vapor and water flying. After he got far enough west to clear Burntjacket and swung south, he had the seas astern, so really could enjoy the night. It was a grand sight with all the frozen scud flying away to leeward, the steam from the exhaust making a white line down through it, the moon popping out once in a while to illuminate it and the spray leaping over the cabin roof, all glittering in the red or green light. Spray from the boat often bounded a couple of hundred yards before it struck water and was frozen into ice before it had gone a third of the way. The waves to windward looked as high as a two-story house. But the engine kept running, and no water appeared in the bilge. At Harford's Point he was able to run into shelter, and the rest of the journey was soon completed. But, arriving at his mooring he found the sheltered part of the cove completely iced nearly to his tender. How get to shore? He headed the boat with all speed into the ice, letting it break toward the shore as long as it would. Now any ice left should be strong enough to hold him. He drained the engine, clambered out, and walked ashore, tying the boat to a tree by a long rope. It was the last trip of the season.

Two days later, Thanksgiving Day, Andrew Kennedy helped him haul out the boat. Cutting two spruce logs from the nearby woods, he dragged them to the shore with his horses, then built a cradle while Doc dug a hole in the frozen ground for a crosstie to form a hitching post. Then they sawed a hole through ice five inches thick, floated the boat onto the cradle, and maneuvered it to dry land. The lake sealed so quickly that year that two of the Coburn steamers were unable to get back home and had to tie up at the West Outlet until spring.

When the district health officer arrived to inspect the stubborn patient, the trip to Beaver Cove was safer but even less relaxing. Doc borrowed a work horse from Mr. Hoskins to haul them over the rocks and ruts of the tote road. Lack of snow accentuated both the roughness and the bitter cold. Doc could run to keep warm, but the visitor refused to leave the jolting pung. Teeth chattering with the double stress of jolts and sub-zero cold, he endured the six-mile agony, told the patient for the second time that he had smallpox and would have to obey quarantine or answer to the judge, and suffered through the return trip.

"Good heavens, how do you stand this country?" he shuddered when Doc delivered him to the station.

"Don't stand it," Doc might have said in reply. "Don't sit, either. Just keep movin'."

Just when the smallpox demon seemed to be yawning toward slumber, a popular Greenville miss who had been teaching in Jackman came home during the Christmas vacation and attended a social, dance, or tree party almost every night of her stay. It was discovered that she had a mild case of smallpox. At least half of the town had been exposed. Doc vaccinated as fast and furiously as he could get materials and time, but before the emergency had passed fifty-five known cases had developed, all happily mild, causing still more exposure. The vaccination involved, literally, a house-to-house visitation. Added to the usual hospital work, office, and house calls, the numerous trips to Rockwood, Kineo, Kokadjo, and other outposts far more distant, it left little time for sleep.

In bed, that is. The new saddle horse offered other services than means of transport. When coming home on many of his long trips he could slide back against the cantle, lay an arm on Cleo's neck using it for a pillow, and enjoy a comfortable sleep while she ambled along.

But there were other times when she returned home alone. Howard would wake up in the middle of the night to hear her kicking on the barn door. If neither Mother nor Carroll heard, he would rouse one of them and somebody, usually Mother, would go down and let her into the barn. A day or so later Dad would return from his call at Rockwood or some place farther away. Perhaps he had ridden to the rails, caught up with the freight that had already left the station before he was called and, before jumping it, would have removed the reins and told her to go home. During Howard's first eight years this happened so many times he couldn't have counted them.

But Cleo seldom gave Doc disappointment. That cold winter, with little snow until well into January, furnished an ideal proving ground for a saddle horse. The tote road to Lily Bay was strewn with broken sleds and pungs. It gave one a smug satisfaction to ride past them in saddle, all warm and comfortable. And there were less mundane compensations. A horse and rider were part of the wilderness life, not an intrusion. One saw deer and bear far more often. The horse traveled so lightly that partridge would flush out of the snow beside the road, whereas the rude noise of pung and bells would have kept them quiet in the deeper snow of their beds.

"Probably think you're a fox, Cleo," Doc chuckled.

· 3 ·

BUT THE SMALLPOX DEMON was a mere imp compared with
the devils of disease actually spawned by the war. For in
1918 Pestilence—that fourth pale horseman of the Apoc-
alypse—came riding out of the trenches of Europe. The
first outbreak of influenza, attributed by France to Spain,
by Spain to France, and by America to Eastern Europe,
exploded in the spring and was epidemic in proportion,
confined largely to those nations in the centers of warfare.
But the second outbreak toward the end of September
was pandemic, sweeping over the world. Even the northern Maine wilderness did not escape.

Doc's first victim of the dread "flu" came in the early
fall. He received a rush call to attend the Meservey boy at
Beaver Creek. Because his own boat was too slow, he was
taken in Fred C. Parke's little fourteen-footer, which made
the trip around Burntjacket, to Beaver Cove. But they
were too late. The boy was dead. A few hours before, he
had been eating dinner, apparently well. The disease had
acted with as deadly efficiency as the poison gases let loose
on the battlefields of Europe. There was but one service
Doc could render. He came home, took his own larger
boat, and brought the boy's body out of the creek into
deep enough water so it could be transferred to Lewie
Mountain's *Priscilla* and taken to Greenville.

It was a new and mystifying disease, but its procedures
were to become all too familiar. A few days later one of
his patients, a girl apparently recovering from "a cold,"
collapsed as she was coming downstairs en route to the
breakfast table. She narrowly escaped death. After that
cases crowded thick and fast, both in town and in the re-

motest lumber camps. The infection spread with the rapidity and intensity of a forest fire. In the four months before the crisis passed, Doc would have treated hundreds of cases, sometimes more than 300 in a single day, and ten of black pneumonia, and would have covered over a thousand miles a month, at least half of them on foot.

This second upsurge of the disease was far more virulent than the first. The symptoms were much the same: respiratory catarrah, headache, lassitude, high fever. But this second wave showed a marked tendency to pulmonary complications often resulting in death. And the young and vigorous were the most vulnerable. A patient might seem well on the road to recovery when intense toxemia would occur, leading to prostration and sudden death. Doc had two patients at Soper Brook whom Mollie Chase, a Registered Nurse, had gone up to care for, one of them the foreman's wife, the other a man in the lumber camp. The latter believed himself recovered, so disobeyed orders. He got out of bed, dressed, and walked through a snowstorm to the cookhouse for breakfast. On the way he dropped dead.

For two months Doc barely slept or ate. The demands on his strength would have taxed the energies of a superman, or of a half-dozen doctors. The dread visitant was no respecters of persons or places. It struck the town's mansions as often as its shacks, the remotest lumber camps as well as the house next door. Doc's only rest was in naps which he could snatch on a boat, on his horse's back, in a lumber camp bunk, or on a floor wrapped in a blanket. People would see him half running down the street, perhaps a piece of pie flat on his hand, eating as he went. Often he would get in around two in the morning, after what he called a "forty-hour day." There would be case notes he needed to make in the office. But he dared not turn on a light. If he did, he would be swamped with patients. He would write out his notes in the dark, then crawl into bed and sleep until daylight.

Patience was naturally stretched taut, and a tongue, never noticeably inhibited, sharpened to a thin point of irony. One of his patients was a wealthy woman in town, not noted for her tongue's inhibition. He entered her room in his usual dress—knickers, wool socks and moccasins, lumberman's shirt and mackinaw, no doubt a bit more rumpled than usual. Always critical of his unprofessional garb, she expressed her disapproval of his appearance in no uncertain terms.

"Good," snapped Doc. "If that's the way you feel, then you're not in very serious condition. I'll go and attend some of my patients who are." And he walked out.

But many of the town's leading citizens were his staunch supporters during the crisis. One of the most loyal was Harry Sanders, Sr., who ran the largest store in the Village. The Sanders had been Dr. Hunt's patients, patronizing Doc in the winter when their own physician was in Florida but returning to Hunt, like most of his other patients, on his return. One year after Hunt's arrival, Doc, as usual, did not resume his calls at the Sanders' house.

"Why didn't you go up to my house today?" Sanders hailed him.

"I supposed Dr. Hunt went," replied Doc.

"You go up to the house and look after the sick ones," said Sanders. "I'll look after Hunt." Later Doc learned that Sanders had told Dr. Hunt, "Pritham was good enough for us all winter, when we're really sick. I guess he's good enough in the summer when we're only half sick." Doc had been their doctor ever since.

Now, during the flu crisis, Harry came to his rescue. Doc made all the house calls possible, but fifty-five a day were all he could manage and still attend to the hospital where he was the entire staff of medical men. There were accidents and confinements as well as flu cases. He was able to visit the daughter of a prominent town attorney once but unable to see her again. Like many others, she died. Her father publicly accused Doc of being a murderer, called a meeting, and ordered him to attend. Doc had no time. Instead he went to call on some patients who had been pleading for attendance for days. Harry Sanders went to the meeting and eloquently defended him. At the time, there was a letter in Doc's office from the state attorney general answering his request for another doctor to assist in the emergency.

"Wish I'd known that," regretted Harry. "That would have silenced your critics for sure." But Doc could not have cared less about critics. He had too big a job to do.

He could have used another doctor, yes, a half dozen of them. But as usual he scorned assistance of most kinds. On his trips into the camps guides had usually proved more trouble than benefit. This period of emergency was no exception. One distant camp sent a burly Polish lumberer to show him the way. The man got lost and had to yell vociferously to find his own outfit.

"I could have hollered myself!" Doc remarked disgustedly.

He could have used more cooperation, however, from some sources. One was his boat. In November he was returning from a call at Grant Farm. It had snowed all the way up from the Lily Bay wharf and back, and, with no heaters and no tight sides in the company cars, by the time he arrived back at his boat at two o'clock in the morning he was thoroughly chilled. A bitter northeast wind was blowing. Since the engine was cold and the wind broadside to the boat and liable to blow it ashore if the motor stalled, he decided to draw the lever and start it in neutral and get the oil flowing before untying. Priming the engine, he gave it a flop, and it started up well—so well that it shook the cam-shaft wheel off into the bilge! Not so pleasant lying down beside a cold engine and timing the valves by lantern light, with the snow falling down your neck, especially when you were so sleepy you could hardly see the lantern and were chilled clear through! But he finally got her timed and the gear on solid, primed her, and away she fired—and shook the gear off again! Repeating the whole process, he jamed the lever into "go ahead" and cast off the lines. This time she went. But it took so much attention getting the drip feeds functioning properly that he neglected to watch his position.

Suddenly he looked out to see land on both sides of the boat. That little island just south of the wharf! Quickly he pulled the switch, and the boat coasted in over the reef and up between a big boulder and the island, then slid up onto a smooth ledge and tipped over against the boulder. Stuck fast! Dropping the lantern over the stern, he noted two inches of green paint out of water. Impossible to move without a push. All right, so be it! He shut down the oil and gasoline, tied the side curtains down aft, drew a camp spread from the bow, kicked off his rubbers, uttered a long weary sigh, and lay down to sleep. A-ah-ah! No knocks at the door, no telephone ringing. For the first time in two months he slept peacefully.

But two o'clock until dawn was not long. With the first light he shook himself awake, ate a lunch from the reserve cans of food he always kept on board, took a peavy from under the floor and, sticking its point between the keel and the ledge, quickly pried the craft loose. Nothing like a lumberman's cant dog for any sort of work needing a good leverage! He wouldn't have run a boat without one. The engine fired quickly. He ran back to the wharf and went to the hotel to get a sick man whom he had refused to take with him at midnight because of the bitter northeaster. A good thing the man hadn't been lying for hours in behind that island with the spray coming over and through the birches to strike the boat, and snow sifting down on him! The whole week was a despicable one for boating, so cold that condensation vapor constantly accompanied the snow and seeing was next to impossible. He was out through the Sugar Island thoroughfare every night of it, and except for this time did not once strike bottom. A good job of navigating with the lake at low level!

Weeks passed, and his request for an assistant was unheeded. It finally took tragedy other than the epidemic to produce results. In the late fall he attended a man at Dulac's camp who had been accidentally shot by a friend with a .35 automatic. The pelvis was smashed, half the bladder ripped to pieces. Doc brought him to the hospital, but he died. Doc was asked to attend a hearing at Skowhegan.

"I can't," was his prompt reply. "I have fifty to sixty patients here with the flu. I can't leave them, and what's more, I won't."

He was sent an assistant, a Dr. Bates who had just been released from the Army. He arrived in January, 1919, and stayed for about a year. But by the time he arrived the worst of the epidemic was over. After four months of "forty-hour days" Doc was glad to return to his usual schedule of being on call for only twenty-four.

The additional medical help was doubly welcome, for Dr. Hunt did not return from his annual respite in Florida with his usual renewed energy. In November of that year he died, after thirty-five years of skilled and dedicated service to the area, not only as physician but as druggist, selectman, superintendent of schools, member of the school board. Though trained in a generation which considered two courses of sixteen weeks each sufficient to qualify a doctor, his keen analytical mind had kept him constantly

alert to new ideas, and he had taken a refresher course
of some kind each winter. Doc would miss him sorely.

But the office in the corner of the cedar hedge did not
remain empty. Happily that very year Dr. Hunt's nephew,
Norman Nickerson, graduated from Bowdoin Medical
School and, after an internship at the Eastern Maine General Hospital in Bangor, he settled in Greenville. Again
there would be two doctors serving the huge wilderness,
working for the next four decades in close cooperation.

Doc had to pay his respects to his colleague in absentia.
The day of Dr. Hunt's funeral he was rushing from a case
in Shirley to a confinement at Ripogenus Dam. A new
road had been built in 1918 to Lily Bay, and it was now
possible to go by car almost the year around from Greenville to Ripogenus. But today there had just been a heavy
snowstorm, and the road was not plowed. The six-cylinder
Overland bought in 1917 was as useless as a pung in summer. Mr. Price, the patient's husband, who had attempted
to drive to Grant Farm to put in the call, had found such
deep snow that he was unable to travel the last few miles,
so had left his car stalled with snow piled to the top of
the radiator and walked the rest of the way.

Cleo was tired from the trip to Shirley and back, so Doc
hired a horse to drive to Lily Bay, changed it there for
another, and from Grant Farm a man with a pair and
tote sled drove him and Mr. Price to the stalled car. Why
in thunder the driver was not asked to stop and turn the
car Doc couldn't figure. He and Mr. Price shoveled the
snow away, but the road was so narrow and slippery they
could not turn the car. After a half hour of labor Doc
picked up his heavy satchel and started to wade the last
nine or ten miles to his laboring patient. He had covered
perhaps half the distance when the car overtook him. Remembering that there was a solid bridge into the woods
some distance back, Mr. Price had shoveled ruts back to
this point, backed his car, and managed to turn.

Even now, three years after its completion in 1916, Doc was still awed by the monumental magnitude of Ripogenus Dam. In the superb gorge, ten or twenty thousand years' grinding toil of the tumbling, foaming West Branch, nature had surpassed herself, and in the monstrous masonry now surmounting it—860 feet long, 92 wide, 64 thick at its base, wide enough at the top for a 16-foot driveway—man had surpassed and conquered nature. No mean engineering feat, forty-five miles from a railroad, building this mammoth structure capable of holding back two and a half billion cubic feet of water and confining it to a new Chesuncook Lake forty-two square miles in extent! That red-flaunting ghost of Larry O'Connor, who had been swept away in the boiling cauldron which was now the "dry way," might well have haunted the operation, repeating his favorite appraisal of the West Branch drive: "By Judas' hemp, it ain't no holy Sunday school!"

Certainly it had not been a job for weaklings. Drunken men, shanghaied in the Bangor saloons and taken in to work, had preferred to make their escape and walk out fifty miles. Nor for the lazy. Henry Bartley, who had bossed the toting from the Lily Bay wharf with a big crew, had helped see to that. Noting one fellow proficient in avoiding labor when the truck was being loaded, Henry had waited for the next empty to back up, noted that the avoidance of labor was repeated, and, rolling his cigar back and forth until the shirker was conveniently located, had hoisted a grindstone over the side of the truck, dropping it with remarkable accuracy on the fellow's toes. The howling victim had been put on the outgoing boat and sent back to Bangor. An effective method of discharge!

Doc arrived in time to deliver a fine infant, lustily healthy as befitted the impressive environs. Fifty years later he would recall the attractiveness of the young frontier mother, possessed of "the handsomest head of hair, chestnut, which hung to her waist." The job finished, he retraced his steps, or rather, the horse's, for he had to travel the last ten miles on foot. The new road was not entirely a boon. In his absence it had been plowed and graveled, so, having the pung, he walked while the poor horse dragged the sled laboriously over the bare ground. With a little forewarning he could have hired a horse to pull the pung over good snow to Shirley and back, and had his own horse for this trip. On Cleo's back he could have covered the ground in half the time.

· 4 ·

THE HELLS WERE NOT all spawned by war. Far from it. One reared its head in December, 1919.

It was morning of Saturday, five days before Christmas. Through the bleak, wild winterland of northern Maine a train with 300 passengers was rushing westward. Many still lay in their berths, but others could not sleep. Eyes stared, fascinated, from the windows, half intrigued, half repelled by the strange new panorama of deep glittering snow, thick jade forests, chains of frozen lakes, bare rugged mountains. For, while a few were returning Canadian soldiers, most of the three hundred were Scotch and English immigrants, fresh from the *S.S. Empress* of France, which had brought them to St. John in a stormy passage from London, and they were bound for Vancouver and Winnipeg to seek their fortunes in the new world. Clutched in hands or in bags under seats or trunks in the baggage car were most of their worldly possessions, valuables as well as trinkets, for there were both prosperous and poor among the hopeful adventurers.

At the same time a freight train of forty-one cars was moving east. The engineer, Bagley, had received orders to pass the immigrant train, which was traveling in five sections, at Morkill siding, eight miles west of Onawa. He remained on the siding while two sections passed; then, it was believed later, he forgot the third section. Expecting to reach the next crossing point before the fourth, which was running a half hour late, he proceeded.

The passenger train with its eight coaches pushed leisurely by a fringe of mountains, came past Benson and over the trestle—passed the flag station of Onawa and moved toward Bodfish, two and a half miles away. Beyond the foot of Boarstone Mountain, a bare upthrust of rock, was a steep upgrade. To pull his load of eight coaches up the incline, engineer Wilson fed his monster engine every ounce of power possible. Meanwhile, on the downgrade, engineer Bagley, with his forty-one loaded freight cars, was rushing toward a curve, able to see less than two hundred feet ahead. They rounded the curve at the same instant. The grinding of brakes, the blaring of whistles, the rending of timbers and snapping of steel, the swift lashing of flames—all blended with the sickening crash and the frenzied shrieks of human fright and agony. Freight cars were tossed on end, to fall with a resounding roar at the base of the mountain range. Passenger coaches, splintered by their own locomotive, reared up for an instant, then toppled over a thirty-foot embankment.

It was a holocaust—an inferno. Passengers still able to move struggled blindly through the limbo of fire, steam, smoke, to the rear of the wreck, to emerge faint and gasping, paralyzed with shock. Some of the cooler-headed, among them the Canadian soldiers, attempted to quiet the panic-stricken and within a few minutes were battling through the mass of tangled steel and splintered wood to reach the dying and injured pinned under the wreckage before they were burned to death by the spreading fire. As the charred and mutilated bodies of the dead were taken out, they were laid in rows beside the tracks to await identification—in many cases impossible. Frantic calls for help were dispatched from the nearest station, and relief trains were soon rushing from Megantic, Quebec, St. John, and Greenville Junction.

Doc, of course, was one of those summoned. With Dr. Bates and several nurses from the hospital, he was soon on his way. Most of the injured, at least fifty, had been taken to an improvised hospital in the woodsmen's Y.M.C.A. in Brownville Junction. Six had died on the way. Though Doc had been appointed in 1913 First Aid Man for the CP railroad serving the Greenville area (a position he would still be holding fifty-seven years later), this was Don Harden's section, so he asked his old classmate for orders.

"Just go ahead," was the simple direction. "Do what needs to be done."

Heaven knew there was plenty that needed doing! Everywhere there were burns, cuts, bruises, broken bones to be set and splinted. Doc found most of the victims incredibly brave. None of those having bones set indulged even in a whimper. But in one room he found two little boys crying lustily and in another a woman weeping because her children were missing. Uniting her with the boys was to see heaven emerge in the midst of hell. She lay down in the middle of their bed, her head at their feet, giving all plenty of room, and they were soon asleep.

The tragedy had its Janus face of comedy. When Doc stopped by the bedside of a boy with a splinted leg, a nurse standing nearby curtly informed him that her friend, Dr. So-and-So, had just set that leg.

"Well," Doc commented dryly, "guess I'd better fix it it up a bit. The way it is now it'd be hard tellin' which way the boy was traveling, with one foot pointing ahead and the other astern."

While she looked on, mutely gaping, he turned the foot

Fred J. "Doc" Pritham and Sarah Ring Pritham on their
wedding day, June 20, 1906.

Young Doc in his early twenties.

Sarah Ring in her late teens.

Street view, Greenville, Maine, just after World War I.

Railroad Junction. Greenville Junction, Maine.

Doc's boat landing at Coburn Wharf.

(At left, above) Doc and his jerry-built snowmobile, circa 1930.

HE WAS BORN IN FREEPORT MAINE.

IN 1901 AFTER A TERRIBLE BLIZZARD HE HAULED 55 LOADS OF HAY FOR THE HORSES IN BRUNSWICK

DR. PRITHAM GRADUATED FROM MEDICAL SCHOOL IN 1905, AND IN 1918 DURING THE "FLU" CRSIS, HE COVERED 2500 SQUARE MILES THROUGH ALL KINDS OF WEATHER

BOB WARE

DR. FRED J. PRITHAM A GREAT MAN IN HIS PROFESSION!

"Dr. Fred J. Pritham. A Great Man in His Profession!"
Pencil sketch by Bob Ware of the *Moosehead Gazette.*

Oil portrait of Doc by Albion Ende.

Doc at his desk-safe, 1943.

Portrait of young-old Doc.

Doc and alto horn in the Greenville High School Band.

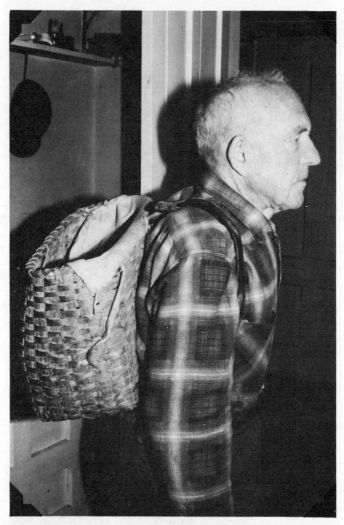

Doc with his backpack setting out on a call.

Front and side view, the Pritham house, their dwelling since 1906.

The Pritham house, Maine winter.

Doc's son Howard, also a doctor,
with his mother Sadie.

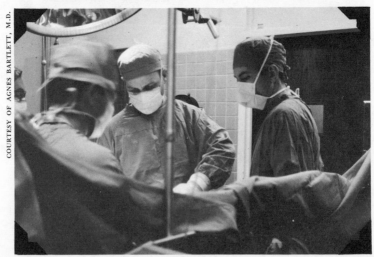

Dr. Howard G. Pritham (Doc's grandson) at surgery,
Veteran's Hospital, White River Junction, Vermont.

Young-old Doc at his medicine cabinet.

Doc and Sadie today.

around and resplinted it. "There. Now maybe he can walk natural."

Another woman who resisted examination sat continually in a rocking chair, maintaining stoutly that nothing ailed her. Later in Montreal it was found that she had a broken hip.

In the late afternoon a train was made up to carry passengers to Montreal. Many of the injured were put on board for transportation to the Royal Victoria Hospital two hundred miles away. Doc returned home on this special train, re-routed over the Bangor and Aroostook tracks as far as Greenville Junction, while two of his best nurses, Grace Blanchard and Jessie Shirley, accompanied the injured patients to Montreal.

For hours, days, search for the dead continued. That night the charred remains of fireman Hudson were extricated from the tangled mass, following the fourteen other bodies already stored in a freight shed in Brownville Junction. But engineer Bagley's body, jammed under a tender fifteen feet from the track, still had not been reached, and not until two days later would that of engineer Wilson be found crushed under a freight car, bringing the final toll of dead to twenty-three.

The day before Christmas a contingent of military police from Montreal might be seen standing guard over a pile of treasures and trinkets raked from the charred and twisted wreckage.

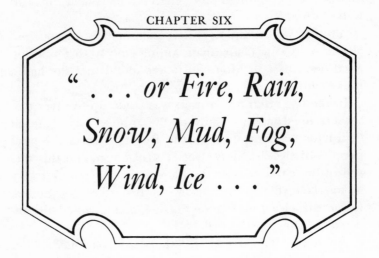

CHAPTER SIX

" . . . or Fire, Rain,
Snow, Mud, Fog,
Wind, Ice . . . "

. 1 .

*Oh, come all ye young hellions, and gather
    around,
I'll tell you a story of twenty men drowned;
A story that's fit to be made into a book,
Of almost a whole crew that was lost on
    'Suncook.*

So STARTED A BALLAD of nearly thirty stanzas, reputedly
by the "Old Moosehead Guide," which was sung for many
years around the deacon seat, a soloist intoning the lugu-
brious verses, the other lumbermen occasionally joining
in the chorus with a gusto which would fairly lift the
"splits" off the roof.

It was November 18, 1920. There had been about a foot of snowfall, and the lakes were skimming around the edges. The Great Northern was cutting around Cuxebexis and Umbazooksus, and about four-thirty that afternoon Alec Gunn loaded thirty-six new lumbermen—Poles, Russians, and "Canucks"—into his motor launch at Chesuncook Dam to take them and their supplies to the camps at the head of Chesuncook Lake.

"Mebbe this boat's last trip this season," he commented cheerfully. "Lake's been freezin' fast lately." The words were truer than he knew.

The men crowded into the launch, a sturdy craft with full-length cabin and glass windows. But, as the ballad described it:

> 'Twas colder than hell, for the wind it was raw;
> Each buttoned up warm in his old
>   mackinaw . . . .
> The fumes from the motors made some of them
>   sick,
> But for the most part they were all riding slick.

No one knew exactly what happened. Perhaps a spark from the ignition, or a backfire of the engine, or more like someone scratching a match to light a smoke. But when they were at the entrance to Duck Pond the bilge-gas exploded, and the whole boat ignited in a mass of flames. The front windows were blown out onto the deck, and Smith, who was running the boat, with them.

"Jump!" someone yelled. "Jump for your lives!"

They jumped. Crazed with fear and unable to swim, some sank almost without a struggle in the icy waters. Others, hampered by heavy clothing, floundered toward the near shore for, fortunately, the boat was in the narrows between Duck and Moose Ponds. A camp clerk was so distraught that he removed all his outer clothes, folded them carefully, and put them on the wheel-house roof, then leaped. But a young Pole, nameless, was destined to become a hero. He threw off his heavy coat and moccasins. He cut a piece of the anchor rope and knotted it around his waist. Then, taking the matches from the pocket of his red shirt, he put them in the lining of his cap, jammed it back tightly on his head, and lowered himself slowly into the water. Being a good swimmer, he quickly reached shore, some sixty yards away. There he hastily kicked dri-ki (dead wood) to pieces and with his dry matches soon had a fire going. Then he rushed back into the water and rescued some of the less vigorous swimmers, dragging them into the warm circle of the fire. When they would have lain down and succumbed to unconsciousness in their freezing clothes, he unknotted the rope and, striking right and left, lashed them into unwilling activity, kept them dancing about the fire until icy blood was quickened and half-frozen flesh tingled again into life. Downshore at Moose Pond storehouse Fred Noad and George Cassidy saw the flaming boat, threw blankets into a skiff, and rowed furiously up the lake. Others telephoned for help.

Taking Dr. Nickerson with him, Doc started for the Dam. It was long since dark, but he drove as fast as the Overland six and the pocked and rutted road allowed. Just beyond Grant Farm he thought he had a flat tire on a rear wheel. Dr. Nick jumped out and looked them all over. No, he assured, it was the holes left by the heavy truck horses that gave the sensation. Even a skilled doctor could make poor mechanical diagnosis. They ran the remaining eight miles on a flat tire. Arriving at Chesuncook Dam, Doc phoned home to have a new tire and tube sent up for their return trip. Going up the lake they had to swing cant dogs to break the rapidly forming ice.

They arrived finally at the scene of disaster, but there was little they could do. The dead were past help. The others, thanks to the young Pole as well as their own resilient hardiness, were restored to comparative normalcy and soon proceeded to their camp destinations for the winter's work.

About dawn Doc and Nickerson arrived at a Great Northern lumber camp at Moose Brook, at the head of the lake. Breakfast was waiting. Dr. Nick watched with mounting incredulity while Doc filled his tin plate with oatmeal, beans, stewed corn, raisin pie, beef, everything on the table, then poured molasses over it and mixed all together. A nourishing conglomeration, certainly! Later Dr. Nick stopped at the store and bought a dozen chocolate bars, his meals for the rest of the day. He offered Doc half of them.

"No, thanks," Doc shook his head, "couldn't. I wish I had a strong stomach like yours, but I have to be fussy what I put into mine."

Doctor Nick opened his mouth, closed it. His silence was more eloquent than words.

They returned home shocked and sobered by a tragedy that would be chronicled, deplored, remembered for the next half-century as the "Chesuncook Lake Disaster." For both living and dead it had been indeed a trial by fire.

> *For just as a fire took the lives of a few,*
> *Not a man might have lived out of that whole*
> *   crew*
> *If they'd made no fire to warm them that night,*
> *When ice made 'long shore, before dawn's early*
> *   light.*
>
> *Among the survivors were Gunn, Smith, and*
> *   Snow,*
> *And about twelve more whose names I don't*
> *   know.*
> *They recovered the drowned men with grapples*
> *   and hooks;*

> *Then looked up their names in the company's*
> *books.*

Some of the names, that is, and they were inscribed on the eighteen small identical granite stones erected in two long rows on a lot bought by the Great Northern in the Greenville cemetery. Many of them were eloquent with strangeness, strange lands, the strange fate which had brought them to this Yankee enclave of Browns, Smiths, Sawyers, Crafts, Sanders. *Peterson, Carlson, Maki, Stowski, Bulkovitz.* And even more eloquent of pitiable strangeness were those with other markings. Unknown Number 1 ... Unknown Number 2 ... Unknown Number 14.

Impressive in their stark simplicity, almost as impressive as the three mausuleums! In the next half-century they would draw many visitors, the curious, the compassionate, the sadly reminiscent. One of the latter was Hugh Desmond, a Great Northern employe well acquainted with the details of the tragedy. From there he went to Doc's office to have an arm infection treated and mentioned where he had been.

"So you spend your day off visiting cemeteries!" scoffed Doc as he rewound the bandages. Then he sobered. "A pity," he thought aloud, "that when a doctor is most needed, he's often fifty miles away!"

> *So ends my song of the 'Suncook Lake crew,*
> *Who gave up their lives as some lumberjacks do;*
> *For there is no calling that tested men more*
> *Than getting out lumber in the old days of yore.*

. 2 .

SNOW. For half the year it was seldom absent in this north country for a whole month. A year's fall might run to 150 inches, averaging well over 100. Bane and beauty, it clogged roads, buried ugly slush, coated thin ice with treacherous camouflage, turned pointed firs into diamond-studded spearheads, stalled cars, transformed modest mountains into white-capped Alps, strained the guts of horses and aging shovelers, hung the noble 67-foot spruce up at Squaw Brook beside the Rockwood trail with the glittering festoons and baubles of a giant Christmas tree.

'Twenty-one was a bad year for snow. Paths to the entrances of houses were like tunnels, their sides higher than a man's head. Louis Oakes, one of the town's prominent men, was having a house remodeled opposite the high school. As Doc rode along West Street on Cleo, a workman carrying sheets of veneer into the house for repairing suddenly lifted his load so that it reared above the high side bank of the path just as the horse came abreast. Frightened, she reared. Doc, a little disgusted with her, gave a yank on the reins. It threw her to the ground. He leaped from the saddle, but not quickly enough. She fell on his leg. The injury, though painful, was not incapacitating. He coaxed the horse up, mounted her, and continued with his home visits and hospital work.

In the evening a call came to go to Rockwood to John King's. He boarded a thru freight and jumped off at Somerset Junction. He could walk to King's, he thought, then walk back in time for the four A.M. train, Number 16. Usually an easy jaunt, a mere seven miles, tonight for some reason it took him a heck of a long time. True, it was hard footing, with a good twelve inches of loose new snow, but even so he couldn't understand his slowness. It was two in the morning before he reached King's. Mrs. King made him sleep there. Then someone drove him to the station with a horse and pung in time to meet the train to Somerset.

That afternoon as he was scrubbing for an appendectomy his leg felt a bit queer, and he looked down at it. There was a seam across the tibia a good quarter-inch wide. You could have laid a lead pencil in it!

"Look," he said to the nurse, "what do you make of that?"

"Oh, F.J.!" She uttered a shocked scream. "It's broken! You must X-ray it right now!"

"No time." He continued to scrub. "We must get that appendix out."

"But—a broken leg—!"

He never did find time. If it had stood jumping from a train and wading seven miles through snow, he reckoned, it could likely take care of itself. It did, healing without further incident.

It was in the fall of 1923 that he bought his first snow-mobile, a Ford Model T coupe connected to caterpillar treads constructed of canvas, with a metal shoe to give a toehold. Though the Great Northern had one, it was still such a curiosity in town that both children and adults flocked to inspect the new contraption.

His first trip to try it out came on January 28, 1924. Deputy Sheriff Dell Rogers called him. A man had phoned from Chesuncook, claiming that his sister had been murdered. At that time Doc was the medical examiner, so it was his duty to accompany the deputy on his investigation. They took the new machine and started. Progress was good but slow, and it was after dark as they rode along the winter road which passed Deer Pond and skirted the lake through the woods. It was the first time a car had traveled this road, though cars had been driven to Chesuncook Village over the ice. As they approached the village the brilliant headlights on the white snow turned night into day. News of their coming had preceded them, and the village was agog with excitement. For once Uncle Anse was not asleep behind his stove. He was out on the piazza of his hotel, bare-headed and in shirt sleeves, bubbling with his usual enthusiasm, eyes almost as bright as the headlights. As the strange vehicle ground to a stop, he fairly danced up and down.

"I told 'em," he shouted, "I told 'em we'd see the bright lights comin' up the road!"

They stayed at his hotel that night, Dell picking up all the news possible about the suspected crime. Locating the accused man in a nearby house, he listened to his story. It was candid and straightforward. The man was accustomed, it developed, to spend an occasional evening with a certain lady who lived on the island, taking with him several bottles of home brew. This time he slipped on a strip of glare ice and broke the bottles. But the lady was equal to the occasion and produced a jug nearly full of a similar concoction. They consumed the contents, and she was so overcome that she fell at the foot of the stairs and could not rise. Nor was he able to lift her. Finding a number of spreads, he covered her, then went upstairs to the loft and fell asleep. Returning to consciousness the next forenoon, he descended to find to his horror that she was dead. He went to another house on the island where the woman's brother lived and told him of the tragedy. Immediately the brother accused him of murder by supplying the liquor and permitting his sister to freeze to death.

In the morning Doc and the deputy took a pair of horses and drove to the island. The accused man, who accompanied them, showed them his pack filled with broken glass and rank with the stench of liquor. But the brother was there also, hot with accusations. It was easy enough to see how the death had occurred. The woman lay about six feet from a door which opened to the north and had a good inch of clearance between bottom and sill. The temperature had been minus thirty. Doc made his examination. So far the facts checked with the accused's story. He

had a hunch that the man was telling the truth. But—
where was the jug he had mentioned? Doc began looking
around. Out in the woodshed he found a jug that seemed
especially well concealed. He brought it into the house.

"That's it!" The accused hailed it excitedly. "That's
the jug she brought out!" Grabbing it, he pulled out the
bung and passed it to the deputy. "Smell it!"

Dell sniffed, looked doubtful, and handed it to Doc.
"What do you think?"

Doc frowned. There was no noticeable odor. But, the
jug was cold.

The brother was exultant. "See? The (blank) is lying.
What did I tell you?"

Doc gathered a good lungful of air, then blew vigorously
into the jug, warming it thoroughly. Then he passed it to
the deputy, who gasped and almost choked from the
fumes.

"That settles it," pronounced Doc. "I'll make out the
death certificate."

"Wh-what do you mean?" demanded the brother bel-
ligerently. "A certificate?"

"I'll give you a certificate of death from intoxication
and freezing. Accidental death. My work's done. No
further need of an inquiry."

The brother exploded. "I—I'll get you for this! I'll
haul you into court!"

"Do," replied Doc equably. "All I need for evidence is
this jug you so carefully washed out and hid. You're the
one to worry. This man you've accused of murder has a
very good case for suing."

Sobered by this prospect, the brother gave the necessary
information, and Doc and the deputy were free to start
for home. They almost failed to get there. Between Deer
Pond and Grant Farm the runners slewed, striking the
battery which was mounted on the side of the chassis, and

knocked it off. Haywire, the woodsman's eternal panacea, to the rescue! Doc always carried a plentiful supply. It was good for almost all emergencies, from mending a harness to establishing an electrical connection, as in the present instance. There was even a legend that a Greenville dentist had once constructed a neat bridge of haywire and the molars of a fawn, which had served its owner's masticatory needs for eleven years!

But the side battery was not the contraption's only liability. Its low gear was extremely slow. Doc found that out on a trip to Sandbar one winter day soon afterward. Thirty miles of holding one's foot on an iron pedal at 20° below zero was enough to disillusion anyone with such a rigging! The next summer he installed a set of Warford gears. Not only did they give more power, but the neutral gear was a great convenience when cranking the cold motor. Then he could drive in Ford high and Warford low and leave his feet free to keep warm. Summers he used the machine with wheels instead of the canvas treads. He also added a water pump to the side of the motor to help cool it. For dry snow the canvas belts worked well, but on the lake one might run into slush and get them wet. Then on a zero day they would freeze and break. A bit later he added the improvement of an all-metal belt which, like an iron chain, shook itself free of accumulating ice. True, it broke occasionally, but he carried enough spare parts for easy repairing.

He was soon setting other records with his snowmobile. "Dr. F. J. Pritham," recorded *The Northern* in February, 1927, "who was the first to drive a car into Chesuncook Village by the tote road, has set another record. On January 10 he filled the tank of his snowmobile with 30 gallons of gasoline and started for Chamberlain Lake. He drove to Grant Farm, Deer Pond, and Chesuncook Village; here he crossed Chesuncook Lake and Gero Island and went up Umbazooksus Meadows past Longley Pond to the head of Umbazooksus Lake. The doctor left his car here and proceeded to the camp at the mouth of Ellis Brook on Chamberlain Lake on snowshoes, a distance of five miles. The doctor had run his car farther north than anyone had ever gone before in this country with a motor vehicle. The return trip of about 70 miles was made in seven hours."

One of Doc's improvements on the snowmobile had serious drawbacks. In fact, it almost cost two lives, to say nothing of his own. He made a wooden frame with his own hands and covered it with sheet iron to make a warm cab. It was built with only one door.

It happened on Washington's Birthday. Doc had been called to Shirley, about six miles to the south, to attend a girl with appendicitis. Finding that she needed immediate surgery, he put her and her sister in the cab of his snowmobile and drove back to Greenville. The road between the Village and the Junction was bare, so it was necessary to transfer to the lake to get to the Junction.

"Why don't you take Bartlett's taxi to the hospital," he suggested to the girls, "and I'll meet you there." But they were enjoying the adventure of a snowmobile ride too much to forego its exciting conclusion.

The ice was rotting fast in the sun, and just that morning an automobile that had gone too close to the reef on the east side of the channel at Mile Island had broken through, so Doc maneuvered the vehicle with special care, keeping well away from the fir tree marking the treacherous hole where the car had been pulled out. But as he neared Mile Island he saw just ahead a smooth strip of ice. Instantly he turned the runners toward the center of the channel, but there was no traction, and the vehicle went straight ahead. He saw that if it kept on sliding, it must run onto thin ice. It did.

"Jump!" he snapped. "Open the door and get out—quick!"

But the girls sat motionless, the well one holding her sick sister in her lap. And the only door was on their side of the cab! He could not reach over them to open it. The car broke through and sank, landing on the slanting side of the island and nearly tipping over. At first he was afraid it would tip far enough to cover the door and shut off escape. He could see the rocks of the shore bottom over the top of the canvas which covered the space above the door. But, no, it did not tip completely on its side. It settled to lie on an angle in about eight feet of water.

Still the girls made no effort to get out. Freeing himself from the wheel, Doc doubled up and dove toward the door. As the girls floated upward toward the cab roof, a space opened beneath them, and he dove through it. But when he managed to get through the door, some encumbrance held him fast. One of the girls hanging onto his mackinaw tail! Bracing his feet against the side of the cab, he straightened and pulled free, bringing the girl along with him. Later he would marvel at the composure which had caused the sister to loose her clinging hands. None of the usual panic of a drowning person! It was unbelievable.

He looked about him. No opening above. The fragments of ice through which they had fallen had floated together, hiding their entrance. But it was incredibly opaque and light. He could see fifty feet in any direction. The green grassy growth on the rocky bottom was as bright and well defined as on the bottom of a fish bowl. Such impressions consumed less than seconds. Towing the girl behind him, he swam quickly to the front of the car, then went straight up over the cowl and cab to emerge through the broken ice on top. There was only a foot or so of water above the car. He shoved the girl to the top side of the cab and, dropping to his knees, looked down over the side. There were the other girl's feet protruding through the doorway. Luck, indeed! He wouldn't have to dive into the cab after her.

He grabbed her feet and, using the doorway as a leverage, pried her head and shoulders downward until she emerged from the door, then gave her feet a quick shove downward. Up bobbed her head so that he could seize her shoulders and pull her to the top of the car. Expecting that with so long an immersion he would have to give her artificial respiration, he was amazed when she blew out her breath with a gasp and gulped, "O-oh, it's cold!"

Fortunately there were men near by. They had passed Mr. Boothman and his boys with a sled-load of camp bedding and dishes that they were taking home to wash for the spring fishing season. The Boothmans quickly returned and, lifting the fir tree from the hole on the other side of the channel, made a bridge of it from solid ice to the car top. Fred Goven came along and loaned his car to take the girls to the hospital. But instead of driving them he decided that Doc should go along with them. Since it was a one-seater, Doc had to drive. His mittens froze to the wheel so he was unable to move the clutch. Finally he pried his hands out of the mittens, leaving them frozen to the wheel while he shifted, then put his hands back into them.

Mrs. Vere Bradley, a graduate nurse, was in the office when he brought in his patients. Looking up, she gave a cry of dismay. There was a half-strange, half-familiar figure dripping water all over the floor.

"F.J.!" she screamed. "What—"

He wasted no words of explanation. "Get these girls to bed, and give them something hot to drink. If she hasn't caught cold, I'll be operating on one of them in the morning." When morning came, she hadn't, and he did.

"Patient always needs a bath before an operation," he was reported afterward as saying.

Howard had witnessed the accident at a distance. Skating on the lake a half mile away, he had watched the progress of the snowmobile, seen it go through the ice. But, though he had skated frantically toward it, Dad had departed for the hospital with the two girls by the time he arrived. He stood staring at the ice-clogged hole slashed by the rakish angle of the car top almost on a level with the water, and there was a sick feeling in the pit of his stomach. He had always envied Dad his swiftness of motion, felt a tiny resentment because his own pace was more slow and measured. But not anymore! Suppose it had taken him minutes instead of seconds! And suppose he had had the old custom-made snowmobile instead of this homemade one. He could never have gotten the girls out.

Sadie had been to Harford's Point that day over the ice with a group of women. She had her own car now, had owned one since 1921 when she had been visiting in Freeport for a week or two after a bout with cabin fever. Doc had ordered the car for her, a little Franklin coupe with an air-cooled engine, and had it delivered to her there, and she had driven it home. She had long since reconciled herself to the fact that if she wanted to go places, she must usually go without her husband.

She was working at the stove when he entered the kitchen and did not turn around.

"Well," he said, "did you get the car up over the lake and back all right today?"

"Oh, yes," she replied, continuing calmly with her supper preparations.

"Good. I put mine in the bottom of the lake."

She whirled around. There he stood in the doorway dripping icicles. She did not panic. After all, he was alive and, unless pneumonia resulted, the worst was over. She listened to his relation of the episode as calmly as it was related, then continued preparing supper while he changed into dry clothes. Only later when they were in the living room did full realization come to her. Doc was reading his medical journals as usual—they were all he ever read —and she was playing the piano while Carroll sang. Suddenly she stopped playing. Her blood seemed to congeal. Coldness swept through her body and numbed even her fingertips.

"Hey, what's the matter, Mom?"

"Nothing, dear. I—I was just thinking—"

That it might be so different tonight! The words thudded through her consciousness like death knells. But she did not speak them. And presently she resumed the accompaniment as if nothing had happened. Nor did she express later to Doc the flood of emotional relief which sent the warm blood racing again through her veins. She did not need to. The two had long since developed an understanding which relied little on verbal communication.

Perhaps it was this wordless empathy as well as their mutual independence which made some people call them the "queerest couple in town." Ella Gerrish saw both characteristics in full play one Sunday afternoon when she visited the Prithams.

"Is Sadie around?" she inquired.

Doc lifted his face from his medical journal. "No. She's been gone about a week or so. I'm not sure just where she went, to Brownville probably to visit Hallie, but I expect it must be pretty near time for her to get back."

Deciding to wait, and thoroughly at home in this house, Ella sat down. Presently Doc launched into his favorite subject, duck hunting, a familiar one to the girl. In fact, she had gone under ether in the middle of one of his hunting yarns. Now, in the middle of another long one, a car drove into the yard.

"Here she is now," said Doc.

He did not move, and in a few moments Sadie came in and stood in the doorway. They said nothing, just looked at each other. Knowing them so well, Ella could almost translate this silence into words. After all, why bother with any of the silly things people say—"How are you?" and all that? You can look and see how the other person is. If they both look all right, then why waste silly conversation? After some moments of mutual scrutiny Sadie sat down, and she and Ella began talking, Doc retreating once more into his journal. The two talked for perhaps half an hour, after which Sadie went to get her suitcase out of the car. Whereupon Doc turned to Ella and resumed his duck story exactly where he had left off.

· 3 ·

A PLAGUE ON the old snowmobile! It had always been a miserable job, the engine wobbling, nothing hooked up decently. Doc was almost glad when on a trip to Shirley the crankshaft finally broke. He got the machine towed home and bolted the side frame piece to a plank on the front of the barn, the only use he could find for it.

His next snowmobile he built himself, in 1928, using the old one's rear end and cross axle, together with the chassis and engine of the Rollins, which he had bought in 1923 and driven until its rear end broke. As he described the process: "I sewed an extra crossbar across it to anchor the gears and axle to, so it couldn't wobble. This crossbar was attached at the front end and to the rear end of the engine and further back to the tail shaft so it had plenty of bearing. With the Warford gears in behind the Rollins gears, I had two gear shifts tandem, and it gave me nine different speeds and plenty of power. It made a fine rig, for this drum encasing the brake acted as a reservoir of oil that worked out along the shafting to keep it oiled all the time. So you could drive that machine forty miles an hour and hold right to it steady. It would spin that worm on the rear end fast enough to heat the housing so when the snow fell on it, it would sizzle and steam, all well lubricated, the oil going right through the rear axle and out around the wheels. Other folks with snowmobiles couldn't drive their rigs that way. Hilton, who was running for the Great Northern, thought he could drive fast, but when he got up to twenty miles an hour, his rig was wobblin' so it threw its belts off into the woods. That was because he was steerin' a forty-four-inch tread with a fifty-six-inch yoke. It set his wheels so one fought the other all the time. I made a new yoke for mine, made it the exact length it needed to be for my runners. It steered easier than the average auto and was fun to run."

It was good for both summer and winter. In summer the front wheels were normal width and tread, the rear ones narrower. In winter the front wheels were replaced by runners. Another wheel was added on each side, just forward of the rear wheels. Around these an endless metal belt with creepers on it transformed the summer car into a winter one. And, one had better believe, it had a door on either side, one that would shut without being locked. When the rig broke through the ice at Forrest Park sometime later, he was out of it before its rear end hit bottom in four feet of water.

But the virtues of the homemade vehicle were never more fully demonstrated than on a trip he made one wild winter night to Pittston Farm some forty miles north at the end of Seboomook Lake. Arriving at Rockwood, he was told that a plow was working north and some trucks and passenger cars were following it, but the chances of getting through to the farm were poor. Poor or not, he had patients waiting.

He soon caught up with some of the cars, one of which had a plugged fuel line and was unable to move. He ran along the road edge and passed—but not before the driver, needing a tire pump to clear his pipe, gave him a scolding for not having one. A few miles farther on he overtook a truck loaded with supplies for the camps. The driver had lost his fan belt. His motor hot, he was unable to move. He held up his hands and shook his head hopelessly.

"You can't get by me!" he shouted.

Laughing, Doc headed up the sidewall, slid along its top and back into the road.

At Socatean Fill he overtook another relay. Largay's car with a load of men going into the woods was in the ditch. A loaded truck had rammed itself into the side wall so the plow could go through. A ridge of snow three feet deep blocked the road. One of Largay's men ran out in front of the hummock, waving his hat vigorously. Doc tooted his horn and fed in some gas. The man's hair fairly stood on end when the runners popped out of the snow, and he leaped out of the way as the vehicle slid neatly over the barrier. Backing up, Doc gave Largay a pull back into the road so he and his men could get on their way north. Since they had eaten last in Bangor that morning and were cold and hungry, they cheered him mightily.

At the 20-Mile he found the drift so deep that great snowballs big as barrels had rolled back into the road escaping the low wings. Here he overtook a truck stalled in the deep mass. The driver gestured to the side wall rising almost vertically higher than his cab, and erupted into curses.

"Holy (blank)! S'no use, you can't get by! (Blankety-blank), we're stuck here!"

Doc thrust his head out. "Keep your door closed," he shouted. "Don't want to tear off its hinges, case I slew!"

He drove right up the side wall and straddled the top of the plowed mass, then with snow spitting and volleying in all directions, he passed the truck and slid down into the road in front of it. With a wave of his hand toward the gaping truckster he was off again. A little farther ahead he overtook the plow with only one truck behind it. He had passed eleven stalled vehicles since leaving Rockwood.

Reaching the farm, he found the lounging room filled with tired men, all fully determined to stay put, even when he told them about the stranded truck and Largay's car.

"You better toss a coin," he said, "to see which of your Caterpillar crews go to 20-Mile and drag that truck in." All looked stolidly unmoved. "Come on now," he goaded. "There's Largay's car behind it full of cold and hungry men. Want 'em to have to walk in? Judas priest, s'pose it was you!"

A crew was on its way in a few minutes.

Doc attended his patients and returned the way he had come. He couldn't resist boasting that he had beaten a V-8 empty truck over the forty-mile route by an hour and a half!

The snowmobile was as effective on ice as on snowy roads, a vast improvement over a car, since it had traction, did not spin its wheels and dig through the ice, and had span enough to reach across a foot or two of open water. It could also go ashore and around the end of a bad wrinkle, usually impossible with a car. A wrinkle? The word is deceptive. The picture it suggests of a mildly uneven strip of ice, like a fold in a garment, is far from fact. Ice, when freezing, expands, jams up, overlaps. Winds may rip into it and rear the cakes on end, so that they may reach a height of ten or fifteen feet. Then, when the weather moderates, the ice contracts, and you may come on a wrinkle twenty or thirty feet wide with open water as far as you can see. Whether with horse, car, snowmobile, or on foot, wrinkles were dangerous hazards. As long as they remained open you had to try each one as you came to it with a peavey, for though the team or car ahead might have crossed it safely within an hour, they shifted so often that you needed to look them over before attempting to cross.

One year the final sealing of the lake took place on a December night accompanied by a northwest gale. The cold was intense, 30 to 40 degrees below zero, so that between gusts ice would form; then the next squall would rip this new ice to pieces and force it back. Cakes six or eight feet across would freeze fast within the crushed ice. Doc had a call from Camp Ogontz. Arriving at Rockwood after walking in from Somerset, he found that Rollin Spinney had skated down from his Towhegan camps that morning. Doc had never enjoyed skating. He would far rather bucksaw wood. But it was faster than walking. He borrowed a pair of skates from Guy Carleton, also a boy's sled to put his pack on and tow behind. But they were hockey skates, with long straight runners, not the rocker variety, turned up at the ends, to which he was accustomed. However, he worked up the lanes of smooth ice, watching his chance to cross into the next one, and made good time until he reached the old ice at the Toe of the Boot. There the snow was too deep for skating, so he left the skates and sled and walked the remaining five miles to treat his patient.

On the return trip by skates he was not so lucky. He must have followed the lanes too far west and moved unknowingly toward the mouth of Moose River. Suddenly his skates began to cut through the ice and water to fly up behind him. Not a cheerful predicament! The straight runners were likely to catch under the ice and throw him. Falling on such thin stuff would mean a long cold swim at best. For a quarter of a mile he followed Emerson's advice to the letter: "In skating over thin ice our safety

is our speed." Never had he moved faster. For once his
five-foot-five body and scant 125 pounds were blessing
instead of embarrassment. With each stroke the skates
sagged and crunched sickeningly, and water flew and
swished around the sled like the wake of a motor boat.
But finally he reached ice thick enough to hold him up.
As usual, his good luck had held!

Some years later he had to cross this same piece of
water again on thin ice. This time it was on a trip to
Farm Island to see a man in a logging crew. From the report, Doc suspected a case of volvulus, and fairly sure that
he must be moved to a hospital he took several men with
him from Rockwood to help pull the patient out. The ice
was so thin that they kept fifty or sixty feet apart as they
hauled the sick man on a sled by a long rope. You could
look across and watch your companions moving along in
the hollows, waves of ice running along with them as each
one settled several inches with each step. But it was new
black ice and tough enough to hold them. They started
in time to catch the morning Maine Central train to
Somerset and were lucky enough to find a CP freight
there, so that Doc got his patient to the hospital in time to
relieve the obstruction with high enemas and save him
an operation.

Falls and springs were the traveler's nemesis—spring,
with its rotten ice and seemingly bottomless mud; fall,
with its unpredictably freezing lake, sometimes a cove at
a time. Start out with a boat, and within twelve hours the
temperature might drop fifty degrees, entombing your
craft in ice. Trust to a car, and you might be stalled in a
raging blizzard; or to a snowmobile, and be plunged to
your axle in mud. "If you don't like the Maine weather,"
ran the old adage, "wait a minute."

One fall, at "freezing-up time," Doc got a call to go to
the Fox Hole on West Branch between Boom House and

Chesuncook Village to treat a wounded trapper. The man was dragging a deer into camp with two dogs in harness and slipped, discharging his rifle. The ball, striking him in the elbow, plowed through his forearm and emerged to kill his best dog. He managed to bind his arm and unhitch the other dog, which finally arrived in camp. His friends hauled him in and sent someone to telephone from Chesuncook Village. It looked like a cold night, so Doc took Sadie's car, the Franklin coupe with a good heater. Beyond Grant Farm about thirty miles away he skidded off the road on a reverse curve. As usual, he did not even think of seeking help. It took him an hour to pry and lever his way back into the road. When he rounded the end of the curve, there about the roadside spring were six automobiles! His cussed independence again, he thought ruefully.

At the village several guides, friends of the injured man, were waiting to accompany them, and they walked up the West Branch to the camp near Pine Stream. It was after midnight when they arrived, to find the man no longer bleeding and asleep in his bunk. Better to let him sleep until morning. The guides were all hungry.

"Biscuits!" one suggested. "Let's stir up some hot biscuits!"

"Not me," said Doc. "I sleep empty, eat to stay awake. I'm for sleeping."

He was lucky, for the injured man's partner vacated his bunk to help get the lunch, and Doc crawled into his warm bed. He awoke about dawn to find the deposed occupant of the bunk curled up with his back to the stove, minus not only bed but anticipated lunch. The cooks had gone to the wrong end of the camp and procured a pail of lard hanging beside several ripe skunks waiting to be skinned. The resulting biscuits were odorously unpalatable. All hands were hungry with no food in sight. The camp caretaker was now awake, highly indignant at having his house-keeping habits insulted.

"You think I keep my eatables out in the dingle with the skunks? Dammit, go look in the opposite end, you'll find plenty of clean food!"

It happened that every man there, including Doc, had a guide's license, but most of the visitors had lost the culinary urge. They skipped out, leaving Bill Henderson, the owner's nephew, to get the breakfast. Thinking to share the blame should the new biscuits prove a disappointment, Doc volunteered to make johnnycake. He pursued his usual technique in cooking, whether johnnycake, biscuits, gingerbread, mincemeat, or venison stew: "Just make it look suitable. When it looks good, it's all right."

The cooking utensils were all leftovers from the lumber camp, the mixing bowl as big as a wash tub, the baker's sheets about two feet square. He spooned some lard into a pan, melted it, greased the pan well, turned the fat into a bowl, dumped in some corn meal, stirred in baking soda and salt, added water, and looked around for the molasses. He never used sugar in his baking, found it as repugnant in johnnycake and gingerbread as on the outside of doughnuts. Not a gullup in sight! What to do? Spying on a shelf a can of Log Cabin Maple Syrup, he promptly emptied it into the mixture, stirred it all up, and baked it. It emerged firm and fragrant, a beautiful golden color. He cut it into four-inch squares and put the pan on the table. Doc took a large hunk of it, but no one else touched it. Finally Len Smith, probably wishing to be polite, helped himself to a piece and took a bite. Promptly he jabbed into the pan and grabbed another piece. It was well he did, for it was the last chance he got at it.

"They cleaned that pan out quicker'n scat," Doc reported later with a chuckle.

A man came in from Chesuncook early the next morn-

ing with a horse and sled to drive the injured man out.
During the night, ice on Pine Stream had frozen hard
enough to bear the team. Doc dressed the man's arm, and
he made a good recovery. After treating other patients in
the village, he took the last boat trip down the lake. About
two miles from the foot they found solid ice. All the passengers rallied to the emergency, took poles and peaveys
to smash the ice. On shore those waiting to ride on the return trip procured skiffs and bateaux and helped break a
channel from their end. It certainly was the last boat trip
of the season!

· 4 ·

SNOWMOBILE, CAR, horse, pung, snowshoes, skates, motorboat, steamer, train, hand-car, jigger, and, most frequently,
his own two feet . . . All were as necessary adjuncts to Doc's
professional efficiency as his medicine bag and moccasins.

The latter was one of his most prized accessories. Most
woodsmen wore high rubbers in winter. Doc discovered
a better rig. Over his soft moccasins he pulled a pair of
ordinary low storm rubbers, the heels filled with pieces
that Tom Woods had cut out for him from thick sole
leather, so that the rubber, being level, would not crumple
and let snow in. It made for easy travel, leaving the limbs
perfectly free above the ankles. Once after hunting all day
in a foot of snow Andrew Kennedy gave him a scolding
for not wearing leather-topped rubbers.

"Why?" demanded Doc. "My feet are perfectly dry."

When Andrew expressed disbelief, Doc pulled off his
rubbers, and there were his moccasins as dry as when he
had put them on. Oh, of course you got wet sometimes, he
admitted cheerfully. When you crossed the lake up to
your knees in slush and shinned out onto the railroad

track, the water would be running out of the top of your rubbers, but by the time you had walked six or seven miles to Somerset Junction your feet would be perfectly dry, because the whole rigging—rubbers, moccasins, woolen pants, and stockings—absorbed the water like blotting paper, and it soon evaporated.

Doc was immune to such criticism, even to occasional ridicule. Once he attended a big Masonic affair dressed in conventional tuxedo. "Oh, look!" someone whispered, nudging a neighbor. "There's Doc Pritham, and he's still wearing his moccasins—*with a tuxedo!*" But before the evening was over, sure enough, he was called out to go dashing off somewhere into the woods, tuxedo and all, where patent leathers would have been far more *de trop* than moccasins in a ballroom.

Moccasins, plus or minus rubbers, were as practical for summer as for winter, for jumping trains as for wading through snow or slush, for coping with every element, in fact, except the deepest mud. They bore him faithfully by one after another of his multiple media of transportation, sometimes with remarkable rapidity.

There was the time, for instance, when he was called to attend a stricken man in the road-building crew at Duck Pond near the head of Harrington Lake. He drove his car over the new road now passable to Frost Pond, via Lily Bay and Ripogenus. Here he obtained a good fast walking horse and, using his own saddle which he had brought along, started the four-mile jaunt to Duck Pond. By now it was night, but a bright moon illumined the marked trail where a road was being built and turned the dew-drenched leaves to glistening silver. It was one of those hours in a sleepless twenty-four which made all the other twenty-three worthwhile. Coop yourself up in a cussed office with regular calling hours like one of those hi-falutin' city specialists when you could enjoy a treasure trove of sights and sounds and smells like these? He passed five deer on the way, so near he could almost have touched them, so little did the horse disturb their native element. Even his man-smell, redolent of this woodsmen's wilderness, must not seem intrusive. And there on the hill just before Duck Pond was the big patch of blackberry vines where one beautiful October day he had counted thirty-six partridge flying off into the woods. Exchange moments like these for a secure and lucrative berth in some smoke-belching city? Not on your life!

But the high hours were often followed by the low ones, as now, when he found that the sick man had breathed his last just as the anxious crew heard the horse coming down the hill to camp. The ride back to Frost Pond at dawn was an anticlimax of routine.

Orrin Young, foreman at Frost Pond and head of a woods operation at Seboomook, sent word to Greenville that Doc was needed at Northeast Carry. Knowing that he also had patients to visit at Dulac's camp nine miles back of Tarratine, Orrin made plans, unknown to Doc, to ride back with him down the lake to Greenville. Arriving home, Doc departed post haste for Dulac's, via freight to Tarratine, then saddle horse the nine miles into camp where he treated his patients—four of them sick with pneumonia. It was sunset when he started back to Tarratine. On the way he was regaled with the hideous screeching of a loup-cervier (Canada lynx), attracted no doubt by the smell of fresh meat from Freeman Tyler's recent butchering at Dulac's and resentful of this unwelcome interruption of its stalk. Instantly Doc tensed with expectancy and tried to rein in his horse, for as usual he carried his .33 with him and he had longed to get a bead on one of these big cats for years. But its tan color blended so neatly with the autumn foliage that he failed to get even a glimpse of it. Just as well, perhaps, for no time was lost.

At Tarratine Doc called Fred Sawyer asking him to come to Moosehead with his boat and take him to Northeast Carry. Now how get to Moosehead, seven miles down the CP tracks? Easily solved. A handcar was standing ready on the rails, all the crew aboard except Fred Girard, the section foreman.

"How about taking me to Moosehead?" Doc asked hopefully.

"Sure. Get aboard."

Doc jumped on behind, and the foreman immediately began to tread the wheel which set the car in motion.

"I say," one of the crew spoke up, "ain't you goin' to ask permission to run to Moosehead?"

Fred pushed down on the handlebar. "We go now," he snapped. "We ask when we get back."

Good old CP railroad! This was the attitude of all its personnel when a doctor needed to get to his patients. At Moosehead Sawyer was waiting with one of his fast boats. They made a quick run to the head of the lake, Doc treated his patient, and by midnight they were off down the lake to Greenville.

The next day Orrin Young came out from his camp at Seboomook in mid-forenoon and paced back and forth in the lobby of the hotel at Northeast Carry, watching down the lake.

"Expecting someone?" asked the manager.

"Why, yes," replied Young. "I'm planning to go back to Greenville with Doc Pritham when he comes."

"Ha! Better not wait any longer. You're twelve hours too late."

Young was a good woodsman and used to lake travel, but he never could figure how Doc could have covered the 130 or more miles so fast. It was a riddle that even Doc found difficult to solve. He only knew that he had to move fast to cover his territory during those years.

Without the service of the railroads he never could have done it, especially in those off-seasons when both lake and roads were impassable. It was at such a time, in April, that a call came from the Harry Johnston family at Rockwood, the same house where he had attended his first patient. The ice was too rotten to travel on, and the woods were full of slush and several feet of melting snow.

Doc took a freight to Somerset, arriving around midnight, then took the CP jigger for the six-mile run over the Maine Central track to Kineo Station. Though the CP section men hid the little machine so no one could use it without their permission, they always let the doctors know where it was hidden. He suspected from reports that the boy, Fred Johnston, had appendicitis. If so, he would get a horse from a neighbor, haul him to Kineo Station, and pump him to Somerset on the jigger in time to ride in to Greenville on the Number 16 express which left around four in the morning, getting him to the hospital in time for an early operation. Arrived at the station, Doc removed the jigger to a safe hiding place, then walked the two or three miles up Moose River to the Johnston cabin. It was cold for April, but he traveled so fast that he was sweating long before he reached the house. Speed was of the essence if he was going to get the boy to Somerset in time to catch the train.

The heat that smote him as he entered the one-room log cabin was not all from the fire in the old cookstove. It was compounded of many human bodies and tense emotions. Apparently every member of the family, those living in the house and others in the neighborhood, had gathered to assist. If the boy wasn't in serious condition, he soon would be. It looked like a wake already! Doc pushed his way to the bed.

It was appendicitis, all right, and such an advanced case that it would mean sure death to move him. Doc cast a

hasty glance about the room, noting the sturdy but somewhat littered kitchen table, the steaming teakettle, the
supply of kerosene lamps. He turned to his old friend
Harry.

"I've got to operate—now—right here. It can't wait.
O.K. by you?"

The big woodsman nodded. His eyes were like those of a
trusting dog's. "Anything you say, Doc. Just tell us what
to do."

Doc told him, issuing crisp orders while he opened his
bag and laid out his few requisite tools. "Clear the room.
Get everything off that table. Pour some of that boiling
water into a kettle. And send one of the other boys for
Walter Maynard. Tell him I need him."

He prepared for the operation with as meticulous care
as in the hospital; boiled his instruments in two pie
plates, one covering the other; scrubbed; applied the
favorite lotion to his hands; saw to it that the kitchen
table was covered with a blanket, topped by a sheet
("Softer for a feller to lie on!") and the boy lifted on it;
that all the lamps available were brought and lighted. By
now Walter Maynard had arrived from his house about
a third of a mile away—an alert, intelligent trapper and
guide, perhaps in his late fifties, with more skills than one
could count on one's fingers. Glazier, wrestler, Sunday-
school teacher, sheriff—at one time he had been all of
them. And already, a few years before, he had founded the
sporting camps destined to become famous as Maynard's-
in-Maine. Now, Doc informed him, he was to add to his
many skills that of anesthetist.

There was a quarter-pound tin of ether in his pack.
While Walter coolly administered it to the patient via a
small towel, Doc proceeded with the operation. Outside
the house, grouped at all the windows, were the peering

relatives, the boy's father Harry among them, three or four at each one. The mother and sister had gone upstairs to the loft, which was floored with a single layer of boards shrunken from many years of hot fires. Nerves on edge, they kept walking back and forth, sending showers of dust down through the wide cracks.

"Quiet up there!" Doc shouted once. But after a few moments of calm the pacing resumed.

The fire died down, and the room quickly grew cold. Even Doc, intent on his surgery, which involved complications, began to feel chilled. And for the patient—!

"Get somebody to put wood on that fire," he ordered tersely.

Walter shouted to the men outside, but not one of them moved. They continued to stare as if transfixed through the windows. He called to the women upstairs, but again no response. Only the slight moaning and pacing, and the intermittent showers of dust.

"Danged fools!" muttered Doc. "Scared. Superstitious about something."

Always swift of motion, he worked even faster, knowing the danger of the increasing cold to the patient. Just as he was cutting off the appendix, the worst happened. The boy stopped breathing. Instantly alert, Walter started giving artificial respiration, pumping the arms vigorously. Now Doc's motions became lightning swift. Knowing that they could give no more ether, he must work against the time it would take the patient to rally and come out of the anesthesia. Using a soft rubber catheter cut in two for drainage, he finished the suturing and closed the incision. Then he put wood on the fire.

"It's all right," Walter reported presently. "He's breathing regularly. And I think he's beginning to come out of the ether."

"Worst operating conditions I ever worked under!" Doc was often to recall later. Yet in spite of the cold, the sprinkles of dust, the poor lighting, the superstitious relatives, the gangrenous state of the appendix, the patient would make a good and quick recovery.

But the difficulties of the trip were not yet over. The river was running full of ice, and the men could not make a crossing until daylight. It was seven o'clock before they crossed over to bring back Mrs. John King to attend the boy. Until she arrived Doc could not leave. By the time he walked back to the station it was mid-morning. The section crew was at work, and to his dismay he discovered that the roadmaster was in town. And here he was with a CP jigger on the Maine Central tracks! Oh, well, the showdown must come sometime. At least the blame was all his. He would be getting no member of the train crew in trouble. Retrieving the jigger from its hiding place, he pumped steadily toward Somerset.

The roadmaster was waiting for him at the American Thread siding, West Outlet. Sure enough, he stopped him, informed him curtly that he was taking away the jigger according to the company rules.

"A shame," Doc retorted cheerfully, "to take such an old shaky one. If you'd only wait a day or two, you might catch me with a nice two-seater. They've just got in a dandy one at Somerset."

The official showed distinct symptoms of apoplexy. "You —you mean you intend to ride over our rails again?" he spluttered.

"It's very likely"—Doc was coolness personified—"since it's the only feasible way for me to attend many sick ones— like the boy whose life I just saved."

"You—you—I'll take you into court for this!"

Doc laughed. "Go ahead. I promise you there isn't a

judge in the state who would consider you have grounds for action."

The man's flushed cheeks looked ready to burst. "I—I tell you I've had men watching nights just out to catch you!"

"So? It would have looked better for your company if you'd set them to repairing the rails and checking the gauge, so their trains wouldn't drop down between the irons the way one did yesterday only ten miles below here."

The red turned purple, ascending from cheeks to scalp. Since anger had apparently driven the official speechless and banished all thought of confiscating the jigger, Doc bade him good-by until the next time and rolled away to Somerset.

The interview was not unproductive, for an arrangement was soon made with the railroad company whereby doctors could obtain the motor car manned by the section crew, and so make a quick emergency trip. Far better than the jigger which was likely to slip badly if the rails became covered with snow, so that one might have to push it all the way to Somerset!

Doc's next service to the Johnston family was more tragic. Harry collapsed while guiding a young woman on a canoe trip. A four-mile paddle to Canada Falls, a motor trip to Seboomook, a steamboat ride to Kineo, and another steamer trip down the lake to Greenville were all in vain. He was dying when he reached Doc, and nothing could be done.

Such emergency operations in the woods as the Johnston appendectomy were by no means unique in Doc's case book. Ruth Vickery, wife of a civil engineer for Great Northern, had good reason to remember another one, which probably saved her life.

It was the winter of 1925. Taking her young children, Ruth accompanied her husband Earl to a camp in the woods up in Allagash country, on Chamberlain Lake. Then, after arriving in the wilderness outpost, she discovered she was pregnant. On January 4 Doc received a frantic telephone call from Vickery. His wife was having pains, a miscarriage. What should he do? Try to get her out?

"No," said Doc. "She might hemorrhage to death on the way. I'll come."

He drove in his snowmobile to the Great Northern company camp on the Ellis Brook operation. There Vickery met him with snowshoes. No big chore hiking six miles through winter woods in the dark—unless you tried balancing snowshoes on another man's trail! They were some of the longest six miles Doc had ever traveled.

Mildred Bridges had come down with her husband from their camp at the head of Chamberlain to be with the patient. "Will you have lunch first?" she asked Doc, obviously anxious to be of assistance but not quite knowing how. "I brought some molasses cookies that I made this morning."

"No, thanks." Already Doc was preparing for the curettage—boiling, scrubbing, issuing orders. A lantern was hung on a wire above the patient's couch. Good! He always used a lantern for surgery in the woods when possible. It gave better light than a kerosene lamp. Chimney a bit blackened, but better not try to wash it. With his mirror for a reflector, it would give adequate light. Once he had gotten the patient to sleep, Earl Vickery would be able to handle the anesthesia.

"Oh, I can't stand this!" exclaimed Mildred Berry, wringing her hands.

"Then go upstairs," Doc ordered cheerfully.

There was an audience. The Vickerys' two boys lay on the floor above and watched the whole proceeding through the cracks. But at least it was quiet. There was no tramping down of dust! The job was finished with thoroughness and dispatch.

Ruth Vickery emerged into consciousness to the sound of Doc's hearty voice.

"Now I'll have some of those molasses cookies!"

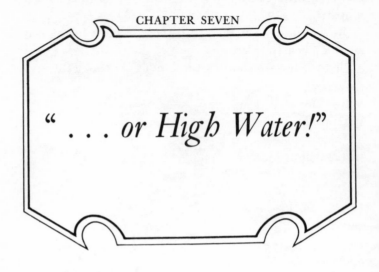

CHAPTER SEVEN

" . . . or High Water!"

. 1 .

H<small>E CALLED HER</small> the *Noname,* fitting designation for an object which in a profane man would have inspired unprintable expletives. How anybody with a canniness for boats since babyhood could be lured into such a dubious investment was a mystery even to Doc. But necessity dictated the purchase. During the exigencies of the flu epidemic he knew he must have a faster boat.

The *Noname* was a racing craft built for the Sheaffers, summer visitors from Philadelphia who patronized the Kineo hotel. Its reputation was not good, for one man had been tossed out of it and had died from pneumonia as a result of the chilling. It was thirty feet long, four wide, and had a six-cylinder Stearns automobile engine which must have weighed nearly a ton mounted high above the floor. Doc bought it in the winter of 1918 and had it ready to go in the spring. Henry Bartley went with him on the first trip to Lily Bay.

"Twenty-one minutes," marveled Henry, "from wharf to wharf!"

But Doc's satisfaction was short-lived. He was going so fast on the return trip that it was impossible to avoid an old deadhead which loomed up ahead six or eight inches below the surface. It rolled the propeller into a little round ball about six inches across. He paddled to the Night Hawk Club on Sugar Island, where Theron Heald helped him touch her stern on his cradle so they could haul her far enough to remove the propeller from its shaft. Then Doc and Henry spent the rest of the day alternately holding the propeller against a stump while the other pounded it with a maul. Judas priest! He could have made two trips with the old boat!

The *Noname* was fast all right! All you could see was the spray, a huge wave on either side and a rooster's tail behind. In May he ran her to Camp Ogontz on a rush night call, making the thirty miles from Greenville in a hundred minutes, with the motor throttled down as slow as possible. It was a dark night, with a high lake and lots of drift, the air so cold that the spray froze. Not a comfortable feeling, knowing there was only a quarter inch of mahogany planking between you and that boiling drift-laden spume. What a solid four-foot pulpwood log could do to that frail wooden skin! But it wasn't *Noname* which lost him time on that trip.

"You must stay for breakfast," insisted the kindly woman who was cooking at the camp. "It will be a substantial one."

It should have been! She must have been two hours trotting back and forth before setting him down to a bowl of oatmeal, some doughnuts, and a slice of bread! Once off, he reached Rockwood in seventeen minutes, all the time wondering why in thunder a man should sit around and lose hours trying to please somebody instead of going about his business.

His troubles with *Noname* were only beginning. In midsummer he was called to Rockwood to treat a man who had been hit in the head by a breaking sweep as a logging crew was winding a towboat out of Brassua. Doc took Father Poirier along, since the frantic caller was uncertain whether a doctor or a priest would be more needed. They made good time until they crossed the wake of a steamer going into the West Outlet. The cleric called Doc's attention to a bit of water on the cockpit floor.

"It's all right," Doc assured him easily. "The boat's flat. Doesn't take much water to show."

But when they crossed the other wake a mile farther on, he saw the boat was filling rapidly. Doc thrust a large pail into the priest's hands, and he bailed furiously but to no avail. By the time they were a mile from the Rockwood shore the boat's stern was submerged. Happily the magneto and carburetor were both mounted high on the engine, and it continued to function even though the end of the exhaust was three feet under water.

"Get ready for a swim!" snapped Doc grimly. The priest said nothing, only continued calmly to bail.

The last half-mile was a toss-up. As they plowed slowly toward the shore by the station, they were standing waist-deep in the cockpit. A dozen strong hands seized the hull before the engine stopped, holding it from sliding back into the water. Doc and his companion jumped ashore and hastened to the King home, where the patient had been brought. The services of both were needed, for in spite of all Doc could do through the night the injured man died soon after sunrise.

Returning to the wharf, Doc found his boat high and dry on a cradle. With the help of a Great Northern tractor the many willing hands had hauled it out and repaired it. The trouble was not, as he had suggested to them on landing, a loosened drain plug. Instead of being fastened to a mooring, where it was free to swing about, the *Noname* had been tied at the float broadside to the sun, so that its planking above water line had shrunk and cracked. Now that the wood was swelled tightly, he returned home without further mishap, henceforth to keep the ill-fated craft secure at its mooring.

"We were in no real danger," Doc told Father Poirier. "Some of the guides were waiting with their canoes, paddles in hand, all ready to come to our rescue. A good thing, for as soon as the engine stopped and her nose fell, we'd have sunk like a rock. We might have had quite a swim."

"Not I," returned the priest calmly. "I can't swim a stroke."

"Well," Doc was said to have reported later, "he was sure no Baptist!"

Fortunately Doc was alone when he had his next and final misadventure with *Noname*. He was traveling up the lake on a fair summer day the following year with a fresh southwest wind blowing. The best of conditions for any normal and sensible craft! But in the two-mile stretch north of East Outlet the wind was working up quite a sea. As he came alongside of Sandbar it rolled in under the stern of that miserable rig, always topheavy. She went over on her beam ends, and there she stayed. Get her nose into the wind, he thought, and lie out over the side, and perhaps he could yank her back on even keel again. So he swung around in a circle, then when she came into the wind he climbed on the uphill rail and swung over as far as he could. No use. He couldn't right her. O.K., so he must do the next best, keep her from running off into deep water before she sank. On her next circle when she cleared the upper end of the island, he swung the rudder down and sank her on the north extension of the bar. He stood on the top rail until the craft's nose went under, then jumped. It was a hundred yards to shore, as George Mountain measured it later. Not far when he had "swum natural" as a boy, but some different in soaked clothes. However, he made it, then walked to the Sandbar camps. Al Cripps, who was staying there that summer, greeted the dripping apparition with amazement. "How in heaven's name did you get here?"

"I swum," replied Doc calmly.

He hired Harry Davis to run him to Rockwood, trusting nature and the southwest wind to dry him off. It did— eventually. Arriving at the patient's house and diagnosing the ailment, he telephoned to Sadie and gave her directions for packing another bag with the needed items and sending it up the lake by Fred Sawyer. George Mountain, one of the guides at Sandbar, went to Kineo for the proper rigging and dragged old *Noname* out of the water, using exactly 300 feet of rope to reach from cockpit to shore. Doc had it towed to the Junction. His friends were vociferous with advice.

"I'll burn that old hull if you try to use it again!" threatened Andrew Kennedy.

Doc might have done so himself. He started the building of a new boat immediately. The keel was laid at St. Germain's boat shop, and the design was by Defoe of Bay City, Michigan, though many of his own ideas were incorporated in its interior arrangements. The hull was thirty by seven and a half feet on the water line and eight feet across the deck. White oak was used for the frame, planked with seven-eighths-inch cypress, and the inside was ceiled with the same wood. A heavy white oak keel was reinforced by iron and had a bronze skeg designed to protect the propeller from drift. Now he could run over a few logs in the night as easily as in a sled over snow. He could feel them as they bumped along the keel and see them boil up in the wake astern, but keep right on his way. He also had a set of celluloid panes set in a drilling backing that he could batten on the outside cabin windows in cold weather so they would not ice over.

He made only one big mistake—using the old motor out of *Noname*. He found that out one foggy summer afternoon when he made a rush trip to Rockwood, where a woman had taken a poisonous dose of belladonna, disregarding the plain directions: FOR EXTERNAL USE ONLY. Howard and Sadie's father, who was visiting, accompanied him on the trip. In his attempt to speed he worked the motor too hard and snapped a piston in two. But he must not stop, the case was too urgent. Feeding an extra amount of oil, he kept the engine going for about ten miles. Then close to Sandbar he saw Fred Sawyer returning with his swift taxi boat from taking a party up the lake and hailed him. Yes, of course Fred would take him to Rockwood.

"Let her drift with the south wind," Doc told his father-in-law, "until you get in under the island out of the direct route to Kineo. You'll be out of the way then when it comes dark, and you can anchor."

While he was attending his patient a thunder shower burst with a terrific southeasterly squall. Drifting in the fog, the two in the boat were caught wholly unprepared. Though they were close to the island and ready to cast anchor, the bottom was soft sand and the wind so strong that the anchor did not even snub the boat. She was tossed high on the beach with a hole in her bottom as big as a waterpail. Howard, though only six, was as coolly capable as his grandfather. He located tins of crackers and cookies in the cabin and helped pile life preservers to make a comfortable bed.

Knowing the treachery of the lake in storm, Doc was tortured with anxiety. Once his patient was out of danger he rushed off, secured Bob Stein to take his boat, and together they ran down the length of Sandbar and up into the cove, but the fog was like soup and visibility zero. Throwing anchor, they lay down on a camp spread and slept until dawn. At least, Bob did. Doc got little sleep. But with daylight and the fog lifted, it was easy to locate the boat. Doc had a temporary patch put on and got the craft towed to Greenville. Howard was with him when he drove over to see how Will St. Germain was repairing the broken plank.

"Why does he have to haul it out of water?" asked the boy suddenly. "Why can't he just stick a pole through her deadeyes and careen her?"

"A good idea," agreed Doc, regarding his offspring with some surprise. Sure, enough, they found that Will had a pole thrust through the rear set of ports and the boat careened just as Howard had suggested. Doc chuckled. Not bad for a six-year-old!

Even with new pistons Doc did not trust the old engine. The next Memorial Day on a trip to Rockwood with two passengers he had trouble again. He was stooped over trying to get it to function properly when a connecting rod broke, knocking a piece of metal as large as a dinner plate into the bilge, and passing too close to his head for comfort. He stopped the engine just as another crank started to break its way out.

"Guess the old engine is done for," he remarked, going aft to shut off the gas.

"I thought I heard something break," said one passenger innocently.

"You sure did," said Doc dryly.

He sculled and paddled to Rockwood, and again had the boat towed home. The next morning he was on board at dawn and, paddling the boat ashore, started unbolting every bit of the engine and throwing it out of the hull. Then he ordered a good Lathrop four-cylinder forty-horse-power motor which gave him some real power and made boating again a pleasure.

But he still wasn't through with being towed. The next time he could not blame the engine. It was late in the fall, and he had been hunting with the boys all day at Bear Brook. A call came in the evening from Rockwood. Up since before dawn, he was so sleepy when he arrived home about midnight that he could hardly make it to the house, only to be met with news of another urgent call, this time from Seboomook, where a man had been accidentally shot. Too stupid with drowsiness to think, he grabbed a pail of lunch and, stumbling back to the boat, headed again up the lake. The lunch kept him awake for a while, but by the time he got to Hardscrabble he had to keep walking to stay awake, even with the window open and the ice cold wind blowing straight on him. He fell asleep on his feet, to be rudely awakened by a sudden jar and the roar of the motor released from its load. Swiftly he threw the engine switch. Looking over the side, he saw the shore line of Toe of the Boot. He had run over the gravel bar and was floating off toward Smith Farm. He pumped the bilge dry, watched anxiously to satisfy himself that there was no leak; then threw the anchor. Again it was Fred Sawyer who rescued him when the mists lifted the next morning. He took Doc to Greenville, then back to Seboomook, where Doc found to his infinite relief that the wounded man's life had been saved by the timely intervention of a doctor from Buffalo.

The boat was towed in on the steamer's Monday run,

and the machinist at the Great Northern shop made a new flange coupling for its tail shaft. Though much of the bronze skeg was scoured away by the gravel, the propeller was unharmed, and the craft was soon in running condition. But Doc berated himself soundly. Except for a lucky circumstance, his patient might have died. A couple of hours' sleep, and he could have reached him in less than half the time! As stupid to run a boat as to drive an automobile when sleepy!

. 2 .

IT WAS IN those years of the twenties that, much to his astonishment and somewhat to his distaste, Doc became known far beyond the 5,000 or more square miles which constituted his area of medical visitation. A journalist named Alfred Elden, familiar with the Greenville section, discovered seeds of drama in the exploits of the little north woods doctor, planted them in a series of newspaper and magazine articles, and reaped a surprising harvest of publicity. "MAINE'S MOST REMARKABLE COUNTRY DOCTOR OFTEN RISKS HIS LIFE SAVING OTHERS," screamed a headline in the Portland Sunday *Telegram* for May 6, 1928. "For A Score Of Years Dr. Fred Pritham Has Tramped The Great North Woods And Sailed The Iceland Seas To Succor The Sick And Injured——He Travels On Foot Or Horseback, By Automobile, Motor Boat, Snowmobile, Snowshoes And Skis."

Portland was only the beginning. The articles caught the fancy of the Associated Press and were syndicated over the country. Similar headlines sprouted in newspapers from Maine to California: Springfield, Massachusetts; Kansas City, Missouri; Jackson, Michigan; Niagara Falls; Chicago; New York City; Oakland; San Francisco.

"Wilderness M.D. Saves Many In Arduous Practice . . ."

"Maine Physician Is Blessing To Rural District..."

"Woods No Terror To Maine Physician..."

"Hero-Surgeon of Moosehead Dares Any Danger With His Snowmobile To Save Lives..."

"He Scorns Guides"... "Ticklish Situation"... "Swam Ashore"... "Knows Country Intimately"... "Adventures Are Countless"... "Experiences of Modest Doctor Read Like Romance"... "Called the Grenfell of the Moosehead Lake Region"...

Doc read the captions, as he was to read other such extravaganza through the years, with tongue in cheek and dour amusement. Except for the abundance of hyperbole the Elden articles were fairly accurate. And he could chuckle over their lurid excesses of language. Not so with some articles which were to come later from other pens.

"All poppycock!" he was to splutter indignantly at an article appearing in a widely read national magazine. "Didn't happen that way at all! Not a word of truth in it. Somebody's fool daydream!" He was always a stickler for details, as his biographer would long afterward discover.

Doc studied Elden's descriptions of himself with interest.

"A small, wiry man in his early fifties perhaps." (Ha, not so good! Oh, well, he'd only missed it by about five years.) "Dr. Pritham is unconventional as to attire and opinions. In summer he may be found clad in flannel shirt, knickers, woolen stockings, and moccasins. Capless, his graying hair is tousled by the breezes from Moosehead, Maine's greatest inland sea." (Who in tarnation would care what he wore!)

"The consciousness of duty is strong upon him. He believes it his duty to keep in prime physical condition. He uses no liquor, tobacco, tea, or coffee. The great out-of-doors is his heaven." (Hell, too, sometimes.)

Of far more interest to Doc was the spate of letters received from strangers, former patients, old friends.

"I have never been in your glorious Maine, but have hopes. If you have never been *west* and slept under the stars on our Great Deserts, you have missed something in your young life. Come on out."

"You are a most wonderful man if this little sketch of your life is true. God will bless you and you are making a heaven on earth. Some day you will receive your reward. I live in the best and most wonderful state of all, Dear Old Texas."

From Kansas: "I read enclosed clipping about you in my home town paper, and the thought came to me that one so interested in the welfare of humanity might help one so unfortunate as I . . . old frame house . . . had little repairs . . . . If I could get help, I could put a roof on. . . ."

From Michigan: "You have no idea what a feeling of warmth came around my heart the other night, when I opened my Jackson paper and your face greeted me."

"I am enclosing a sheet of the Oakland California *Tribune,* just to show you that even California knows of the good work you are doing. I am well aware what you have to contend with, for I practiced medicine in Hartland and Pittsfield for over thirty years. If you ever tire of snowmobiles, come out where there is no snow."

Also from California: "I wonder if you still remember me? Do you remember when you pulled me out of a bad case of pleurisy and pneumonia back in 1916 in the Y.M.C.A. Hospital?"

Again from California: "Do you remember going deer hunting one night at midnight? I am the awful girl that played the joke on you. (Rose Churchill, nurse.)"

From Springfield, Massachusetts: "It says you have given up tea, coffee, and tobacco and liquor, and I admire you for it. Now I have given up tea and drink a glass of milk at noon and night. I still take a cup of coffee in the morning. Had I ought to drink water in the morning, or would it do any harm to drink milk in the morning? Do you think it advisable to open windows at night in the winter? First to let you know I am thirty-seven years old and still unmarried as I am a bookkeeper and don't earn enough to support a wife. Would it be advisable to give up pie and cake? I have a very good set of teeth but a weakness for sweets. I have given up doughnuts in the morning. If you can spare a moment please write giving me a little advice . . . ."

And so forth, and so forth. Doc chuckled, then sighed. The wages of fame.

· 3 ·

HIS CORRESPONDENTS were not the only ones influenced by his somewhat rigid regimen of health.

"Ugh! Salt!" exclaimed young Howard with shock and disgust. "There's salt in these here peas!"

Ella Gerrish, who was keeping house for the Prithams during one of Sadie's visits in Freeport, felt herself shriveling beneath Doc's amazed glance. Salt in peas? it questioned with wordless scorn. Who would be so stupid as to use salt in cooking? Ella said nothing. Doc said nothing. He did not need to. Ella was properly squelched. She should have remembered that Doc never used salt in his food if he could help it. He thought it contributed to the hardening of the arteries.

The following afternoon she was given an exhibition of Doc's techniques of discipline as well as his emphasis on sanitation. Howard was visibly sniffling.

"So?" said Doc. "Got a cold, have you? Didn't I see you and Jimmy swapping spit over that bottle of pop?" With no further ado the message was communicated.

There were some disadvantages in being the son of Frederick John Pritham, but the lack of salt in one's diet was not one of them. Howard had been reared saltless since babyhood, also tealess, coffeeless, and, for the most part, sugarless. It was a greater deprivation that for long days at a time he was almost fatherless. Dad was seldom home for long at a time. When he was, meals were usually interrupted, since people knew that was a good time to catch him at home. Many times he would not sit down to a meal but take a few handfuls of food and eat on the go. Mother was the coordinator and a very efficient one, serving not only as housekeeper, chief disciplinarian, playmate on walks and picnics, stern mentor over homework and Sunday school attendance, but also as medical assistant, frequently giving advice or even medicine in an emergency and making trip after trip to Lily Bay to meet Dad, who would have gone by boat to Rockwood, taking him to calls on the east side of the lake and then returning home.

Howard also was at times pressed into medical service. Someone had to be at home to answer the telephone and doorbell and take down the calls. He did not accept this responsibility gracefully. In fact, for the rest of his life he would shy away from the telephone like a horse from its first automobile. His involvement with the functions of a doctor came early. One of his prime recollections was of going to the head of the lake with Dad, then across to Seboomook, where there was a guide in camp with an infected finger. With a morbid fascination and intense admiration he watched Dad open and dress the wound. But his interest in the medical arts soon faded. He saw how hard Dad had to work. Not for him, this business of being a doctor! Noting that education was a prerequisite for such professional skill, he was careful not to get high rank in school, not fail exactly but merely to get conveniently by. If he received 69 in a test, he would try to make 71 in the next one, so his average would stand at a passing 70. His supreme ambition was to live in the woods as a guide with his idol, Andrew Kennedy. Later Ella Gerrish was to remind him of this early aspiration.

"I think maybe my first idea was the best one," he would reply half jokingly.

Not that great effort was required to get mediocre rank! From the time that he started his education in the two-room schoolhouse on the next street he found school and everything connected with it as repulsive as the telephone. Everything, that is, except its pre- and post-activities. Once promoted to the big town school with grades five to eight on the lower floor, high school on the upper, extra-curricular excitement heightened. The friendly (?) feud between Village and Junction boys, with its ammunition of mud, ice pellets, stone-loaded snowballs, increased the glamor of education. But aversion to study remained constant. He was even slower at learning than Carroll, though he remembered what he did learn longer. Without the stern and persistent tutelage of Mother, who was bound that her two boys should be educated, his school record might have been even less than mediocre. Mercifully she had given up on music lessons after battling over them many years with Carroll.

And fortunately Mother's austere self-sacrificing New England puritanism was tempered by a remarkable sense of humor and ability to enjoy life. Once she got her own car she took the boys on frequent trips to Freeport, to Brownville to visit Aunt Hallie Greeley, to Massachusetts, once even to Philadelphia; no mean feats of courage in those days of poor dirt roads! Not until 1927 was there any attempt in winter to plow the road which led to Monson and out to civilization. Oddly enough, in July of that same year the first airplane appeared in the area, a hydroplane used by the Maine Forestry Department for spotting fires. All the townspeople, including Howard, flocked to the lakeshore by the old Y.M.C.A. to gawk at the sight and marvel at how up to date they had become.

"What next?" was the incredulous query on every lip.

But in spite of his eternal preoccupation with his job, it was Dad who furnished the ultimate joys in recreation. Saturday, when possible, was his day off, and he would take the boys hunting in season, occasionally fishing. One of the trips Howard liked best was to York's camps on Daicey Pond in the shadow of Mount Katahdin. They would leave Greenville in the dark and drive to Ripogenus Dam where the gate was kept locked. It was Howard's duty to jump out and run about a quarter of a mile to get the key from Joe McInnes. Joe would send one of his big St. Bernards to bring it back. It wouldn't leave your side until you had unlocked the gate and placed the key between its teeth.

Twenty-two miles beyond the Dam where the road met Sourdnahunk Stream car travel ended, and there York would meet them with a buckboard and they would jounce eight miles to the camps over a tote road so rough you had to keep a good grip to keep from falling off the seat. But Howard reveled in this trip down the valley of the Sourdnahunk with Doubletop Mountain on one side and the Travelers on the other. They would spend the day fishing; then, since Dad preferred walking to the buckboard, hike out to the car about daylight the next morning, perhaps seeing a dozen deer during the eight miles, and arriving home by midmorning or noon in time for Dad to make his rounds of patients.

The boy often accompanied his father on professional

trips, especially by boat, and for the sake of the ride, not because of interest in medical problems. Sometimes he would get up in the middle of a bitter night to go. During his high school years, when Carroll was at the University of Maine majoring in electrical engineering, their relationship became even more close. Dad would let him pilot the craft, and he became fairly expert at navigation, even at night, with Dad giving him a compass course to steer if the lights at Capen's on Deer Island or at Rockwood or Greenville were not visible. But never as expert as Dad, who seemed to have both compass and timing in his head! Once, coming down the lake in a snowstorm, Howard was in the cabin steering a compass course and Dad was in the back working the anchor line. Presently Dad came into the cabin.

"It's about time we got to the tip of Harford's Point," he said, slowing the engine and putting the gear in neutral.

Just then the snow whirled around, clearing the air, and sure enough, there dead ahead was the high gravel bank on the tip of Harford's Point.

The lake could change from flat calm to raging storm in minutes, and the trips would often be rough going with everything buttoned up and solid water rushing the length of the boat. No fun then when rust and dirt would be stirred up in the gas tank and the engine would miss and you would have to stop and clean the gas line, especially if it was the middle of the night after a long day in the camps or woods!

Part of his enjoyment on these trips derived from the host of colorful characters they ran across. At Rockwood, for instance, there was Billy MacDonald, a guide and trapper, who had actually been scalped by Indians in the Kineo Hotel Guides' Camp. One night during an argument one of the Capino boys had Bill's scalp nearly off before onlookers intervened. It was Dad who restored the ravaged pate to near normalcy. Howard regarded the treasured scar with acute fascination. Future forays of Billy in the resulting feud had gained him a ripped abdomen. Someone had fastened the escaping intestines inside the wound with a horse-blanket pin, and he had been brought to the Greenville hospital to survive for future skirmishes. Long afterward Howard would see Billy again on his deathbed in the same hospital, head beaten almost to a pulp with a large flashlight.

But it was Chesuncook that yielded the most intriguing roster of characters. There was Uncle Anse, of course. And there was Dan Smith, who had once been a woods cook and, though he had stopped cooking long ago, still always wore an apron and a paper bag hat, and chewed tobacco. He tried to teach Howard to make custard over an open fire, but it came out more like soup. When there was no preacher, Dan would hold services in the church-schoolhouse. Though sometimes all alone, he would proceed just the same, singing the hymns solo and giving a sermon.

"I advertised there would be a service at ten o'clock," he told Howard, "so I had it regardless." The highlights of his life were the visitations of a bona-fide preacher, be he Catholic priest, Protestant parson, or rabbi. "When the great man came, the whole town was there to meet the boat and escort him to the church!"

Since Dad had treated almost everyone in the area, Howard heard scores of tales about his father's exploits. Though he was a husky youth, some of Dad's exploits made him tired just to think of.

"Once he made a tremendous trip to Chesuncook," he recalled long afterward. "Left Greeenville in the late afternoon and drove to Grant Farm by snowmobile, thirty miles, walked to Chesuncook over the old winter tote

road which is twenty-two miles, did a Caesarean section
in a home, walked back out, drove to Greenville, and
operated on schedule that morning in the hospital. That
Caesarian baby's the McBurnie that now runs the Chesuncook Hotel."

Be a doctor like Dad? Not on your life!

In 1930 Howard graduated from high school at sixteen
(with Mother's help), but lacking one or two subjects to
meet college entrance requirements. So he was dispatched
for a year's further torture at a good prep school, Maine
Central Institute in Pittsfield. It was during that year
that he decided to study medicine.

· 4 ·

IN THOSE YEARS of the twenties and early thirties the lake
was still center-stage, both for recreation and transportation. Even the Depression year of 1931 saw 5,000 people
gathered on the shore to watch the annual Fourth of July
drama. Howard, prepped for Colby College, was among
both audience and actors. Doc marched and played in the
Marine band. There were swimming contests, motor boat
races, tilting contests, aquaplaning, bateaux competitions.
The prizes were free boat rides on Andrew Cannon's Baby
Gar speed boat, and—those marvels of the present but
commonplaces of the not too distant future—airplane
rides.

With roads not yet tarred and the automobile route to
Rockwood not to be completed until 1936, the lake remained the chief thoroughfare. The big old steamers, converted about 1922 to diesel power—the *Moosehead,* the
Marguerite, the *Katahdin* with its spread-winged eagle
on the pilot house—were still the gay, flamboyant queens
of *Mspame,* large water. Canoes, motor taxis of all sizes,

row boats, bateaux, sportsmen's yachts—Doc rode them all, mingling indiscriminately with hotel patrons, sportsmen, guides, lumberers, and easily mistaken for either of the latter.

"Here, guide," a city fisherman bound for a sporting camp near Rockwood addressed him peremptorily. "Would you change the water in our pail of live bait there?"

"Sure," replied Doc agreeably, and did so.

"Thanks," said the sportsman, and handed him a half dollar.

"Thank *you*," replied Doc, unsmiling, and slipped the coin in his pocket.

When they reached the camp and discovered their mistake, the visitors were chagrined. Not Doc. He felt highly complimented. He was constantly being mistaken by summer visitors for a guide or woodsman. Why not? He was both. Even the unmistakable skepticism with which prospective patients eyed his unprofessional appearance disturbed him not a whit. They usually changed their minds. For instance, there was the woman who had been summering on the Allagash.

Her husband, telephoning from Caucomgomook, sounded frantic. Would Doc hire Fred Sawyer and come to the Rockwood wharf to get his wife, who was very ill? No, said Doc. He would be waiting as requested but not in Sawyer's boat. He preferred his own for carrying a sick woman, with the weather blowing up heavily to the south.

The woman arrived at the wharf, half dead with pain and nausea. She had walked across the Carry from Round Pond to Caucomgomook Lake, where her husband had hired the Great Northern's bateau to take them to the head of the lake. Lying on the bottom of a craft used all summer to carry meats, hay, and other odorous supplies, with the spray gathering enough to make a wash in the bilge, and already nauseated, she must have suffered the torments of hell. Then sixty miles in the car over a bumpy road!

Doc made her a bed on the top of the engine box, placing her above the heat of the engine and amidship, subject to the least motion if the boat pitched, then opened the engine just enough to time the rise and fall of the boat with the waves. About halfway to Sandbar, Sawyer's boat came tearing past them down the lake, striking terrific blows on each sea, cabin roof buckling an inch or two over the engine every time she pounded.

"Glad we're not on that boat," said the woman's husband with profound relief.

"Thanks," said Doc, then could not resist adding, "That's the boat you wanted me to bring." He turned to the woman. "How are you riding?"

"It's like heaven," she murmured. "At last—warm and comfortable."

At the hospital Doc examined her, diagnosed acute appendicitis, advised immediate surgery. The man's eyes narrowed. His thoughts were as obvious as if expressed in words. Entrust his wife to this little backwoods runt in work shirt and sneakers? All right for the native hicks up here, no doubt, but for city folks who could afford the top-priced specialists of Beacon Street?

"We'll take her to Boston," he said abruptly.

About one in the morning Doc received another frantic call. His wife was worse. Would Doc come and operate? Would he get the best help possible to assist?

Doc would. Waking another nurse to replace her, he secured Eleanor Hamilton, the night nurse on duty, as skillful and sympathetic an assistant as any city hospital could provide. He removed a gangrenous appendix, then, finding a suppurated gall bladder so filled with pus that its walls were like wet newspaper, he carefully removed that also. The woman made an excellent recovery. When the man bade Doc good-by, there was in his eyes no hint of skepticism, only the most grateful and profound respect and admiration.

The summer people seemed prone to accidents. One day a young man from Portland disregarded the advice of his guide and tried to carry a 20-foot canoe up in the Umbazooksus region. A gust of wind upset him and he fell, dislocating his shoulder. The guide went out to Mud Pond Carry and tried to phone, but the line was not working. Finally he succeeded in getting a call through to Greenville by way of Patten.

Doc drove to Chesuncook Dam, where Alec Gunn detailed a man named Ed Hall to take him in the *Little Joe* to Umbazooksus Meadows. Heavy seas stirred up so much dirt that they had to clean the pipes three times before reaching the head of the Meadows. Arriving in camp, Doc found a boy stretched on the bed with a very bloody leg.

"Ha! Thought I came to treat a dislocated shoulder!"

"You did. Me," said the boy's companion.

Doc listened with grim incredulity. After the guide left, the two boys were cold. The uninjured one tried to split wood for a fire as he had seen the guide do, but split his leg instead. His injured companion, viewing the blood with alarm, tried to tell him how to pad and bandage it, but without much success. He decided he must do something. He took off his belt, a strong leather one, and twisted it about a round in a chair, one of the kind woodsmen make out of crooked limbs and a stump, weighing about two hundred pounds. Securing the belt to his wrist and keeping a steady strain on his arm, he weakened the muscles enough so that by twisting his body he finally felt the bone slide back into the joint. Then he bandaged the leg.

"Good boy!" commended Doc. Pretty good work for one of these city dudes!

Boiling up a few tools, he sewed the wound together and prepared to start for home. Home? Hardly. His work was only beginning. Presently a party of returning sportsmen and guides arrived, having made the Mud Pond Carry from Chamberlain, and asked Hall to take them to Chesuncook. They had four canoes, which the guides proceeded to tie fast—or so they thought.

"Those ropes won't hold in the heavy seas we'll meet after we leave the shelter of Gero Island," Doc warned them. But they only laughed.

Doc steered while Ed Hall nursed his engine. The Meadows were full of floating dri-ki. And sure enough, a gust of wind swept in from the gap between Gero and shore, parting the delicate rigging, and away went three of the canoes. This time, after corralling them, the men tied them securely. The high seas had stirred up the gas, making the engine miss and backfire, but they managed to deliver the parties, canoes and all, at the Chesuncook wharf. By now it was supper time, but Doc and Ed, anxious to get down the lake with all the daylight possible, pulled out and headed for the Dam. Down about four miles, off the old camp ground, dirt plugged the pipe again, and the engine stopped. Hastily they threw anchor, and luckily it held. Cleaning . . . stopping . . . throwing anchor . . . cleaning . . . . On the third sequence the bow fell off with the sea, lifting up on a wave, and the craft rode it in beautifully to strike the entire length of her keel on shore, so far up on the beach that they were able to jump right out of the cabin windows onto dry land!

So . . . a four-mile trek back to Chesuncook. This time they sat down to a good supper. While they ate, Alec Gunn rounded up a crowd of guides to go down with

them on the *Thetis* and drag *Little Joe* back into the
water. Since the lake was falling six or more inches a day,
being drawn heavily to run the mills at Millinocket, there
was no time to lose. *Little Joe* would soon be completely
high and dry.

Alec nosed the *Thetis* in, and a man carrying a light
rope jumped on the *Joe*. Then somebody flubbed. Too
much hawser was played out and got wound so tightly
into the propeller that the engine stalled. All hands
grabbed oars, pikepoles, whatever would reach bottom,
and managed to hold the boat from blowing around while
Alec and the engineer cut the rope away as far under
water as they could. They finally got back to the wharf.
Nothing doing now until morning.

Doc awoke early. The wind had shifted, and the fields
were white with frost. A cold northwest wind was blowing. Knowing that the propeller must be cleared in time
for the mail run at seven, he went to the wharf, removed
his clothes, and waded in with a jackknife. By grasping
the propeller blade with one hand he found that he could
hack at the rope with the other. The water was over his
mouth but under his nostrils enough to permit breathing,
as long as he watched the waves and timed it correctly.
Alec soon came down in bathing trunks to help. The job
took them three-quarters of an hour in water close to
freezing. Haste was important, for Alec wanted to haul
out the *Little Joe* on his down trip, the lake was dropping so fast. But they were ready to go, with breakfast
eaten, by seven. Or would have been except for dallying
passengers.

"Want you to meet Reverend Hempstead, Doc," said
Uncle Anse, breaking off a jolly and leisurely conversation. "The Reverend is the new Superintendent of Social
Service for the Great Northern. Swell guy. We're old
friends already."

"The Reverend," a big man with a genial manner and twinkling eyes, greeted the newcomer with keen friendly interest. "Well, well! I must say you look more like a woodsman than a doctor!"

The familiar words, usually so innocuous, sizzled against Doc's raw impatience like water on a hot stove. The icy immersion, the enforced delay, the necessity for haste, all set his nerves jangling. "Hold your sarcasm," he heard Henrietta Bigney's cool admonition, and nodded, biting his lips to hold back the brimstone. He waited, fuming, while the jolly conversation continued for another quarter-hour.

They drove the *Thetis* wide open down to the cove, ran a rope over to the *Joe,* and happily twitched her into the water on the first try, leaving Ed to clean out her pipes for the nth time and get her going. Doc's choler slowly subsided and by the time they reached the Dam, nearly on time, he was warming to the new social worker's winning personality, and a friendship of many years with Alfred G. Hempstead was in the making, years in which he was to remove the genial cleric's appendix, travel many miles to save his life in a bout with pneumonia, and bring his youngest daughter, Betty, into the world.

The occasional publicity given Doc's exploits on the lake aroused in him fully as much choler as a factor which slowed his tempo. Such was an item which appeared on March 23, 1933, in one of the state's newspapers:

"The birth of twins recently to Mrs. Albert Gaudette of Rockwood," it ran, "revealed another epic in the romantic history of medical science, the story of a physician who risked broken health, possible death, to answer the call of professional duty.

"Summoned to Rockwood about 7 P.M., Dr. Pritham

left Greenville in his snowmobile to make the twenty-
mile trip, extending the distance seven miles to take advantage of twelve miles of road to Lily Bay. At Lily Bay
he headed across the ice and proceeded safely until within
eight miles of his goal. Suddenly his heavy vehicle crashed
through the ice and catapulted the physician into seven
feet of water. Although soaked from head to foot by icy
water, the doctor groped and recovered his medicine kit,
clambered upon firm ice, and started on foot to finish his
trip. His clothes were nearly frozen on him, and, nearly
exhausted by his exertions, the physician arrived at the
Gaudette home about 2 A.M. just in time to minister to
Mrs. Gaudette in the birth of twins. His duties completed,
Dr. Pritham stopped only long enough to change and dry
his clothes, and then turned back on foot on his long trip
back to Greenville. To all the urgings of friends that he
wait until morning the physician turned a deaf ear. His
duty still called. He had a surgical operation to perform
at eleven in Dean Hospital. He kept his appointment and
performed the operation successfully."

Other papers printed the story with considerable ampli-
fied details.

"Not the way it was at all," fumed Doc. "Fact was I
got too close to shore, that's how the rear end of the snowmobile broke through into four feet of water. The front
end didn't go down at all. I could easily have hauled her
out, had power enough, but she broke her rear spring.
That left the rear wheel to come ahead, so had no contact with it. It was written up in the papers. Some danged
fool had me wallowin' around in the water with the car,
me with an inflated inner tube floatin' around in the
water! Now what in heck would I want with an air tire?
The rubber on the rear wheels was solid, and the front
end was wooden skis. And as there was no water on the

car floor, I couldn't have got wet. I stepped out on the ice and took my satchel to Rockwood.

"But the thing the feller missed was that there probably wasn't five men in the state, five doctors anyway, who could have made the trip across the lake that night. The air was all full of drift, what they called on the Grand Banks 'thick o' mist with the stray under.' One minute it was going to the south, then in a minute to east or west. Anyone tryin' to follow that stuff, he'd simply have turned around in a circle. A feller had to make up his mind where he was goin' and hang to it. I headed for Cowan's Cove because it would keep me in sight of that high ground between Spencer Bay and Kineo, and when I got to the Cove I found the wrinkle had opened and there was a channel forty or fifty feet wide of water. I walked clear to the foot of Sandbar to get around that water. But from Sandbar to the Moody Islands the snow was almost to my knees, with about a half inch of crust. I had to break a hole. It wouldn't hold me up, leg would go down in almost to my knee, and the crust was so hard that you couldn't break it with your leg. You had to bring your foot out the way it went in. Slow and awkward. But when I got to the wrinkle, I soon made Rockwood.

"I knew the Whitten boys would be playin' cards in the roundhouse, and the wrinkle rounded right there in front of it. I went up over the bank and asked one of the Whittens to take me up to Gaudette's. So he got out his car and run me up there. Before morning she had the twins. Then I took the morning train to Somerset, picked up a CP freight and came on home. Didn't walk on the return trip at all, except from the station to home. That's just how some fool wrote it up in the paper!"

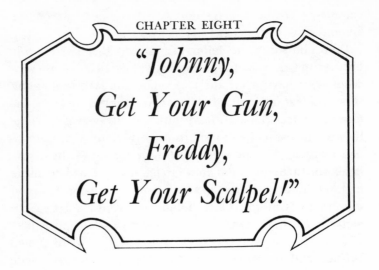

CHAPTER EIGHT

"Johnny, Get Your Gun, Freddy, Get Your Scalpel!"

· 1 ·

THE EMINENT AND AFFLUENT doctor from Portland who had been called to Greenville for a consultation descended from the Bangor and Aroostook's eleven o'clock train and rode to the hospital. Dr. Pritham would be there presently, he was told. At the moment he was out hunting deer. Doc soon arrived, cheerfully apologizing for his delay, but satisfied expression belying his regret. He looked like the proverbial cat licking cream from its whiskers.

"Sorry, didn't mean to be late, but ran into a nice little doe. Had to stop and dress it."

The city visitor regarded his country colleague with undisguised envy. "Want to know something?" he asked

242

ruefully. "You're a king among hogs, while I'm a hog among kings."

Doc nodded. The more eminent and affluent his brother physicians, the more of conflict he seemed to discover in their harassed and complicated lives. Duty versus pleasure, busy-ness versus family enjoyment, mounting fees versus mounting demands of prestigious living. He wanted none of it. During the years he had had many opportunities to become one of the more eminent and affluent. "Runners" from drug manufacturers had repeatedly painted glowing pictures of bigger communities short of doctors. Offers had come to him directly from former patients or other physicians cognizant of his skill and reputation. But he was never tempted. Why in thunder should he be? He already possessed the two assets which he considered essential to a happy and successful career: plenty of work where a man was needed, and—*freedom.*

No conflict in *his* life between duty and pleasure, office and home, months of harassment and weeks of jealously hoarded vacation! For him life was all of a piece. Much of the time he could travel with a doctor's bag in one hand and a hunting piece in the other; like the trip he once made to a camp up on Ellis Brook operation.

It was late in the fall, close to freeze-up, snowing and pitch dark. Ice was two inches thick on Black Pond, but fortunately Alec Gunn's boat was protected by iron plates along the water line and powered by a Diesel 100-horse-power engine. Alec handled the boat while Doc worked the hand pump. The boat twisted so badly in bucking the ice that it opened seams, and water squirted halfway across the engine room. When they got about halfway up Black Pond, they couldn't go any farther.

"Where's the tote road?" asked Doc. Alec pointed out the direction as well as he could, and Doc stepped out on the ice. "If you can make it, come back for me day after tomorrow."

He found the road and walked about four miles, arriving at five in the morning at the small cabin where the camp foreman was living with his wife and children. While spotting trees the day before, the foreman had opened his knee joint with his axe as neatly as a surgeon could have done it, cutting every ligament on the outside so that one could swing the leg inward and look right into the joint and see the crucial ligaments, cartileges, happily uninjured. He had been alone about two miles away in the woods. Binding the wound as well as he could, he had hobbled back into camp and put in a call for help. Bad, thought Doc. Securing two pie plates from the cookee at the main logging camp, he boiled up a few instruments and prepared to put his patient to sleep.

"Careful, Doc," warned the foreman. "When I go to sleep, I often choke, have to be rolled about to wake up."

Bad? Worse! Doc contemplated the situation with even less optimism. Here he was nearly a hundred miles from competent help, faced with the prospect of turning ether over to a cookee who had likely never even smelled it, plus operating on a man liable to choke to death, with a knee joint open to the weather for sixteen hours and traumatized by two miles of travel! O.K., amen, so be it.

As soon as the patient relaxed, he turned over the job of pouring ether to the cookee, hastily splashed his hands through soap and water, then into a Dakin's solution. Painting about the knee with McDonald's solution, he swung the leg sideways and mopped out all the dirt he could see, using more of McDonald's to dampen the gauze. While closing the wound in four layers with catgut, he kept one eye on the cookee and the patient's respiration. The man couldn't have breathed more than a dozen times while he was at work! His face was as black as ink, the cookee's white as putty, beads of sweat dripping off his chin. And no wonder! Doc hoped the man's wife and two little children, who sat watching the whole performance, couldn't see the blackened face and infrequent breathing. But at last it was over, and the patient soon roused, not even nauseated, to make a perfect recovery.

A good chance to get a deer! thought Doc as he retraced his steps to the shore, carrying his .33 along with his medicine pack. He counted twenty-five different-sized tracks of deer which had stepped into his footprints made some four hours before. Reaching the bank where he could see the landing, he sat down on a dead tree to watch for both a deer and the boat. But after the sleepless night he could not keep awake. He was roused by a loud snort, only to see four white tails disappearing into the woods. No boat in sight, and of course no deer. Throwing his mackinaw on a tree for a signal, he hustled the four miles back to camp, ate a good dinner, and hurried back. Still no boat. Again he fell asleep, then awoke to see a dandy buck standing not sixty yards from him eating beechnuts! No sooner seen than shot. Just as he made the last sweep of his knife to sever the gullet and remove the intestines he heard the boat whistle, and at the same moment on the other side of him the camp clerk swung around the bend in the road with the outgoing mail. While Doc wiped his hands, the clerk seized the deer and dragged it to the wharf. With the weather moderated and the channel open, they made good time out of the ice with no working of the hand pump.

He had treated his patient, had a nice nap in the sun, and shot a deer. An unusually successful trip, that! Nothing unusual, of course, finding a blind tote road in a snowstormy night. Hadn't Alec told him the direction to go?

This built-in compass with which nature had blessed him was a boon to others beside himself. Once a neighbor expressed a wish for one of those toadstool fungi which grow on the trunks of trees and are ideal for decorative purposes.

"I saw a dandy," Doc told her, "in the woods about two miles in from Bear Brook. If the boys are home and we go hunting next Saturday up there, I'll go knock that thing off the tree and bring it to you. It's got a pretty red top. Just what you want, I reckon."

"But, how in the world could you ever find it?"

"Easy. I'll go right to it." He did.

And of course the built-in compass was supplemented by that other natural endowment of inestimable value to a doctor-woodsman-hunter: those cat's eyes that could see in the dark.

"How in heaven's name did you get here?" he was greeted when he arrived late one night at Fred Park's camp two or three miles off the river at Machamp. "We thought you'd come by the 'Way-freight' in the morning."

"Found there was a train coming soon after you called and got 'em to drop me at the dam."

"But, how in tunket could you find the camp in the dark?"

"Simple. Followed the tote road, of course, same as to any camp."

"Simple! With drag roads all the way, how could you tell which was the right one?"

Doc regarded the questioners with indulgent patience. "You telephoned me, didn't you? All I had to do was follow the wire."

They were no less dumbfounded. How could anybody see a little eighth-of-an-inch wire in the pitch dark! Doc understood their skepticism. Most people were night blind, couldn't have seen the thing twenty-five yards away. If open to view, he could see it easily at two hundred. He had run on to few men with night vision. Fred Bigney had it. So did Fred Sawyer. (A special endowment of people named Fred?) What caused it? Vitamin A, maybe, perhaps B also. Or, more likely, it was just born in you. But, like the built-in compass, it was a mighty handy gadget. Even on the one occasion in his life when he was reported lost, both mechanisms were apparently still working.

"Wasn't lost at all," he maintained stoutly. "We had a very heavy rainfall. The country around Burnham Pond there was all flooded, about three feet of water in the main road that came out at the head of Squaw Bay. I got across on a fallen tree and started a nice big buck in on a side hill. Couldn't get a sight of the tormented thing but was within easy gunshot half a dozen times. Just glimpsed his head once, but he was gone before I could cock the gun. I followed the darned thing till it got pretty near dark. Then I had no notion of wadin' out through all that water. So I swung round to hit the Moosehead height o' land which extends from the northwest corner of Burnham Pond out to the railroad track. I followed this along, but it got dark and it was cloudy, and I drove through a thicket and then I'd have to wait till I could glimpse the moon to get direction right. Traveled along and come out on the height o' land just where I expected to. Luckily an auto came along just about that time and give me a ride in. Fools all thought I was lost, but I wasn't. Knew where I was all the time."

Sadie, less happily endowed, was not so fortunate. At least once she got herself lost, and thoroughly. She and Doc were hunting one November from the one-room log cabin at Bear Brook which Will Redmond and Andrew Kennedy had built for trapping on Great Northern land in the early twenties. It was a quarter-mile walk from the road, on the East Branch about three miles from Grant Farm. Sadie knew the country well, for she had spent many days and nights there with the boys in summer, since they, especially Carroll, enjoyed the fishing, and the whole family often went up on a Friday for the weekend.

"It's Sadie's camp," Andrew Kennedy insisted, refusing to let even her sister Viola and a teacher friend use it for a holiday.

Along with her many other adjustments Sadie had become a fairly proficient hunter. That she had never shot a deer was due not to lack of skill or opportunity but to the sudden burst of admiration for the grace and beauty of the intended victim. On this day in November they were hunting deer separately in the Bear Brook region. Somehow Sadie got into a beaver flowage in a thick swamp and could not find her way out.

"If you ever get lost," Doc had often warned her, "stay where you are. Wait for someone to find you."

It was sound advice, for in this wilderness of forests, lakes, and mountains one could easily travel a hundred miles without encountering a human settlement. Not a pleasant prospect, however, on a cold day in late November with night coming on! But Sadie was not one to panic. And she had not spent the last quarter-century in this country of guides-woodsmen-hunters for nothing. If she must spend the night in the woods, she would do so as comfortably as possible. After building herself a neat little shelter out of evergreen branches, she collected as much wood as she could find and made a fire. Just as she had coaxed it into burning and it was too late to gather material to start it again, a heavy rain came pelting down. The fire smoked and sizzled and gave every indication of demise. How protect it enough to keep it going? Suddenly she saw an old tree with a huge piece of loose bark. Tearing it off, she held it over the fire until the shower let up and the wood was burning enough to hold its flame even in the rain. Somehow, huddled in her makeshift shelter, she got through the freezing night.

When she did not show up at dark, Doc went to Grant Farm for help. He was not really worried. Sadie was perfectly capable of handling almost any emergency. A search was started immediately. Somehow the news reached Greenville that "Pritham," as Sadie was popularly called, was lost, and the town roused itself en masse to action. It was said later that two hundred people went up to join the search. The next day, with snow threatening, Doc decided to explore the swamp, even though he had warned Sadie time and again not to cross it.

"If you find her, don't make a big fuss," he told the men with him, "just be casual."

Albert Spinney was the one who found her, looking a bit dazed and sitting beside the embers of her fire. Doc saw her for the first time back in camp. Unlike many husbands, he expressed his relief with neither embraces nor kisses. If there was sentiment in the look they exchanged, it was not revealed in his greeting.

"Well, Sadie," he observed dryly, "I see you've burned a hole in your pants."

Nor did he bother to express thanks to the scores of townspeople who had rushed to the rescue. After all, it had been their idea. He hadn't asked them to come. He hadn't been worried. Neither had Sadie. Why should anybody else have been?

No, Sadie hadn't been exactly worried. But the next year about Thanksgiving time, when everybody went hunting late in the season so the meat could be frozen for winter, she found a good reason for visiting her relatives in Freeport.

This brief hiatus in deer hunting did little to interrupt Sadie's outdoor activities. She was a good all-round sports-

woman, a valuable asset in a vacation paradise and a
household of two growing boys. She hiked, picnicked,
fished, boated, snowshoed. And she climbed mountains.
Not Doc. He might run like a goat through the woods,
but he was no ardent mountain climber, for two reasons:
poor hunting in the higher altitudes, few patients. But
at one time or another Sadie climbed them all: Squaw,
Little Squaw, Katahdin, Spencer, Rum, Elephant, Lily
Bay, Number 4, Kineo.

There were three ways of climbing the stark headland
on which the lookout had once signaled danger to Chief
Kineho: the Bridle Trail, used in early years by horseback riders, the Indian Trail which followed along the
edge of the cliff, beginning at the lake shore, and the
Chain Trail on the south and steepest side of the sheer
rocky cliff, so named because a chain was usually fastened
to the climber in making the ascent. Once Sadie went up
by the latter, climbing by a rope hitched at the top. It
was when Carroll was working on the New Haven railroad and had brought a friend home with him. A pity
her distressed in-laws, worried over her delicate physique,
could not have seen her then!

It was because of Carroll that she also climbed Soubunge, the two-thousand-foot mountain on the north
shore of Harrington Lake. During the Depression of the
early thirties, between his job in New Haven and one
with the water company in Caribou, Carroll marked time
as fire watch on Soubunge, and Sadie spent some days
camping there with him. To while away the monotonous
assignment Carroll amused himself by asking every
climber who signed the register to state what brand of
toothpaste he used. Sadie never did find out which brand
came out ahead, or whether the unsolicited research resulted in a grateful subsidy from the favored company.

. 2 .

DOC WAS AS FASTIDIOUS about the choice and custody of his guns as of his scalpels. When his .33 Winchester became obsolete during the early thirties, he turned it in for a .308 Savage. Dr. Nick, who was taking a short study course in Boston that year, took along the old .33 and brought back the .308. Doc chose a Savage rather than a Winchester because hunters were likely to leave the latter's box magazine at home or on their car hood and find themselves in the woods without ammunition. The Savage had a roto magazine that was solidly installed. You always had it with you, and you almost always had ammunition in your pockets if you had a holder to put it in.

He got .32 specials for the boys. Will Redmond had a .32 special that he liked because it had an auxiliary clip that would hold revolver shells, so when he was in the woods hunting deer and wanted to get a partridge without making too much noise, he could slip one of those revolver shells into his rifle, and it would discharge with a mere pop, not audible more than a hundred feet away. Sadie, as well as the boys, used one of those rigs. But after he got his twelve-gauge shotgun, Doc often used slugs in that to hunt deer. It was equally effective for birds or heavier game. As he grew older and this became too heavy for him, he would use a twenty-gauge. Seldom would a year pass from 1905 to 1970 that he would not get his full quota of deer. An exception was 1968, his eighty-ninth year, when there was such a tremendous fall of snow, two feet at a time, that it would have been hard finding game even after shooting it.

But ducks, not deer, would always be his favorite quarry. The loft of the old barn, workshop as well as storehouse, slowly filled with floats, sculling paddles, decoys, all made with his own hands. The lake game was much the same as he had bagged in Freeport—scaup, scoters, black duck, occasionally a mallard. His favorite was the little hairy-headed hooded merganser, the best eating of them all. He usually prepared them himself, roasted and stuffed some, fried a good many. Sadie seldom ate them. She found the wild, fishy taste of all but the black duck offensive. In fact, Carroll was the only one in the family who shared Doc's fancy for all kinds of wild meat. Venison, bear, coons—Doc preferred all of them to beef, and could cook them to perfection. To his knowledge he assisted at various times in the consumption of nine bears and at least a half dozen coons.

"How do you cook coon?" some of the nurses at the hospital asked him curiously. Soon he brought one which he had cooked for them to sample. They pronounced it good . . . until in his detailed account of its preparation he enumerated certain savory innards which had been left in for added flavor. Then more than one made a hasty exit.

In spite of his skills as a woodsman Doc took his turn at spending a night in the woods, involving Sadie in the adventure. It happened in a strange way. One early morning in 1934 Doc was coming up from the shore of Burnham Pond, where he had gone hunting ducks. Suddenly pain, sharp as a dagger-thrust, split his head. The world reeled. As it slowly righted, he realized what had happened. Somehow he had walked head on into a pointed dead cedar limb, and it had run right through his ear drum. An accident not likely to happen once in a hundred years! He staggered to a fallen tree trunk, sank down, and held his reeling head. Fortunately it was his dead ear which had been pierced, the one deafened by the exploding nipple in the old gun forty-five years before. After the pain slowly subsided, he rose shakily to his feet and started again toward home.

But something strange had happened. Instead of the shock impairing his hearing, as might be expected, small sounds had suddenly become magnified: his feet crackling through dead leaves, the snapping of a twig, the scurrying of a squirrel. And above all the small sounds there was a peculiar silence, as if the world, still charged with the chaotic vibrations of creation, had subsided into peace and quiet. Then all at once the significance of the change smote him. *The ringing in his ears had stopped!* The dull humming resonance which constantly, day and night, for forty-five years, had strummed and jangled through every conscious moment of his life, was no longer there. He felt like a man released from prison. In spite of the continuing pain, all the way home he walked on air. But he dared not take the new freedom for granted. A little cedar stick the cause of a miracle? It seemed too good to be true. So he told no one of the accident or its apparent result. He would wait and see.

A couple of days later he and Sadie went up in their favorite Bear Brook country hunting. The weather was disagreeable, drizzly after a light snow, but excellent for tracking deer. Sadie had wanted to start early, but cases prevented their getting away until noon. It was mid-afternoon before they got into the woods. Doc found a good place to plant her, in the hard wood, where she could see a good distance. He would circle around her through the thickets, hoping to scare out any deer that might be in shelter.

"I'll be back by four," he told her. "Be sure and wait for me right here."

The weather was moderating, melting the inch or two of snow hanging on all the trees. At about three a thick fog set in. Doc kept traveling in wider and wider circles, the wet snow making travel more and more difficult. By late afternoon the water was running out of the tops of his shoes, drenching his clothes, seeping into his pores, running down his neck, and, yes—probably working its way into the injured ear.

"Time to go back and get Sadie," he decided. "Must go straight east up the hill."

He started, shook his head to avoid a limb, came very near running into another, and suddenly found himself in a merry-go-round of dizziness. All about him were rings whirling, intermingling. He could not even tell where east was. He tried to get up the hill by sighting a tree which he thought was in the right direction, then staggering to it and grabbing it before falling down, then picking another one. But he found he wasn't holding his direction well. Deciding to use his compass, he found the deuced contraption was broken. In two or three tries he was back down at the foot of the hill. Traveling along its edge for a little, he came to a fallen log with little firs and spruce growing all around it, and he crawled in on top of it. Wet through, not a dry thread in his clothing, head still whirling, he yielded himself gratefully to the warmth of his little shelter. He would stay here ... just long enough ... to get dry ... clear his head ... then must get to ... Sadie ....

He awoke with a start, feeling light on his face. The moon rising, he thought, must be close to midnight. Shocked into full consciousness, he dragged himself to his feet, discovered to his horror that it was not a moon, but daylight. Sadie! She had been out in these cold wet woods all night! His head was still whirling, but he knew he must get to her, or at least where she had been. He moved gingerly. The flat expanse of thicket at the foot of the hill looked to be about half a mile across. There was a pine tree on the further side of it. If I can just cross that half mile of thicket and hit that tree, he thought, I'll be back on my compass points. If I can only hit that tree . . . . He hit it all right. It was smack in front of him, had been only about ten feet away when he saw it. He managed to cross the brook and get up on the knoll, stood there and hollered. A voice replied, some man right handy, must be alongside of the brook. He hollered again . . . and again. But to get that feller to reply a second time, he couldn't. Nor could he make Sadie hear.

What to do? The dizziness had left him, but he knew it might come back at any moment. If he went back and tried to find Sadie, he might not get back out. He dared not chance it. The temperature was plummeting. He could not run the risk of Sadie's being left in the woods for another even colder night. So he started back home. Arriving at Kokadjo, he telephoned to Perley Redmond, explained the situation, and asked him to come up and get Sadie out. Viola and Hallie both came with him, and Doc met them at Lily Bay.

"Where shall I find her?" asked Perley.

"Remember that place where I got a deer once?" Doc described the occasion, and his brother-in-law nodded. "You go there and holler. She'll answer you."

Meanwhile Sadie was experiencing mounting terror, not for herself, for Doc. She knew something must have happened to him. Before the fog set in, she could easily have gotten out and made her way back to the camp at Bear Brook, but she was afraid he would come back and find her gone. By four the fog was so thick she could see scarcely ten yards away. There was an old stump nearby. She picked up dead branches and piled them around it, hoping she had enough to last through the night, for if she went far enough to find more she knew she could not find her way back. She made a fire around the stump and did have enough to keep a small one going. At periodic intervals she shot what cartridges she had in an attempt to signal, but they brought no response. It was cold, and as night approached it became colder. She was wearing only a jacket, not the heavy coat she usually used for hunting. During the night her hands became so swollen with cold that she had to use both of them to lift a piece of wood. Rain began to fall. But somehow the night passed. She even slept a little.

"There was a nice thicket you could have gotten into within seventy-five yards," Doc reminded her later in mild rebuke. "But, no, you sat out there all night in the cold."

The worry was far worse than the discomfort. With the coming of dawn she was nearly frantic with fear. Then finally came a shot. She knew instinctively it was a signal. Her cartridges were gone. She could not signal back. But she could yell, and did. Viola said they could have heard her five miles away. There was little relief in being rescued. Like Doc when reported lost, she had known all the time where she was. It was the sight of Doc, safe and apparently sound, which restored her world to normalcy.

The attacks of dizziness did not recur. After the inflammation caused by the cold water in the ear subsided, Doc's hearing was as good as formerly. A thorough examination by an ear specialist revealed that he could locate sound perfectly with the one ear. That was no news to Doc. "When I'm out hunting," he told the specialist, "if an old partridge gets upon a log and drums, he comes home to dinner with me."

And—the ringing permanently ceased. It was like being born into a new world, of sound, of serenity, of—best of all—silence.

"People must have thought I was an awful cranky old thing," he said once to Ella Gerrish, "but that cussed jangling in one's ear for forty-five years without a minute's letup might make even a plaster saint cantankerous!"

· 3 ·

THE YOUNG NURSE rushed from the operating room, weeping.

"He—he called me an *idiot!*" she wailed.

"Not F.J.! He couldn't have!" The girl's cousin, Nellie Morrell, a graduate nurse employed at the hospital, looked shocked and incredulous.

"But he did! I heard him. He said, 'Idiot, idiot'!"

"I still say he couldn't have," Nellie insisted stoutly.

She was right. The misunderstanding was soon explained. These were days before the designation of a particular "instrument nurse." The attending nurse actually assisted in the operation. As the girl's hand held an instrument, in her nervousness it must have shaken a bit.

"Steady it, steady it!" Doc had urged in his low even voice.

It was true that sometimes the nurses, especially the new ones, were a little afraid to work with him. He was extremely exacting, with them as with himself. A perfectionist in sanitation, lightning-swift both in motion and decision making, he expected his assistants to be equally alert and circumspect. It was also true that his orders occasionally lacked specific detail and clarity.

"I followed him clear down to the outside door at his heels to be sure that I was getting his orders straight," complained one nurse.

This lack of clarity was known to have resulted in the giving of wrong medication, as with Albert Gonyer, a French Canadian who had been thrown from his bicycle. Fearing that he had a concussion, Doc had ordered him to bed with directions that he must not sleep. One of the nurses gave him a sleeping pill by mistake. Instead of rebuking her, Doc congratulated both her and himself on the error.

"It worked out all right," he chuckled. "Albert's up there snoring away as peacefully as can be. That's just what he needed."

On at least one occasion Doc himself was guilty of administering the wrong medication. Paul Sawyer called him to make an appointment to have his ear washed out. Soon afterward his brother Charles called arranging to have a shot for bursitis. Paul arrived first, and Doc automatically gave him the shot.

"What's that for?" demanded Paul.

"Your bursitis, of course."

"But I came to get my ear washed out!"

And there was no denying that Doc took the knowledge and understanding of his colleagues too much for granted.

One day when Nellie Morrell was relieving the administrator the phone rang. It was Doc calling the upstairs nurse. I think I'll listen in, thought Nellie, knowing the nurse was new. "I'm sending in Mrs. So-and-so," Doc announced tersely. "I'm going to operate on her this morning for the same job we did on Mrs. John Doe." The actual names specified were as vague entities to the bewildered nurse as these substitutes. She came running down to Nellie in a dither. "How does he expect me to know what was done to Mrs. John Doe!"

Fortunately Nellie remembered the case. She looked it up in the records, and the operating room was properly prepared by the time Doc arrived.

Nellie came to Greenville from her home in Rumford in the twenties to visit an aunt. She liked it so well that she stayed. Though she had planned to become a teacher, she changed her mind and trained in nursing, graduating from the hospital nursing school in 1929.

Since the building of the new hospital in 1918 the new

nursing school had grown and thrived, first under the super-
intendency of Miss Grace Batson, who was followed by Mrs.
Mildred Clark and Mrs. Vere Badley. To finish all their
requirements, students affiiliated at first with the Newton
Hospital in Massachusetts, of which Charles A. Dean was
a trustee, later with the Eastern Maine General Hospital in
Bangor, enabling them to take their state board examinations in Augusta. Doctors Pritham and Nickerson assisted in the nurses' training, giving lectures and practical
demonstrations. Many girls trained here went on to distinguished careers, like Eleanor Hamilton, who served in
the armed forces in Africa, Italy, and on transports, and
retired from Fort Dix with the rank of major.

Nellie was long associated with the hospital and nursing
school after her graduation. She worked for some years
in the Carey Memorial Hospital in Caribou, then returned to Greenville, married William Morrell, telephone
foreman for the Great Northern, and in 1935 became a
relief nurse in the hospital, working there periodically
for many years, to become supervisor in 1954. She knew
F.J. as a doctor as few other persons could.

But she did not always find it easy, taking directions
from Doc. One morning he decided that he would put a
pin through a patient's knee, an orthopedic procedure
not yet standardized by equipment and techniques which
would come a generation later. While he was inserting it,
the brace and bit which he used did not seem to be
answering his needs.

"Go down to my garage," he told Nellie. "Up in the
loft over where I have my decoys, you will find a brace
hanging on a wall. Get it for me."

Haste was imperative. Nellie ran to her car and drove
down the hill, thinking with some trepidation, "Suppose
I don't get the right one. He'll be pretty disgusted."
Arriving at the garage, erstwhile the barn, she had other

worries. She looked with horrified dismay at the sole means of ascent to the loft. She was mortally afraid of ladders. Gritting her teeth and clinging for dear life to each rung, she climbed through the small opening, and crawled out on the splintery floor. No time to more than glance at the fascinating medley, the tool bench, the gunning floats stacked one on the other, the baskets and cartons of decoys—ducks of all shapes and sizes wound round and round with string! Above them on a nail hung a brace. Let it be the right one, she prayed, and somehow managed the even more terrifying descent. It was. The patient was still under anesthesia when she rushed back to the operating room. Employing the makeshift implements, Doc successfully completed the operation.

Except for rare exceptions—the incompetent, the slow, the super-sensitive—the nurses who trained or worked at the Charles A. Dean Memorial Hospital soon became as staunchly loyal devotees of the meticulous, sometimes crusty little doctor as was Nellie. Like Bernice Smith, who had grown up in Greenville and came back in 1937 after training at the Eye and Ear Hospital in Portland. She found him so different from the doctors she had known that she often wept. But frustration soon changed to admiration. True, he wasn't so sophisticated, and he didn't always go by the books. He used common sense instead. If a mask made his glasses steam up so he could not see properly, then why wear one? If he could feel around better in a body cavity with lotion on his hands than rubber gloves, why not use it? Once when Bernice's brother was having trouble with his legs and she tried to straighten them, Doc gave her hands a gentle slap. "If they feel better that way, then why not leave them?" Well—why not?

And if a half-dozen instruments were sufficient for an operation, then why use half a hundred? With a knife and scissors and two or three clamps he could perform almost any of the surgical feats for which other general surgeons required a growing multiplicity of tools. He had his own little kit, the basic instruments which always traveled with him, scarcely bigger than a manicure set. When he operated in the hospital, it was always opened up. Then usually 75 per cent of them were pushed aside on the table, there if he needed them. And so neat he was! The nurses marveled because when he finished in surgery there was hardly a spot in the place. One of his colleagues was different, and they used to tease him. "Too bad," they jibed, "that F.J. couldn't do them all!" After an operation, especially at night, Doc would stay and help you clean up. Perhaps by the time you got the patient upstairs for recovery and came back, the work would be half done.

And, once you got accustomed to his tempo, his speed of operation was a delight—provided you were able to keep up with him. Bernice was. Other doctors seemed intolerably slow by comparison. And of course they did to F.J. himself. He always hated to assist. Once when a fellow physician seemed to be taking an unconscionably long time to develop a prognosis for one of his patients, Doc's patience was honed to a fine edge.

"She may get well," he observed in a pungent aside, "if she doesn't die first of old age."

Beneath the apparently crusty surface there was often this sudden bubbling up of humor when you least expected it.

"Yes," he was heard to comment about a girl who had started training in the school of nursing, "she began to work here, but she was pinched too many times in the elevator, so she decided to transfer to Portland."

"Too bad," he commiserated with a patient who had been brought in with a badly cut foot. "And a brand new boot, too!"

Later, when Bernice was living in Connecticut, she wrote Doc asking if she could come home to have her baby. It was during the Second World War, when he was again alone and working almost around the clock.

"Are you too busy to bother with me?" she asked.

"Come home by all means," was his reply. "You flatter an old duffer."

She was not the only one whose faith in Doc transcended time, space, and experience. For some time Nellie Morrell lived in Portland, and her daughter had what she presumed were attacks of appendicitis. "I just can't have her done down here," thought Nellie. "I've got to get back to Dr. Pritham." And in due time she did. Much later, when Nellie's daughter had her children, she was living in Connecticut, where the most skilled medical service was available. But did she take advantage of it? No. It was Doc who delivered her babies.

Of course this faith was not always rewarded. Ella Gerrish was visiting the Pritham house one Sunday and heard Doc telling some friends about a woman from Monson who had refused to let anyone else operate on her. Though arrangements had been made for her to go to a Bangor hospital, she had insisted on having Doc as her surgeon. She had been brought to Greenville. Something had gone awry with the operation, and she had died. It was one of the rare occasions when Ella had seen him show emotion. Never had she known him to be more sober or depressed.

Ella's mother had this faith to an excess. When Ella was teaching out of state and her mother was living with her and fell sick, no other doctor, even the best qualified, would satisfy. But as soon as Ella brought her back home, all Doc had to do was come in and look at her, and immediately her health improved. Doc had no "bedside

manner." Often he asked few questions. He seemed never
in a hurry. There was not too much bothering to take
pulse and temperature and blood pressure. Not at first,
that is. He would sit down, start talking perhaps about a
duck hunt, all the time looking keenly at the patient,
noting any changes in face, eyes, general appearance, and
getting a very good idea of his condition before starting
any sort of examination. But for those who knew and
trusted him his very presence set the healing process in
motion.

Such respect for his skill was not always shared by
his brother physicians. One year when there was an
epidemic of polio he thought he had a case of it and notified the state board of health. They sent up two experts
with a microscope to verify his diagnosis. "We'll let you
make the tap," they offered magnanimously.

"Ha!" thought Doc, quite aware of their secret smiles
and smug expressions. "Plenty willing, aren't you, to let
old Pritham get that fluid out! Afraid you can't do it the
first time and will have to try, and try again. Think an
old fellow like me can't do a difficult job like that, and
you'll have a grand time watching!" Well, it wasn't easy,
the way it was usually done, the tap being made in a
straight line through that dense, tough ligament that
hooks the spine and the spinal column together. Many
times the ligament would prove so hard and tough that
the needle would skate off to one side, and several attempts
would have to be made.

Doc considered. Why on earth couldn't you tap that
column from a sideways position and not go through the
ligament at all? No sooner thought than done. He picked
up a syringe, chose a point about half an inch to the side
of the ligament at center point, and made one stab with
it. He felt the needle go through into the space, drew back

a little on the plunger, sucked some fluid into the syringe. "Here you are," he said, "Come get your fluid." They did, the smugness quite gone from their faces.

"You know," said one of the experts, looking at the sample under the microscope, "that's a perfect tap. There isn't even a drop of blood."

Fortunately the test was negative. But Doc could never understand why the old method persisted in use, when simple common sense and a slight change in technique made the process so easy. But the profession had always been resistant to change. Look at Semmelweiss, with his well-proven hypothesis that childbed fever was the result of dirty hands! It had taken almost half a century for doctors to accept the most rudimentary laws of sanitation! And how long would it take for them to do the sensible thing and get a post-operative patient out of bed and walking around within a day or two, a beneficial practice which he had discovered for himself back in 1905 and had been using on his patients for more than twenty years? He had other little surgical tricks of procedure also, like turning the peritoneum up so that both cut edges were on top and facing upward. This made it certain that there were no raw edges underneath to form adhesions.

Doc was a "maverick," yes, unbranded by most symbols of conformity, whether professional or human. But the "back-woods" from which he issued was one of the Rivieras of the world. Since Thoreau the Moosehead-Allagash country had been increasingly invaded by a steady influx of the great. His famed Indian friend Joe Attean had been only the first of a long succession of able guides to list in their wilderness safaris some of the world's most famous names. The legendary duchess at Kineo Hotel, who each night had worn a different gown, necklace, and bracelet, all fabulously precious, but always a huge emerald on a finger of her right hand, and who had been found crumpled one morning on the sharp flints of Kineo, jewels never accounted for, had been but a prototype of the area's noble clientele. James Russell Lowell, Holman Day, Ted Williams, Eileen Farrell, as well as more local celebrities like Bud Leavitt ... they were only samples of the names inscribed on the guest books of Kineo, Squaw Mountain Inn, Maynard's-in-Maine, Seboomook Hotel, The Birches, Lily Bay House. They went into the woods, and they came out—sometimes to land in the Greenville Hospital or Doc's office.

There was the man from New York who had received a fractured femur from a hunting accident. He was brought to Greenville by the CP train, to be taken off at the station on a stretcher by some waiting men, one apparently a hospital orderly. But when he arrived at the hospital he found to his intense dismay that the shabby, slightly stooped little fellow who had directed his transfer was not an orderly at all, but the operating surgeon! "I just knew my end had come," he confessed later. "That man would never be able to save me!" But he did, and the visitor never tired of singing his praises.

It wasn't the only time he was taken for a lesser menial. A boy who had been lost on Katahdin required the amputation of a toe. When Doc arrived at the hospital on the morning of the operation, he found that the young man's fiancée and her mother had just arrived on the train from Quebec. Shocked by the patient's condition, the mother stepped from his room into the hall just as Doc was emerging from the room of another patient.

"Orderly, get me a glass of water," she commanded in the tone of one used to obedience. Then, as he made no move to comply, her voice became more peremptory. "Boy, get me a glass of water. I feel faint."

Doc looked her up and down with dispassionate interest. "Madam," he said with cool politeness, "nobody faints in Greenville."

Doc was by no means immune to insinuations of contempt or patronage, either because of his stature or because of the way he dressed. But there was another sort of patronage which he found even more distasteful, the intellectual or professional. He intensely disliked being "talked down to." His weapon against such forms of condescension was either silence or indifference, sometimes both. A man who was installing an X-ray machine in the hospital and trying to explain its mechanism almost developed nervous prostration in the process. Because he was using language appropriate to a half-witted child, Doc wandered about the room doing other things, apparently oblivious to all that was said. The man came out wiping the sweat from his face.

"I don't know whether he'll be able to run it or not," he confessed wearily to the head nurse. "I tried to explain it to him, but I'm afraid I didn't get through."

The nurse, knowing Doc, only smiled.

The minute the man had gone Doc began inspecting the machine. From the first he ran it without any trouble. In fact, he had absorbed every word the man had said.

Evidently he thought the city woman with the dog bite was patronizing him a bit also. At least she addressed him in tones one might employ toward the elderly or deaf. She found him in the basement of the Methodist Church peeling carrots for a church supper. Her dog, she explained, had gotten into a fight with another dog. When she tried to separate them, the strange dog had bitten her hand. Doc glanced at the hand, then resumed his peeling, the same motions he would use in whittling a stick. The woman leaned over and spoke even louder. What should she do?

Still Doc did not raise his eyes. He had seen the grazed
hand, and he knew all the dogs in town. "Oh, just take it
home and wash it out with soap and water."

The loud voice subsided into meekness. "Thank you,
Doctor. And, how much do I owe you?"

"Nothing." The peeling continued without interruption, and the woman hurried home to follow his pre-
scription.

Payment for his services was always the least of Doc's
concerns. He was a doctor, and it was a doctor's business
to make and keep people well, not make and keep himself
well-to-do. When a doctor became the richest man in
town, like some he knew, owned the most pretentious
house, drove the biggest car, there was something wrong.
Not that Doc belittled the value of his services or was
indifferent to the making of a decent living. He charged
reasonable fees and expected them to be paid—if or when
possible. He made no difference in prices for those who
couldn't pay. But he rarely sent a bill. Edna Gunn, who
worked in the post office for thirty-seven years, could
vouch for that. All through the years he took much pay
in kind, perhaps more than in actual money: firewood,
farm products, pork or beef when a farmer butchered, hens,
eggs. People would bring what they had. He never put a
monetary value on the goods received. He let the donor
do that. And he made a sufficient living, enough to supply
the simple wants of his family, to send Carroll to the University of Maine and Howard to Colby College during
the Depression years, later to Tufts Medical College—
yes, and, as treasurer of the Methodist Church for at
least fifty-seven years, to keep the succession of ministers
paid on time and the Conference bills discharged in full,
often to the consternation of parishioners, who were expected to reimburse him later. As to other funds ac-
cumulated or where they were spent or interred, that

was his business and his alone. All the town knew was that they were not spent on his house or person.

Many paid their back bills, and many never did. One woman married during Depression years, who suffered a case of hepatitis, must have owed him large sums for his many visits. It was a long time before she could pay anything. Finally she brought him ten dollars. "I'll pay more when I can."

"No, that's fine," replied Doc. "I'll look up my records. If I find you owe me anything, I'll tell you. Otherwise we're all square."

"Do I owe you any money, Doc!" another man asked him.

"I don't know."

The man gave him ten dollars, then went back home and discovered that his wife had already paid their bill. He went back to claim a refund.

"Well," said Doc, "some don't pay at all, some pay twice. It sort of evens up in the long run."

Another debtor went into the post office and asked Edna Gunn to change ten dollars. He wanted the bills to pay Dr. Pritham.

"But Doc has plenty of change," protested Edna. "Why not give it to him?"

"Oh, no," was the reply. "If I gave him the ten spot, he'd pocket the whole of it. But if I give him a dollar on account, he'll be perfectly happy."

Nevertheless, some thought he overcharged. At one time the home office of the Great Northern felt that his fees rendered for services to their employees were too high. They sent a young man up from Bangor to investigate. He went out with Doc on a case. They traveled by car as far as the road went, then used a canoe for a short distance. After treating an injured woodsman at a lumber camp, Doc and he returned to the canoe. While they

had been gone a boom of logs had filled in the space
which had been open water. Carrying the canoe, Doc
crossed the boom, hearing occasional splashes behind
him. When they reached Greenville, there was another
call waiting, but the young man had had enough.

"No amount could compensate," he reported fervently
to his superiors, "for what that man has to go through in
just one day of his life."

There were a few other instances of protest. Ella Gerrish was keeping house for the Prithams when a woman
came out of the office sputtering over the amount of her
bill. Doc was a profiteer, a mountebank! He was getting
rich on the ills of the poor! He—et cetera, et cetera. Ella
was nearly bursting with indignation, but Doc seemed
completely unruffled. He followed the woman to the
door and closed the screen behind her. When she finally
ended her harangue he remarked pleasantly, "Well, that's
the price you pay for having an educated man in your
midst."

Only once did he try to collect old debts.

"Was foolish enough to take on one of those miserable
collecting agencies," he described the incident regretfully.
"Turned over some work to them and was sorry for it
ever afterward. I didn't get much of anything, and they
robbed the people. If folks don't have money enough to
pay, they may as well have what they can save as to have
somebody rob 'em of it. If I started a lawsuit, they'd have
to borrow the money to get them out of it and be forever
payin' up."

People usually paid in time, if they could. Like Henry
Budden, who came in one day after the First World War,
fished out one of those long limp pocketbooks, and pulled
out fifteen dollars, payment for a bill rendered some ten
years before.

"It's the first time I've ever had the money, Doc. Got

it from the soldiers' bonus. I sure appreciate the fact that you've never sent me a bill in all this time."

In 1939 Doc went to Boston again for a post-graduate course in obstetrics. He had a wonderful time. He began to get invitations as soon as friends discovered he was in the city. Former Greenville residents, summer visitors, medical associates—all began calling up and inviting him to meals and rides and parties. Though Stan Walden, a Greenville native, got his invitation in fairly early, Doc had to date him three weeks ahead. Harry and Helen Farrington, who owned camps in Beaver Cove, were especially hospitable in providing entertainment—suppers, theater parties, sightseeing expeditions.

But professionally the period was not too productive. He didn't see a baby born all the time he was there. One of the hospitals he visited in a slum section was the filthiest place of its kind he had ever seen. He had never seen a lumber camp in such condition. And he certainly could not approve of all the techniques they were employing.

"If you were up in my country," he told one of the doctors, "you'd do a job like that just once. You'd never get another. News would travel on the grapevine, and you'd be all through. Up there in the woods you've got to be pretty careful, got to make good. If you can't, everybody knows it, and quick. You'd just fold up your tents and fade away."

CHAPTER NINE

Act Three

. 1 .

CAME THE RED MAN. Came the White Man. Came the lumberer and the sportsman. Came the tourist.

Against the age-old backdrop of lakes and mountains the human drama quickened. As it moved into its third act the stage set swiftly altered. Props and actors were reshuffled, refurbished, replaced with all the revolutionary impetus of the mid-twentieth century.

There remained but a few relics of the first act, the age of the Red Man, vestigial remnants of the once noble Abenaki. A hundred place names, meanings long forgotten, endowed the donors with doubtful immortality. A few descendants of the Capinos still lived on the point of land halfway between East and West Coves. On the

streets of the Village there could often be seen the pictur-
esque figure of old Henry Perley (Chief Henry Red
Eagle), connoisseur of Indian legends, one-time announcer
for Barnum and Bailey ("I was the guy that gets up front
and tells the lies"), and for twenty-seven years a head
counselor for older boys in Y camps. But by the end of
the sixties there were less than a dozen Indians left in
town of a one-time colony of more than a hundred.

Still, of course, there was the Indian Store, sprawled
the length and breadth of the old Shaw Block, luring
tourists with its vast displays of baskets, toy totem poles,
semi-precious stones, and souvenir gadgets, and exem-
plifying one of the old and unique virtues of the Yankee
outpost: honesty. A visitor, it is said, once bought a pair
of moccasins in the Indian Store and left them on the
counter. Two years later he came back, and the Indian
girl clerk wordlessly passed him his package.

The theme of the second act, age of the lumberer and
sportman, rose to fresh climax in the third, but with what
a difference! The old days of lumbering were as defunct
as the ghost of Larry O'Connor and the roaring torrent
which had swept him to his doom in the "dry way" of
Ripogenus. Gone was the old lumber camp with its log
walls, straw-filled bunks, and deacon seat. The new camps
were often portable, made of pre-fab materials, with clean
tiled floors, individual iron beds, hot and cold running
water, shower baths, electric lights, flushes. With bull-
dozed roads running straight into the operations many of
the crew lived at home and drove cars to and from work.
Instead of singing the old ballads, men listened in the
forties to Frank Sinatra, in the fifties to Mitch Miller, in
the sixties to the Beatles. Doc emphatically preferred the
old ballads.

Gone were the double-bitted axes, the crosscuts, the
bucksaws. And while the chainsaws buzzed and ground

and whined, there was talk of a new laser device which would replace all saws, producing a beam of high-energy light with enough heat to vaporize all materials. Struggling to cope with the increased toll of injuries exacted by the chainsaw, Doc shuddered to think of the accident and mortality rate in the age of a laser.

Gone, too, or nearly obsolete were the tools of the river drives—cant dogs, pike poles, peaveys—relegated to museums like the Lumberjack Room of the Bangor House, immortalized in bronze and granite as in Charles Tefft's heroic sculpture of "The Last Drive" near Bangor's Public Library, or merely left to rot and rust under the flapping tar paper of an old camp's skeleton. For the spring drives of long logs ended on the Penobscot in 1933. By 1966 there was only one drive of long logs left in Maine, one of the last in the world, by the St. Regis Company on the East Machias River. From the thirties to the sixties Doc saw it all happen to his big world: the last drive, the last of the fire-belching Lombard steam haulers (you could still see one up at Churchill Depot at the head of Chamberlain Lake), the coming of the tractor, the mechanical loader, the huge diesel trucks with their tandem pulpwood trailers which had revolutionized the big business of lumbering—yes, and turned the old two-fisted, red-shirted woodsman into little more than a grease-monkey.

He saw the end or change of old landmarks, Grant Farm's big lumbermen's hotel become a bony skeleton, Chesuncook Village a ghost town, Harford's Point a continuous array of summer estates, the Lily Bay House, haven for lumbermen since the 1880s, a popular resort hotel. In 1952 he saw the last steam-powered locomotive in northern Maine, Engine 251, make its farewell trip from Derby to Greenville, saddened like all the other citizens, only to have happiness restored when the proud new diesel arrived on its first run thirty-three minutes late. With even more nostalgia he saw the new breed of sportsmen make their hit-and-run forays, roar through town in their high-powered cars, swoop down in their airplanes.

"Those were the good old days," he regretted the passing of the old ways. "Plenty of work, everybody happy. The summer people came with their families. The women stayed at the hotels, the men took guides and went down the Allagash. Now . . . ."

He saw the smashing fulfillment of James Russell Lowell's prophecy, delivered when the poet visited Moosehead on a canoe trip in 1853 and for the first time saw a woman in bloomers. "They will come into general use," Lowell predicted, "when women believe that sense is an equivalent of grace." A hundred years later, except in the black fly season, one could see a thousand or more females in—bloomers? Even Doc knew better than to apply the old-fashioned term to the brevities which abounded.

He saw the Coburn's proud steamboats demeaned or banished, the *Katahdin,* proudest of all, demoted to the status of tow boat for the Scott Paper Company; their places in the coves preempted by shining new Pipers and Cessnas. In fact, he saw the passing of an era.

Doc did not really like the planes. He preferred the old ways of travel. But if they could get him to a patient more quickly, he was all for them. He used them sometimes in getting to Chesuncook and to Jackman and to attend Daicey, who ran the camps at Sourdnahunk. And of course plane trips were required during the murder case in which he was involved.

It was in June, 1943. Again Doc was the only physician in the whole vast area, with Dr. Nickerson away serving in the United States Medical Corps in North Africa and getting himself decorated for bravery in Tunisia. During the three years of his absence Doc was out straight with work, performing an unusually large number of Caesarian sections, hysterectomies, and gall-bladder operations. It was no great job, he reflected wryly, being the only doctor in the five-thousand-square-mile area. It had been much worse during World War I when fewer patients came to the hospital or office. All one had to do was keep oneself well and be on duty twenty-four hours a day!

The call came from David Knowlton, Deputy Sheriff of Piscataquis County.

"That you, Doc? Golly, glad to have found you! There's been a shooting up at Porter's camp on Webster Lake. You know Wes Porter. Seems he's been shot. I've called State Trooper Mealey, and we need you as Medical Examiner. Both of you are to meet me right away."

Doc did know Wesley Porter, formerly a potato inspector for Aroostook County, a very fine guide, and he knew Webster Lake, in Baxter State Park, about twenty-five miles north of Mt. Katahdin. At least fifty miles by car and then another fifteen by foot! If poor Wes wasn't already dead, he might well be by the time they got there. But fortunately Knowlton had called the Civil Air Patrol, which provided two amphibian planes. An hour after the message was received they were on their way. It was not a pleasant ride, in pitch dark with wind rising and a storm in the offing. And, worse yet, the pilot, a lieutenant of the Civil Air Patrol, did not have night eyes! When they came in for a landing on Webster Lake, Doc could see the water perfectly. He kept telling the pilot their height above the water—"a hundred feet" . . . "fifty now" . . . "forty" . . . but the lieutenant paid no attention. He was obviously trying to let the plane down by watching the dri-ki along the shore, its bleached tangle a white vagueness in the night.

"You're only ten feet!" Doc yelled, then as he still paid no attention, "Lift her nose!"

The warning blast hit the pilot so suddenly that he obeyed automatically, but too late. The plane hit the water with a blow that sent it bouncing some seventy-five yards; then it struck again with a bang that set every bone shivering.

"Gracious!" The pilot winced. "That's the worst jolt I ever got in a plane!"

Doc said nothing. No further vindication of his judgment was necessary.

The three sportsmen met them, full of relief and explanations. Porter had prepared supper in his fishing camp, and they had all eaten to satiety. Aromas of coffee, bacon, fried potatoes, and fish still clung faintly to the small camp's interior. Hardly had they finished eating when a rustling noise outside roused their attention. "Sounded like a footstep," one of them had remarked, but Porter had disagreed. "More likely one of those cussed porcupines. Better go out and look."

They had gone out, the three Massachusetts anglers ahead, one carrying a .22 revolver, Porter a little behind. Three shots had come in rapid succession, and with a strangled cry Porter had fallen.

Doc did not wait for explanations. He found the victim alive but unconscious. After a swift but thorough examination he lifted a grave face.

"It's bad. I'm afraid he won't pull through. But we'd better fly him back to the hospital."

"Where was he hit, Doc?" asked Knowlton.

Doc tersely explained. He had been shot three times in the head. One of the shots had hit him on the lower lip, shattering his teeth and jawbone; the second had ricocheted off the skull behind the left ear; and the third had come within an inch of the second and apparently penetrated the brain.

The deputy whistled. "Some shooting! He aimed to kill, all right!"

Wrapping Porter in blankets, they carried him to one of the planes. There was a buffeting wind, and thunder was rolling ominously, but haste was imperative. Getting Porter to the hospital swiftly was his only chance. They got up off the lake and rode into the teeth of the storm. Doc hoped heartily that this new pilot had night vision. Whether he did or not, he put the plane down safely in West Cove.

As expected, Porter lived only a few hours. Doc wrote his report and sent it to Augusta: "This man was shot by an unknown assailant hidden in a pine grove by the house, and he was shot with an unusual pellet." Unusual was right! One of the holes had been made by something Doc had never run across in all his experience with shot, and he had seen a good many different sizes, from buck-shot down to Number 8's.

In Augusta an autopsy was made. It was indeed found that one of the pellets had penetrated the brain. Immediately the medical officer telephoned Doc and told him to come down. What in thunder for! wondered Doc silently. But the state sent a plane to fly him down and back, and he interrupted one of his wartime "forty-hour days" to make what he was sure was an unnecessary trip. It was. When he got through with this further examination, he made his report: "This man was shot by an unknown assailant hidden in a pine grove by the house, and he was shot with an unusual pellet." One interesting detail emerged, however. The unusual pellet had been cut from a lead pipe, which had been chopped into slips and rolled into shots. No wonder the ragged thing had made a different kind of hole!

Meanwhile search for the murderer continued. That

the shooting had been deliberate was evidenced by the three dead-accurate shots to the same mark from a spot roughly forty yards away. But why Porter? He was a respected, kind-hearted man with no known enemies. His sixteen-year-old son Clint was permitted to join the searching posse. In subsequent days signs were found of the marauder: camps broken into, windows smashed, ashes of old campfires. Bloodhounds were employed without success. The man was obviously a crack woodsman as well as a crack shot. He doubled back on his tracks, waded through lakes and rivers to elude pursuit. But on August 1 planes spotted him between Eagle and Churchill Lakes, sixty miles northwest of Webster. Then when Bert Duty, a fish and game warden, and a forestry fire watcher approached a cabin, they were welcomed by a fusillade of shots. Again the clever criminal escaped, this time through a rear window. But Bert Duty, warden for years and a woodsman who knew every inch of the country, was one of the worst enemies a man could have. That evening he was telephoning the posse from his cabin, telling them exactly where they could find the fugitive the next morning.

"You hide around that little clearing at nine o'clock," he said, "and I'll wager this fellow steps out of the woods and you can get him."

As Duty finished talking, he lit his pipe and stepped back, just as a bullet came through the window and stove the phone in pieces. The murderer had been watching him. That ended all telephone calls. But the posse had received the message. They were waiting the next morning in the specified spot. As predicted, the man stepped out of the woods. Instantly he swung up his gun, but one of the posse was quicker. His shot from a .35 automatic shattered the man's right thigh.

The murderer was identified as Alphonse Morency, who had fled into the wilderness from his home in Quebec

Province to escape the draft. His motive for killing Porter had been merely to frighten away the sportsmen so he could plunder their camp.

"What a hell of a thing to do!" ejaculated one of the state troopers.

Again Doc was flown to the scene. He put a tight bandage on the ugly wound, and they flew the injured man back to the hospital. While agreeing heartily with the appraisal of the trooper, Doc dutifully attempted to save the man's life. But there was more than a stern sense of duty in his approach to the task. There was deep respect for the innate potential of a human being, plus a compassion which seemed oddly at variance with his rigid Yankee rectitude. Perhaps its flowering had come with the mellowing of maturer years, yet it had sprung from a strong, sturdy plant of early growth. His sons could vouch for that.

"Despite his rigid personal code of conduct," Howard could remember, "and his impatient and critical reactions to other people's less than perfect actions, he still had an amazing tolerance of people's faults. I recall chronic alcoholics with unreasonable demands that he put up with for years and years and never turned away. Some of them would have tried the patience of a saint."

So now Doc set himself meticulously to the saving of a mean, trigger-happy murderer. Prospects were doubtful. So many vessels had been blow open in the thigh that you couldn't go in and tie them. He wouldn't have stood the anesthesia. The chunk of thigh displaced by the bullet could have weighed one and a half pounds! But by this time the hospital had stores of plasma, and Doc prepared to give him a dose. He was in the utility room standing at the sink dissolving it when the alarm sounded. He rushed to the patient but was too late. A nurse, thinking to facilitate action, had seized the shears and cut the ban-

dage open. With the pressure removed from the blood
vessel the man was dead in less than two minutes. There
had been only a remote chance of saving him, but Doc
would like to have tried. Happily, however, there was
use for the plasma. There was a patient in the ward who
needed it badly, with no money to pay for it. Doc continued to dissolve it, and the poor fellow got the benefit.
More deserving of it, too, by a long shot!

The story was written up, luridly and with some exag-
geration, in *Detective,* under the title of "The Sinister
Secret of the Draft Dodging Killer," along with such ex-
travaganzas as "The Crime of the Jealous-Mad Lothario"
and "Unholy Horror of the Screaming Woman." Doc had
no use for such a tom-fool yarn. He would not give it
house room. It was his sister-in-law Viola Redmond who
preserved it for posterity.

. 2 .

Doc's LITTLE WORLD changed also. As decades passed, from
the twenties to the fifties, the little frontier town "two
hundred miles from nowhere" became more and more
cosmopolitan. Thanks to the Shaws, who had hauled,
sawed, and sold lumber for three generations, it acquired
a sturdy and beautiful public library. Through the gen-
erosity of the Crafts family it boasted an imposing brick
Masonic Building. Doc interrupted his post-dawn wood
splitting and gardening to help grade and landscape its
grounds. And, by an accident of fortune quite remote
from lumbering or sports, the town spawned another
philanthropic millionaire.

Louis Oakes had come to Greenville as poor as Doc,
and as frugal. He became the chief fire warden and one
of the most respected men in town. Sadie was a close

friend of his wife. Doc brought his daughter, Edith, into the world and continued through the years as the family's physician. More thrifty than his brother Harry, Louis Oakes was continually helping the latter recoup his business failures. "This is the end," he declared firmly with the investment of a few thousand in a mining venture in Canada. It was the end of poverty for both of them. The company struck gold, and the frugal Louis became a multi-millionaire, faring better than his brother, Sir Harry, who was murdered in Nassau in 1943. He continued to live simply and without great ostentation. His town was as much the beneficiary of his fortune as he himself. His spacious new home, between Village and Junction, lent the whole area dignity and distinction, and the new high school which he donated, dedicated in 1935, just a little too late for Howard, raised the town's educational standards by 100 per cent.

But if some of his fellow townsmen revealed the growing affluence of the community in their manner of living, not so Doc. Except for necessary repairs through the years, most of which he made himself, insulation after about thirty years of drafty ventilation, a coat of asphalt shingles which obviated the necessity of painting, the house next to the Methodist Church remained almost in its pristine condition of the early 1900s, a sturdy monument to Yankee frugality. Save for a shining new maple chair donated by the Moosehead Company for services rendered, the offices remained in 1970 much as they had been in 1910: same low couch for examinations, same round-backed wooden chairs (still "cussed uncomfortable"), same medicine cabinet with much the same medicines, same roll-top desk, same small white sink in the corner (installed when running water was put into the house), same little table made out of a supply box and covered with Lilla's oilcloth. True, after half a century of coping with the old black kitchen stove, Sadie finally acquired a long-coveted electric range, and there were other kitchen improvements which facilitated her constant baking for church, Masonic lodge, hospital, D.A.R., woman's club, literary union, and other community suppers and food sales.

"I couldn't be too active at first," she regretted, "with the boys growing up and being always on duty at the office." But the roster of her community activities through the years reads like a prominent listing in "Who's Who." She was president, Secretary of Promotion, District Promotion Secretary of the Woman's Society of Christian Service, delegate to the Methodist Conference, president of the Missionary Society of the Union Church, president, secretary, and historian of the Woman's Club, president and secretary of the Onawa Literary Union, regent and chaplain of the D.A.R., all offices up to the worthy matron of the Eastern Star, plus installing Grand Chaplain, High Priestess of the White Shrine of Jerusalem, chairman, treasurer, secretary, and food project leader of the Extension Service, town and assistant county chairman of the woman's division and teacher of first-aid classes during the war. In fact, whenever competence and responsibility were requisites for a particular job or office, the judgment was often "Let Pritham do it."

But, as with Doc, first allegiance was always to his professional obligations. She was in the house when needed to answer telephone, admit patients, even dispense advice and medicines if occasion demanded. She was there when a reporter from a prominent national magazine arrived for a scheduled interview, expecting the subject of his projected article to be waiting in panting but humble eagerness for the publicity he was generously to bestow. It was Sadie who answered his ring.

"I've come to have a talk with a real *man!*" he announced with gusto.

"I'm sorry," replied Sadie, "but I'm afraid you'll have to have a talk with a real woman, because the doctor has just got a call and he's gone to the head of the lake to be gone for some time. In fact, I don't know when he'll be back."

The reporter gasped. This obscure little backwoods doctor breaking a date which would reap him national publicity just because of some ailing country bumpkin? But— he considered—there might be news value in just such eccentricity. Meekly he scheduled another interview, depending of course on the doctor's convenience.

But, like Sadie, Doc found time for other than professional service to the community. Favorite of all his avocations to both himself and the townspeople was that of musician. His alto horn was almost as familiar an accessory to his person as his back pack or medicine bag. He played in every town band which was organized, participated in summer concerts for tourists, marched with it in every Memorial Day and Fourth of July parade, until each one petered out for lack of interest. Then at about age sixty-five he became a member of the high-school band!

He loved it. Except for white hair and slight stoop, his lean short agile body blended into the group like one of themselves. Most of the boys outstripped him in height and weight, but he could outrun, outblow, outmarch any one of them—and did. For twenty years he attended rehearsals, accompanied the band to basketball games, marched in all their parades. Three times he marched with them down Bangor's main street, Skowhegan's four times, Madison's three, Millinocket's at least once. The young people accepted him as one of themselves, and he took vast pleasure in giving them hints about playing, buying their lunches when he knew they could not afford to, taking pride in their superior skill.

"Ha!" One night as they entered the new Bangor auditorium he heard the announcer let out a whoop. "We're going to have some music tonight, folks! Here's Greenville coming in!"

At Waterville in 1965, when Greenville won the basketball trophy for eastern Maine, Doc helped lift the shingles off the roof. It was an immense satisfaction that his alto horn, giving the after-beat, supplied the final tone color without which no band was quite complete. Few of the forty or fifty high school bands playing in the tournaments could boast an alto horn. One night in Bangor he was approached by an official on the floor, an expert musician, who, noting his white hair, assumed him to be the band leader.

"You know your band sounds the way a band ought to sound," he enthused. "It's the only one here that sounds correct." Because, Doc prided himself, it had the after-beat. He was as triumphant as his band-mates when Greenville scored a victory.

Far more than the adulation of grateful patients Doc treasured the accolades of his teen-age associates. A trophy for good attendance was carefully preserved. And when they presented him with an award, signed by every member of the band, it was accorded a place of honor in his office as distinctive as his medical school diploma and framed accreditations.

He was eighty-five when he stopped playing with the high-school band, chiefly because he did not have time to attend rehearsals. Then, too, his lip was beginning to fail him. But horn, as well as player, was destined for honorable retirement. Plans were soon made for its preservation in a glass case among the high school memorabilia, with appropriate plaque commemorating both instrument and player.

Another Greenville landmark which remained as unchanged as the Pritham house was the little Methodist Church just across the side street. Except for an occasional coat of paint its modest but solid structure had altered little since 1900, when Walter Gerrish and the dozen other members of the flock had sweated it into being. Ministers came and went, the younger on their way up to larger and more remunerative parishes, the older on their way down to hard-earned retirement. Doc seldom attended religious services except on Boy Scout Sundays. But he was a faithful trustee and appeared at official board meetings in time to read his treasurer's report, then slipped out. Occasionally his plans went awry, as when he attended church one evening to see an advertised program of pictures, and the young minister, Ralph Barron, preceded the entertainment with a worship service.

"Spinach first, dessert afterward," he commented with an ill-concealed glance of glee at Doc, who countered with a good-natured chuckle.

But Doc rendered the church far more sacrificial service than many of its more pious devotees. He mowed its lawns, shoveled its paths, sawed wood for its furnace, baked bushels of beans for its suppers, and for more than half a century saw that its bills were paid.

"We closed the year in the red both for the repair fund and the budget, too," he wrote Chauncey Wentworth, a former minister who was Conference treasurer, in 1957. "But I paid all the bills, so all they owe is me, and we will hope that as time runs along they will catch up. They have before, and I tell them not to worry too much about it."

He saw that the ministers were promptly paid, unusual boon for a small-town cleric, especially in the Depression years. But the service was more to his liking in some cases than in others, with young Ralph Barron, for instance. Every Monday morning at eight o'clock he would climb the seventeen cement steps to the parsonage front door, and when Lucille Barron opened it, he would say, "Hmmm! It's always a pleasure to come up here and pay a preacher who isn't lazy."

And he ministered tenderly and scrupulously to the physical needs of its parsonage families. One Sunday morning just before church, George Bullens, one of the "on-the-way-ups," who suffered from an allergy, saw him charge into the church, seize a bouquet of roses from under the pulpit, and bear it away with indignant mutterings. "Here I'm trying to cure this man of hay fever, and some fool comes along and sticks a bunch of roses under his nose!"

And one morning Jane Tolman, newly arrived young wife of another cleric, was roused from sleep in the pre-dawn by a strange sound and frightened half out of her wits by the sight of a dim fur-clad shape creeping stealthily up the back steps and onto the porch. Bear? Burglar? No. Only Doc choosing his own time and method to deliver a welcome donation of fresh vegetables.

But if his small material world remained nearly static, his intimate human world changed profoundly. Did the years spawn more of comedy or of tragedy? It was hard to tell.

The grandchildren were all comedy: Freddie, Carroll's boy, whom Doc delivered in January, 1938; Howard, Jr., born in 1940 while his father was an intern in Waltham, Massachusetts; his sister Merrill, usually called Merrie; Howard's four other children, Charles, Andy, Sarah, Robin. But their own children .... Did tragedy and comedy run so all-of-a-piece in other families, so that one could hardly tell where one left off and the other began? Yes. A country doctor knew well enough that they did. During the forties and fifties, it seemed, Doc and Sadie plumbed every emotion of pain and pleasure to the dregs.

Pride in the success of both sons, with Carroll in a good electrical job at Aroostook, Howard finished with his medical training at Tufts and practicing in Brunswick. Anxiety, with Howard serving in Europe in the Army Medical Corps, at the front in the Battle of the Bulge, wounded and awarded the Purple Heart. Satisfaction, when he came back home to practice with Doc in Greenville. Shock, shame, sadness, self-reproach, their rigid code of conduct violated, when both boys' marriages were shattered by divorce. (Where had they failed? What had they done wrong?) Pity, forgiveness, resignation. And then again distress and anxiety.

It was 1949. Howard, married in 1947 to Lenore, a native of Chesuncook Village, was still practicing in Greenville. He had learned to fly a plane and often hired one from the two local services for attending distant cases. Late one afternoon Dick Folsom, who operated one of the services, called from Chesuncook. A messenger had come in from Oscar Gagnon's lumber camp requesting medical aid for an injured man. There would not be time for Dick to fly from the Village to Greenville, pick Howard up, and get back before dark.

"Get a plane from Ray O'Donnell's," he suggested, "and fly in. You can pick up the messenger at Nick Mulligan's in Chesuncook. He can show you the way to camp."

Howard took his bag and secured the plane. It was a dark overcast day, spotted with snow flurries. Just as he reached Spencer Pond he ran into a storm so heavy that he could not see the ground for visual flight. Fearing to run into Little Spencer Mountain, he turned left and came back over Moosehead Lake. Here the snow was not so thick and the shore made enough contrast so he could follow it to Northeast Carry, then move down the West Branch to Chesuncook Lake and around the point to the

Village. Landing in front of Nick Mulligan's cabin, he picked up the messenger and started the four-mile flight to camp.

It was still snowing and nearly dark when he prepared to land at the mouth of the road on the shore of Umbazooksus Meadows. Just in time he saw the "boil" in the ice, a smooth spot where freezing had occurred later than in surrounding areas. Impossible to tell where the high banks began and the level ice lay! To scout the landing area, he made a pass at low altitude, intending to land on the way back or circle and land in the same direction, but in making the pass and looking back to judge the landing area, he allowed the plane to get in a nose-high attitude and to lose flying speed. It went into a terrific stall and spin. They crashed. Both of Howard's ankles were broken. His passenger's feet were also injured, but he was still able to walk. He managed to get ashore and build a fire, but Howard had to remain in the plane. With the pain and cold, for it was below freezing, the night was torture. Hours later Oscar Gagnon and Ben Spear, thinking they heard a plane, came looking for them. Both camp tractors were broken down, so the only transportation was a large hand-drawn "moose sled." One of the men returned to camp to get it, and Howard was hauled out first to Nick Mulligan's cabin. He told one of the men how to dissolve a morphine tablet and at last got some surcease from the pain.

Doc heard the news when Dick Folsom, preparing to fly him out the next morning, came to the hospital for some splints. When Howard arrived, Doc was shocked at his son's condition. The right foot was completely severed at the ankle, hanging only by a little stub. There were four different kinds of wood and all kinds of dirt in the wound! It was decided to drive him immediately to Bangor. Doc was never satisfied with the result. Howard was in agony and fever for three months; then the leg had to be amputated clear to the knee.

"If he'd stayed here," Doc regretted, "I would have amputated it within an hour, a nice sound tissue that would have healed kindly. But, no, they tried to keep the blamed thing on. Horrible mistake!"

Howard returned home, to spend long months in a wheelchair. Even when able to get around, he found it impossible to maintain his balance because of a misplaced astragalar bone and had to be assisted at every step. Still he managed to act as anesthetist at the hospital. Though the condition was corrected by an orthopedic specialist and with the help of a prosthesis he was finally able to walk without difficulty, the accident discouraged him from pursuing the career of a physically active country doctor. In December, 1949, he entered the employment of the Panama Canal as a medical officer in the Canal Zone.

Disappointment for Doc. It had been a dream to have his son follow in his footsteps. Grief was soon to follow. On Labor Day, 1951, Carroll came up from Springfield, Massachusetts, where he was employed, to spend the holiday with his parents and his son Freddie. Long afflicted with ulcers, he started bleeding. But in spite of Doc's protests, he refused to stay. He must take Freddie back, to get him in school. He'll never get there, worried Doc. The two left on Monday. It was Saturday when Doc received a call from a hospital in Newton. Carroll had collapsed on his way home and been taken there for treatment. "And they waited four days to let us know!"

Doc and Sadie started at once for Newton. An operation was performed, but too late. Carroll died on Tuesday.

Not only grief: frustration and agonizing regret. "If we'd only known! If they'd only operated earlier, instead of waiting 'til they knew he was a goner! If they'd opened him up and given him drainage at once, he might have recovered!"

Grief, yes. A raging torrent of emotion which might easily engulf a man! But there were patients waiting. The day after the funeral he was back at work.

"You don't give way to grief, do you?" commented Mrs. Anderson, the Greenville librarian, when he came to visit her mother.

"No need of it," replied Doc, and immediately launched into a leisurely and pithy duck-hunting story, all the time keenly eyeing the patient's familiar features for indications of her state of health. Along with the sparkle of amusement in her eyes as she gazed with appreciative understanding at the little doctor there might also have been detected a trust and affection almost akin to worship.

· 3 ·

"YOUR GRANDFATHER is a big man, a very important man. Remember, you must be very obedient and respectful."

"Yes, Mother." Six-year-old Howie nodded soberly. He had vague memories of his grandfather from a visit long ago, when he was three or four, memories of a somewhat frightening giant about ten feet tall who had scolded him soundly for trying to put some rubbish in a big black kitchen stove. He might burn himself, the giant warned. But he had only done what he had seen lots of other people doing! Why pick on him?

It was 1946. Howie and his sister Merrie were going to Greenville to spend the summer with their grandparents. They rode on the train to Newport, where Grandfather met them. Giant! Ten feet tall! Howie could not believe his eyes. Why, this was just a little man, not much taller than some of the boys at school. And how could he be important, wearing clothes like that, just a short sleeved colored shirt and wool trousers? Howie felt vaguely disappointed as well as relieved.

But not for long! Grandpa, he soon discovered, was the best playmate a boy could have. From the time he got up in the morning, around seven or eight, Howie would follow him around like a puppy. Already Grandpa would have been up for three or four hours, sawing wood, working on his boats or in the garden, or maybe mowing the church lawn with a scythe. Very likely he had been up during the night, too, as he always was if the telephone rang. Howie would hear it sometimes and wish he weren't so sleepy, so he could get up and go with him, but instead he would burrow more deeply into sleep and dream he was on one of the exciting trips Grandpa had told him about, before the days of fast cars and trucks and tractors and airplanes. Howie did go with him on rounds during the day. There was always a whole string of calls. Grandpa would pull up to a house, reach behind the seat and bring out his black bag, which looked almost as big as he did, then tramp into the house without knocking. Then Howie would sit in the car until he came back out, and away they would go.

"Bad case of sciatica," he might say, launching into a confidential recital of symptoms and remedies while the boy listened, wide-eyed and intent, feeling very wise and important.

Revelations might be even more graphic, to say nothing of more luridly fascinating, when Grandpa returned from the hospital after, say, performing an appendectomy. His descriptions were forthright and pithy. "Want to know just how I did it? Well, that belly was stiff as a board, and I just took the scalpel—like this—and stabbed it right there in the right place." Other earthy details might follow, ending with a chuckle. "But I decided after awhile that I'd better stop while his ears were still pink."

One didn't have to look up far to talk with Grandpa. He even seemed to stoop down a little to be nearer one's level. Perhaps it was this lack of disparity in size which gave them such an affinity from the first. More likely it was an innate concord of interest stronger even than ties of blood. Avidly Howie watched Grandpa clean up his decoys, modify them to make them sit just right, paint them, perhaps add a piece of cedar underneath to make one float higher, spend many a leisure moment in summer getting ready for the fall hunting; listened with thrilled attention to stories of the early Freeport days. And something in his small body leaped and vibrated to the lure of salt mists, wild honkings, whirring wings.

That summer was only the beginning. The boy spent most of his vacations between ages six and twelve in Greenville. And again his image of Grandpa changed. Not a giant, at least physically, but certainly a figure to inspire respect and a bit of awe! He had such wonderful confidence, such strong assurance in his opinions, and he seemed to know everything about everything. Hardly a question which he could not answer! And yet such a simple man! Some people thought him queer because of his clothes and eating habits, but he chose clothes because they were comfortable and easy to work in. He ate the food he did because he liked it and it kept him healthy— and he sure ate plenty of it! And used up every calorie. He was a hard man to give a present to. He had everything he needed. The family tried hard for years, at birthdays and Christmas. Consequently he had a bushel or two of handkerchiefs and ties and socks that he would never use. He would never have occasion to.

"All these fool bottles of after-shave lotion!" he once

commented. "I've had this one for twenty years and am still using it."

Some people thought him gruff, too, because he was short and terse of speech. But if they did, they sure didn't know him! They should have seen him the time he and Howie were driving back from fishing. Maybe seven miles out of town they came on this man walking along the road dressed in rags, somebody Grandpa knew.

"I s'pose we ought to give him a ride in," he said, "but he prob'ly hasn't taken a bath in a month. I hate to pick him up, but I hate not to." They picked him up. No bath in a month? More like six months!

And some people thought him stubborn. If getting strong ideas and sticking to them was stubborn, then he was. Like the matter of smoking. The sign in his office, NO SMOKING, was at least a foot high. On another trip they picked up a hitchhiker, and the man had a cigarette in his mouth. "You won't need that weed in here," said Grandpa. Then, as the fellow looked bewildered: "May be good for keeping the mosquitoes away, but we don't have any in here." The offending brand was extinguished.

After his parents' divorce Howie saw little of his father, and Grandpa became a sort of father figure in his life. At eight the boy was aping his every gesture. At ten he was talking with a Maine twang and spinning duck yarns. And at twelve he had decided to become a doctor. He never changed his mind.

At twelve also he started hunting. Grandpa always bought his license. The lessons the boy learned were not all in the techniques of gunning. Grandpa, he soon discovered, was scrupulously law-abiding. Never did he subscribe to the common practice of shooting a deer and having friends or members of the family tag it. Never did he permit anyone else to tag a deer he shot. "If a man can't shoot a deer himself, he don't deserve one," was his inflexible reply to a woodsman he treated who was unable to pay and offered him a nice buck he had strung up outside the camp. Howie went hunting with him every fall from age twelve to about twenty and got his first deer when he was seventeen.

When Howard Junior was about seventeen and Grandpa was in his late seventies, they often hunted ducks together. Howie would come up from Massachusetts Friday night after school, and Doc would meet his train at Freeport. He would have a mattress in the back of his Willys jeep, the decoys and shotguns stacked in the rear end, and the gunning float on top. They would drive to Merrymeeting Bay or Muddy River and sleep in the back of the station wagon. Rising before dawn, they would eat the lunch Grandma had packed in some old lard pails, maybe sausage, ham, sweet potatoes, mince pie. They would shoot ducks all day Saturday, then on Sunday morning Grandpa would take him back, and he would grab the train.

Howie was lean and strong, well on his way to six feet and 175 pounds, but he was no match for Doc when it came to paddling. Arms would be aching, throat burning, heart pounding like a sledgehammer, but he would grit his teeth and keep on paddling, bound not to appear a weakling. Meanwhile Grandpa would just paddle and paddle, easy as a duck swimming, with no sign of weariness.

They did little talking. The communication between them was deeper than words. Each seemed to have an uncanny sense of what the other thought and wanted to do, and they were usually in agreement. Physically they were as disparate as a string bean and an artichoke, the boy long, lean, rangy; the man short, compact, still weighing less than 130, yet almost as tough and vigorous at eighty as he had been at twenty. But in spite of their physical disparity and the span of sixty years they were astonishingly alike in temperament and taste. Both were niggardly of speech and resented people who were overly outspoken, especially if they ventured opinions not backed up by facts. Both were stubborn. Both could crouch happily in a cold pre-dawn mist or tramp through miles of swamps and thickets and knee-deep snow for the thrill of a whir of wings or the flash of a white tail. And both took the cue for their life's marching step from the same drum and trumpet.

It was not because of any urging or encouragement from Grandpa that Howie decided to study medicine. As far as the boy could remember, the matter was never discussed between them. Nor was he inspired to emulation by any dramatic act of healing which he saw Doc perform. In fact, the practice of medicine was only one of Grandpa's many functions. And yet he was definitely responsible for the shaping of his grandson's career. Howie never really considered why. He knew only that he loved and respected his grandfather so much that he wanted to be like him in every way possible.

CHAPTER TEN

Curtain Calls

. 1 .

FIFTY YEARS! The town of Greenville and the five thousand square miles of surrounding country joyfully prepared to pay honor to the beloved little doctor who had served them at all hours, in all seasons and weathers, for half a century.

That year, 1955, was a landmark for Doc in more ways than one. He observed the fiftieth anniversary of his graduation from medical school, was honored by the Maine Medical Association for fifty years of membership and service, and celebrated his seventy-fifth birthday.

"Picked up my fifty-year pin at Rockland," he wrote Chauncey Wentworth on July 11. "Got a handsome cake, a Pendleton shirt at the close of the bawling held on my birthday at the Community House, and got a nylon shirt

296

and a leather belt here at home. The biggest haul I ever made on my birthday. It comes so near the 4th that that day has served very well, and it was pitch hay for many years on both."

But the Dr. Pritham Recognition Day, held on August 13, was the high point of the year, indeed of all fifty years. The town spent weeks in preparation. Numerous committees were appointed: Finance, Program, Invitations, Parade, Grounds, Refreshments, Entertainment. The Maine Medical Association was invited en masse, its president, Dr. Martyn Vickers, to be the principal speaker. A big parade was planned, its marching units to include the American Legion and Auxiliary, the Boy Scouts, a contest array of decorated bicycles and baby carriages, cars with the insignia of all fraternal, civic, and service organizations and, of course, the Band. A Pritham Fund was instituted, its goal $25,000, its purpose the installation of a new heating plant in the hospital. A car was designated to call for the guest of honor and his family and transport them to the athletic field where the program was to be held.

"Not me," refused Doc emphatically. "Send a car for the family if you want to, but I'll be with the band."

Sure enough, when the parade started up the road from the Junction, there he was, tooting his horn, marching on the outside at a fast clip, taking enormous strides to keep in line as they turned the corners. He wore his usual band suit, green trousers, short-sleeved white shirt, and tan visor cap. Scarcely regulation dress for the guest of honor in a formal recognition service, but typically Pritham. Typical also were other features of the parade—the bicycles and baby carriages occupied by segments of the 1500 offspring he had brought into the world, the Great Northern truck in the rear motorcade bearing Doc's first famous snowmobile.

"For the benefit of absentees," reported the *Moosehead Gazette*, "it looked like a mechanized sled, being a Ford body of respectable years mounted on a forward pair of runners and an after pair of tracks. This vehicle, incidentally, was designed by the doctor."

While the band was playing it started to sprinkle, and by the time the judging of the doll carriage and bicycle entries was finished, it was pouring. Spirits as undaunted by the elements as Doc's during a half-century of similar vicissitudes, the crowd adjourned to the school auditorium, where Mr. Hamlin, minister of the Methodist Church and instigator of the affair, flew around getting matters reorganized. When the curtain went up, there on the stage were the distinguished speakers, Sadie, festive and gracious in a dotted pale blue dress with sparkling buttons, Howard, his wife Lenore, and their four children. Occasionally, during the ensuing program, Doc joined them, commuting between his place in the band and the seat of honor.

The speeches, of course, were flattering, extravagant, embarrassing. Fortunately Doc could indulge his frequent impulse to squirm by a sally into the band section after each one. At every such excursion there was a round of applause. Mr. Hamlin stressed his multiplicity of activities. "We may find him splitting wood, mowing his lawn, shoveling snow from in front of the fire station, playing in the band, as well as attending the sick, making his calls, or working in the hospital."

"Yes, or changing my tire ... or taking my clothes off the line so I could get to the hospital quicker ... or sitting up with my croupy baby all night ... or shoveling my walks when I broke my leg. ..." Scarcely a soul in the audience who did not supplement the list silently from personal experience.

Bernice Young, the town's historian, gave an animated

and artistic résumé of Doc's early life. Dr. Nickerson paid brief but sincere tribute to "my competitor" (laughs) "who in all the years has never been too busy or too tired to come and help when I asked him to." Dr. Vickers, who had been born in the county and had heard of Doc since he was a little boy, made the address of the day.

But it was Howard's short speech which pleased Doc most. The boy had never been one to palaver. His dignity, poise, simple eloquence were surprising. A wonderful thing this, he said, for a doctor to have happen to him while he was still alive. Though most doctors made a good living, it wasn't for monetary values that they chose such a career. All the money in the world couldn't compensate for the life and death decisions they had to make, any one of which might mean professional failure. It was the intangibles, the approval and good will of their patients, that were most valued. And this great gathering today was tangible proof of the intangibles, appreciation and approval.

Doc's turn came finally. He mounted the platform from the band section for the last time. He was presented with a check for a thousand dollars, first installment on the hospital fund, pledges for which had already reached several times that amount. He wouldn't make a speech. Too much had already been said. He would just say thank you and sit down. He turned to the audience, opened his mouth.

"My friends, I can't tell you—"

Whatever he had intended to say was drowned in a tremendous clapping. It was such a noise as had seldom been heard in that place, even in the last seconds of a basketball game, with Greenville suddenly breaking a tie score. It kept on and on, for at least three minutes. Doc stood looking down into the faces, hundreds of them. He knew almost every one, and not only the faces, the bodies.

At least half of them he had held by the heels and slapped, eliciting the first protesting squalls. He knew just which ones had incisions and where, which stomachs were squeamish, which livers sluggish, which hearts murmured or palpitated, which smiles hid what aches or pains or fears or terrible knowledge of malignancy. A minister must feel something like this, custodian of people's souls instead of their bodies. No—not the hit-and-run ministers he had known! How could you get to know a person's soul in two, three, five years? Judas priest, he knew these people inside and out, souls as well as bodies! Not like one of these danged specialists, not their hearts, or their eyes, or their bones, or their lower innards. He knew *them*. And he had given fifty years of his life to do it. Not say anything? Just mumble a thank you? It would be like keeping mum at a family reunion!

When the applause died down, he began. He spoke simply, pungently, with rugged candor, as he had lived. He had come to this north country because in those days it had been a frontier, and he had wanted wildness, adventure, freedom—yes, and a place where he was needed. He spoke of the beauty of the lake in the warmth of summer, the glory of autumn, its terrors in the winter's cold or in a storm "which had Kineo written all over it." As he rambled on, his rapt audience heard ice cracking, ducks squawking, winds whistling, smelled pines and lumber camps and new-mown grass and sweat, saw ten thousand suns rise over Elephant and set over Squaw, felt the ache of straining muscles, freezing nose and toes and fingers, and a thousand miles of tramping. A face would remind him of some incident, and he would relive it, chuckling. Like the time he and Dr. Nick had an old Ford. They got way up on the Lily Bay road with it and ran out of gas. "Gorry, we had a good time, had to push the thing to the height of land! I pushed, and Nick drove." There! He had talked too long. But fifty years were a long time, and thousands of miles.

"Maybe some of you folks may wonder," he said at last, "why I should play in the band at my own party. Well, it's this way. Haven't you always noticed that professional folks, doctors, lawyers, preachers, and such, always like to toot their own horn?"

With this peroration he descended to the band once more amid a thunder of applause for his final toot.

Certainly a day of triumph, that August 13, 1955. But somehow he had felt more of exultation on a June day a few weeks before when he had given shots of the new Salk polio vaccine to sixty-two first- and second-graders from Greenville and Shirley.

After the fifty-year Recognition Day their fiftieth wedding anniversary the following year was almost an anticlimax, but an open house was held for them at the Methodist Church, with many friends attending.

"They gave Sadie and I a big hurrah," Doc wrote Chauncey Wentworth along with his Conference payments, "at our fiftieth, the Woman's Society of Christian Service sponsoring it. Around 200 registered in the guest book. Several of Sadie's relatives came from Freeport."

The relatives were nieces, Barbara Taylor and Helen Ring. Viola and Hallie were also there, acting as hostesses. There were many gifts, an ivy leaf dinner set, a gold cutwork tablecloth and napkins, a purse of money.

> *"We've come from up hill, We've come from down glade,"*

began Bernice Young's anniversary poem,

> *"to pay our respects to Fred and Sade."*

Howard had wanted them to come to Panama that year
to celebrate their anniversary and Freddie's graduation
from high school, but Doc would not hear of it. He was
too busy with patients. Besides, Panama was too hot.
"Then you come alone, Mother," Howard wrote Sadie.
She was game, being used to traveling alone. It wouldn't
be the first long trip she had taken. In the forties she had
gone to San Francisco as a delegate to an Eastern Star
convention, one of four from Maine, crossing the country
by train and returning through Canada by the Canadian
Pacific, which had arranged the trip. Though Doc had
not budged from his usual locale, his genie-like influence
had followed, even preceded her on the journey, for news
that the wife of its long-time patron was a passenger on
the CP was magically relayed the length of its rails. How
they recognized her in Vancouver neither of them could
fathom, but from the time she entered Canada she was
treated like royalty. There was a train hand always on
hand to carry her satchel. At Toronto she was given a
lower berth with the finest accommodations. Her companions from the more pretentious Portland area, who
had sent in their applications earlier, were nonplussed.

"I'd like to know how you got better reservations than
we did!"

But Doc accompanied her to Panama neither in body
nor in spirit. In fact, he had a baby with a strangulated
hernia and could not even drive her to Bangor. It was
Perley and Viola who took her to the plane. The Nicker-
sons were away for an indefinite period due to sickness,
and Doc was again the only doctor in the area.

"Seems like old times being all alone," he wrote a
friend. "Being used to it one don't worry."

Undaunted, Sadie got up out of a sick bed to go. The
name of Pritham possessed no magic on the airlines. In
New York she was told she must go back home to get her

vaccination certificate. She refused. "Look at it!" she insisted, pulling up her sleeve. Finally convinced that the evidence was recent and conclusive, they let her go. Over Florida the plane was caught in a storm. Rain poured in torrents. She was three hours late getting into Panama, but Howard was there waiting. Doc was right. Panama was hot in April, but she loved every minute of her stay. Howard, who was at that time school physician, took her fishing after hours. She caught a ten-pound jack in the Chagres River, hooked a big tarpon but snagged her line and lost it, to the envy and sorrow of Howard, who had never hooked one. Sometimes they fished until midnight. She went to Balboa and Old Panama, ate bushels of fruit, trembled for the safety of the swarming children as one of the hospital nurses drove her through the narrow streets at an alarming speed.

She wanted to come back by boat. She had always yearned for a long cruise. But no proper ship was scheduled. "Go up with me," suggested the clerk in the shipping office. "I'm taking my family on a Japanese freighter." Howard and Lenore were horrified. She should return to the States later with them, as planned, by air. But she persisted and had a most enjoyable week's trip on the freighter, which was bringing a load of coffee and oil from Cuba and taking back coal to Japan. In New York there was difficulty in getting cleared, for the captain spoke little English, but he finally got a chance to land. She arrived in Bangor by train at five-thirty in the morning, with no train through to Greenville until six in the evening. But she hadn't come this far to content herself with a twelve-hour wait. She took a train part way and begged a ride to Greenville by the mail truck. At the village she met the connecting truck from the Junction, with the postmaster driving.

"Warren, have you got room for me?" she asked.

He grinned. "Well, Sadie! What in thunder are you doing here, comin' by parcel post? Sure. Jump in."

As usual from a trip, she arrived home unannounced. And as usual, there was little sentimental fanfare of greeting. She and Doc looked at each other, discovered that all was well with each of them, and nodded with quiet satisfaction.

"Well, Sadie! I see you're safe home again."

. 2 .

CAME THE SKIERS. It was Louis Oakes, perennial benefactor, who engineered this, the town's final leap toward the epitome of progress. A group of promoters came to see Oakes on a March day in the late fifties, among them Sal Hanna, a professional designer of ski areas.

"What's a ski area?" demanded Oakes.

Not content with a verbal explanation, he determined to find out for himself. "Pack a lunch," he told Erma Budden, his housekeeper-secretary. "We're going to drive to Sugar Loaf and look into this business." Then in his late eighties, Oakes was still keen and vigorous and as interested in new projects as when, twenty years or more before, he had built two high schools, one for his native township of Dover-Foxcroft, one for Greenville.

They started at five-thirty the next morning and drove the hundred miles or so to Sugar Loaf Mountain in Kingfield, noted for its ski development. Though the skiing was not at its best that day, Oakes was thrilled with the sight of a small seven-year-old girl barging confidently down the slope. From that moment he was sold on the proposition. All the way home and for days afterward he talked constantly about expansion of the Squaw Mountain area. "Can't you see it? Such a wonderful thing for children!"

Oakes owned half of Squaw Mountain, and there was already a Squaw Mountain Association. Plans were set in motion for the project immediately, and the following winter the Haley Brothers built a mile-long road to the site of the future ski lodge. During the sixties the area exploded into a vast complex for winter sports. Two T-bar lifts gave convenient access to the skiing slopes. Instead of the old three-and-a-half-mile trail to the top which had taken Sadie more than two hours of strenuous climbing, she could now, summer or winter, sit comfortably in a gently swaying chair and in a few minutes be hoisted within a short, if rigorous, climb to the summit (a method of transit which, in spite of its disconcerting depths, seemed tame by comparison). The old roads where the belching Lombards had lumbered and horses had sunk belly-deep in mud and snow were now sleekly plowed year-round thoroughfares. A string of exotic little Swiss chalets sprang up along the seven-mile stretch between Squaw and the Junction. Sanders' emporium added a new and profitable ski line to their constantly burgeoning merchandise. In the old Push and Pull, now the Moosehead Lake Hotel, its sawdust-floored bar and "death room" long since converted into a sophisticated cocktail lounge, red shirts and unshorn heads still prevailed, but on long-haired and bearded adolescents, not rowdy, lusty lumbermen. (Sadie wasn't sure she relished the change.) The motel business boomed during winter skiing as well as spring fishing, autumn foliage, fall hunting, and summer touring. And at the turn of the decade, spawned by a new Moosehead Resort Corporation which included the Scott Paper Company, came a multi-million-dollar complex transforming what one sports writer called "this last frontier" into an "eye-popping showplace" of the Northeast: a million-dollar lodge complete with three penthouse suites, sauna, indoor swimming pool, twenty big units with picture windows, wall-to-wall carpeting, and other luxury appointments, plus a nonfail snow-making mill to combat the vagaries of nature. The little town "two hundred miles from nowhere," with no road out in winter, had become one of the lushest and most popular pleasure resorts of the country.

Though the latest breed of tourists whizzed and whined past their house at all hours of the day and night, Doc and Sadie were neither affected nor overly impressed by the new developments. They had seen too many changes in the last sixty-five years. A long-haired, bearded, red-shirted ski-jumper was tame copy of the roistering lumberer, and even the most souped-up jalopy could not hold a candle to the roaring old Lombards. Sadie was far more concerned over the loss of the huge spruce on that same road to Squaw. Sixty-seven feet tall, with a branch spread of thirty-four feet and a diameter of two and a half, its nearly three-ton bulk had been hauled off to New York in 1962 for a Christmas tree in Rockefeller Center. Even a few days' delight for millions of appreciative eyes could not compensate for the destruction of fifty years' magnificent achievement. It was like taking the Great Stone Face to a sculpture show! All the rest of her life she would mourn that "lonesome place against the sky."

Somehow Doc could not observe these portents of prosperity with more than mild and impersonal interest. He had seen too many more momentous changes in his ninety years. Even the town's other major improvement of the decade, that steel-glass-brick miracle at the top of the hill, failed to involve his deeper emotions, as had its humble predecessor back in 1918. Sure, Greenville needed a new hospital, was in danger of having to close the old one for failure to meet with modern standards and to attract the new breed of better-trained doctors. Looking around them at the increasing number of small Maine towns bereft of all medical services, concerned citizens contemplated the future with dismay.

"It's either raise money for a new hospital," they began to voice fears in the mid-sixties, "or find ourselves with no hospital and no doctors!"

They were no novices at money raising. An unflagging hospital auxiliary had labored through the years, via fund drives, fairs, teas, food sales, and numerous other media, to add constant improvements to the old building: new floor tile, stainless steel bassinets, motorized and manual patient beds, microhematoret machines to speed analyses of blood processing, laboratory equipment! But—a whole new building! Heroically the town girded itself in 1966 for the raising of $100,000.

Doc was of course involved in the unfolding drama, but more as audience than actor. He studied and approved the plans. Reluctantly he let Nellie Morrell, the superintendent, persuade him to turn the sod which initiated the building project in the big vacant lot east of the old hospital. Sadie poured at innumerable teas. With curious but objective interest Doc watched the new structure rise, participated in its dedication ceremonies, then occasionally entered its smooth-swinging plate-glass portals to visit patients or act as a consulting physician. It was a beautifully efficient building in spite of its limited space for only 26 in-patients, and its equipment and staff were of the highest quality: up-to-date X-ray machines with an expert technician, a registered physical therapist, data phone connection with a heart specialist at the Eastern Maine Medical Center in Bangor. And the Greenville airport with its two 4,000-foot runways and the multiple flying services were always available to fly emergency cases to Bangor or Waterville.

Doc approved and participated, but always with a certain wry reluctance. He had felt more at home in the makeshift old attic of the Y.M.C.A. than in this gleaming sterile one-floor complex with all its gadgets. Progress by all means, and this was it! Only a fool would go lumbering with a bucksaw in these days of the colossus that could snip off a two-foot pine trunk like a pair of scissors cutting string. He was tickled as the rest of the town when the hospital's first specialist arrived, an orthopedic surgeon of statewide reputation. Heaven knew one was needed with all these skiers busting arms and legs and necks! Sometimes there were as many as five casualties in a single day. Oh, Doc heartily approved of the new hospital! But it did not belong to his world.

· 3 ·

SIXTY YEARS! He was eighty-five the year he picked up his sixty-year pin at the Maine Medical Association meeting in 1965, and medicine was still something to be practiced. Office hours continued to be all day, and he went whenever and wherever he was called, whoever—or even whatever—the patient.

It was perhaps in 1967 that one of the valuable riding horses at Squaw Mountain Inn cut its foot. No veterinarian was available. The groom sent for Doc.

"I sure hated to call you, Doc," he greeted in embarrassed apology, "but somebody said you knew a lot about horses."

Doc unloaded his bag. "Oh, that's all right. I don't mind helping a horse."

He made two trips before the case was successfully closed.

"What do I owe you, Doc?"

"Nothin'."

"But surely—all that way—you can't—"

"I said—nothin'."

This new breed of doctors, some of them he just couldn't understand. On one of his trips to visit relatives, when he was still driving his own car, he was stopping in a large town when a frantic call came to attend a man with a coronary occlusion. His family had called five doctors, and not one of them had been able or willing to come. Doc went and administered the needed treatment. He was still sputtering with indignation when he arrived home in Greenville.

"I don't know what ails this generation. Roads were good down there, and the people seemed like folks who paid their bills. Not that that mattered. I'd have gone if they couldn't pay. Judas priest, in my book a doctor's a doctor, and if a patient needs him day or night, he ought to act like one! I can't understand it."

Change? He had seen plenty of that in his profession. Progress? That, too, of course, yet sometimes he was not so sure. Oh, knowledge and skill had increased a million-fold. The experts knew more and more about less and less: heart, lungs, brain, bones, eyes, ears, innards, and all the rest. But patients weren't just a conglomeration of organs. They were *people*. And they didn't always have their heart attacks and stomach aches during daytime office hours or on the steps of some city hospital or clinic. What about the poor devil who hatched up a red-hot appendix or a strangulated hernia out in some small-town bedroom at midnight with no hospital or doctor within fifty miles?

And here in Maine there were plenty of such situations. The state had far fewer doctors in 1970, than in 1900, when Doc had been entering medical school. In 1900 the Maine Medical Association had included 1,206 physicians, one to every 576 of the population; in 1970 only 969, one to every 1,000. And more and more of these were flocking to the large towns and cities. Dozens of small towns like Greenville had no medical service whatever. In Doc's class of forty-four students at Bowdoin forty of them had

come from Maine towns and most of them had gone back
to practice in them. But the Medical School of Maine had
been closed in 1920. Though there had been a hundred
Maine boys studying medicine in 1969 in thirty-three medical colleges outside of Maine, how many of them would
be returning to their native state? And how many of
these would concentrate in Portland, Waterville, Lewis-
ton, Bangor? And how many of the pitiable remainder
would be willing to rout out at midnight to rush to that
red-hot appendix or strangulated hernia, perhaps in some
tar-paper shack fifty miles away? But, no. He was getting
almost as bad as these brainy experts. A patient wasn't
an appendix or a hernia. He was a person, and he had a
name. Harry Johnston. "Uncle Anse" Smith. Roy Hatt.
"Big Clara". . . .

Sixty-five years. He was honored again by the Association, but this year in absentia. He was not moving
far from his little world these days. Those who had seen
him jump trains and skitter over thin ice and wade
through miles of mud and snow and slush were sobered
by the sight of his slow step and stooped shoulders. But
cheeks remained smooth and ruddy, eyes keen, the good
ear strong and alert, mind almost as razor sharp at ninety
as at seventy, sixty, forty. And the huge woodpile beside
the house diminished steadily, the garden flourished, the
rude ladder leading to the loft, where floats and decoys
were stored and where he often chipped kindling wood,
was climbed almost daily. And patients continued to push
the bell on the front door, or enter and halloo without
ringing.

In July, 1970, on his ninetieth birthday, friends con-
gregated in the Methodist Church to honor him again at
a recognition supper. There wasn't room for all in the
town who wanted to attend. He was presented with a
magnificent cake decorated with roses and topped by a

toy stethoscope, syringe, and thermometer. There were more poetic eulogies and platitudes. And there had been other instances of recognition in recent years.

"To the Pritham family," the Voice of America announced in its international broadcast one day in 1969, "medicine is not something you take, but something you practice." Beamed from transmitters in Greenville, North Carolina, Munich, Germany, the island of Rhodes, and from another station in the Far East, the program was heard in Europe, East and West Africa, the Far East, and South Asia. The sketch elaborated on the medical careers of the two Howards as well as Doc's. Though he did not bother to listen to the broadcast, many of his friends did, and one, Charles Sawyer, made a tape recording which Doc heard, not without a few wry comments.

"The oldest Dr. Pritham still maintains an active practice in Greenville, Maine, the town where he was born." (Ha! Error number one. Why couldn't these reporter guys ever get things right?) "Now in his eighty-ninth year he can look back with pride and satisfaction on the life he has devoted to his profession." (Satisfaction, maybe. Pride, no.) "The doctor over the years estimates that he has logged more than a thousand miles or 1600 kilometers walking through the backwoods caring for the sick and injured." (A thousand miles! He had tramped over twice that in a few months during the old flu epidemic.)

"Country doctors are a special breed, and many others, knowing the hardships experienced in a practice in the backwoods might have turned off into a more comfortable and profitable practice. Greenville in 1969 is still backwoods country." (Ha! Some of his fellow townsmen wouldn't appreciate that!) "In the summer months it is delightful with blue lakes and green mountains, but in the winter the climate is harsh. Greenville is frequently the coldest spot in the United States." (Granted.) "With the bitter cold each winter come many needles of snow, but for more than sixty-four years Doc Pritham has answered each call for help from widely scattered patients. Always of comfort to his patients was the fact that Doc Pritham never had specific office hours. His home was open any time, and never was the weather too bad or a call too far for him to respond." (He should hope so. What in thunder was a doctor for?)

"People say of the Pritham doctors that their devotion to a cause, an independent spirit, and an ability to know people as friends rather than patients are the qualities that make them just a little special."

That same year a woman writer in Maine wrote, asking if she might write a book about him. He knew her slightly. Her husband, a Methodist minister, had been a district superintendent in the area and had presided over meetings where, during his fifty-six years as church treasurer, Doc had presented his annual reports. Of all fool ideas! Who in thunder would be interested in a crazy yarn like that? Sitting down at his old typewriter in the outer office, Doc rattled off an answer so crisply terse that the paper seemed to crackle.

"In reply to your letter asking about writing a book I am not interested. I am losing memory of those days when I traveled." (An overstatement that, as his biographer later discovered. He could recall the name, date, symptoms, and treatment of almost every patient he had ever treated, plus the most minor detail of his incredibly multiple media of getting to them.)

But the woman persisted. She was convinced that he had had a unique and interesting experience, which might not only illuminate a fast-vanishing historical era but highlight the increasingly desperate need for more dedicated medical service in rural areas. Against his better judgment he let himself be persuaded. Reluctantly he sat

down again to the old typewriter and rattled off a resigned but brief acquiescence.

"I will cooperate."

But it was still a fool idea. A book, a *biography!* Judas
priest! Who was he to write a book about? Just a little
backwoods doctor who had tried to do his job!

· 4 ·

THE YOUNG WOMAN wandering through a huge outdoor
art show in Buffalo, New York, stopped short before a
picture. It portrayed a slender, white-haired man, eyes
almost fiercely straight and steady, lips quirked in a mere
hint of smile, hands firmly grasping a big black bag. In
the background was a symbolic medley of logs, snow-spray,
pine trees, a swirling stream, and a· crude sawmill with
chimneys, issuing plumes of cloud-white smoke.

"O-o-oh!" she murmured in an obvious burst of emotion. "A-a-a-ah!"

The artist, Albion Ende, regarded her with some alarm.
"What is it, madam? Is anything the matter?"

The eyes she turned to him were agleam with tears.
"That *is* Dr. Pritham, isn't it? The old doctor in Greenville, Maine?"

"Why—yes. Don't tell me you know him!"

"If it weren't for him," she said simply, "I wouldn't be
here."

She told him the story. Her parents had lived in New
Hampshire, and for two weeks each summer they had
vacationed on Moosehead Lake. One day their boat had
capsized, and her mother had nearly drowned. Near to
giving birth to a child, her condition had been desperate.
They had brought her to Greenville, to Dr. Pritham.
Not only had he saved the mother's life, which had been

in grave danger, but he had done the next to impossible, brought her live and healthy child into the world.

"I was that child," she finished soberly.

The artist nodded. Having spent many summers in the Moosehead region, he was used to hearing stories of Doc's exploits. But not from a chance meeting with a stranger some eight hundred miles away!

"It's a small world," he said with trite but fervent wonder.

When Doc was presented with the portrait he expressed polite and duly modest appreciation. But in private he indulged in a derisive hoot. "Who in thunder ever saw me out at my job in a blamed suit and tie! If I'd gone into the woods in that rig my patients would have laughed their heads off!" Secretly, however, he was rather pleased with the picture.

"It's a small world," Albion Ende had said, really meaning that the world of a little country doctor in a town "two hundred miles from nowhere" had proved unexpectedly big. And just what are the boundaries of that big-little world? Greenville, Maine? The north woods around Moosehead? Towns and cities where his patients have scattered, like Buffalo, New York? The span of a single generation?

Doc was right. It is hot in the Canal Zone, as hot as it can be cold in Greenville. There is often a difference of a hundred and more degrees in their temperatures. Sometimes, remembering the blue-cold-clear lake, the crunch of snow under one's feet, cool winds whistling through pine needles, Dr. Howard wonders, "What am I doing here?" Even that chilly night when he sat in the plane on the ice with two broken ankles does not seem so terrible in retrospect. And his cottage at Harford's Point which can be visited only once in two years seems very far away. But even on the hottest days there is little time for reflection. He has a job to do.

Not the same job as when Sadie visited him in the fifties. Then he was chief of the School Health Section, with four nurses and two clerks to assist with the health services of up to 14,000 students. Though the program he set up at that time is still essentially unchanged, it is conducted under different auspices. He is now "Line of Duty Injury" physician in the General Practice Clinic of Coco Solo, the hospital run by the Health Bureau on the Atlantic side of the Canal Zone. He also takes his turn staffing the emergency room which is open twenty-four hours a day, seven days a week. No more airplane trips, dashes over water, snow, and ice in boat, car, snowmobile to reach a case of emergency! This job is more practical for a man with an artificial leg, but no less rigorous and demanding, especially today, with the hospital staff of twenty-two doctors short by four.

It's a typical day, with samples of the usual run of accidents: foreign bodies in the eye, cuts and lacerations, bruises, sprains, fractures, bee stings, dog bites, burns, chemical exposure, usually on men from the docks where a container may have broken or a chlorine gas cylinder leaked and gassed a few workers. Here is a man who collapsed from heat exhaustion. Dr. Howard gives him resuscitation. A stevedore arrives, like so many, with a bad head injury. He is given first aid and sent on to another clinic. And, as all too frequently, there is a casualty from an auto accident. Here, to lighten routine, is a bit of tragi-comedy. One of the guards on the docks was bitten by a cat! The cat makes its home on the docks and was stealing the guard's lunch. To rescue it, the guard grabbed the cat and got bitten. It's a "Line of Duty" injury since it happened on the job.

And now comes a real emergency, a badly injured seaman. There are many hazardous occupations in the Zone. One is stevedoring. Another is boarding ships, especially when the trade winds are blowing and the water is rough. When it's too rough for the forty-five- or sixty-five-foot launches, tugs are used, with their perilous hazard of a breaking hawser, especially in these days of nylon hawsers, which can stretch like rubber bands. When one begins to "sing," a whole bevy of fast-moving Negroes rush to get out of the way. This man was not fast enough. But he is luckier than the three who were killed last year and the two others who had their legs amputated from hawsers breaking. Luckier than the one boarding a ship a few months ago whose foot got caught in a rope and he went through the winch. The man operating the winch panicked and ran, and by the time someone else got there the victim had gone through the winch three times. Or the stevedore who was killed last month when a sling-load of cargo swung and caught him against the side of the hold. Dr. Howard tests the patient for broken bones, treats his bruises, and sends him in to X ray.

Nine out of ten of his patients are colored, most of them Negroes of West Indian origin with some brown Panamanian or other Latin American nationalities mixed in. Dr. Howard speaks Spanish—self-taught since his arrival —with about half of them. With ship crewmen he sometimes has to resurrect his rusty German or French. A few San Blas Indians speak only their native language and often bring with them another San Blas who speaks Spanish, so there may be two interpreters, one English-Spanish, one Spanish-San Blas. About half of his fellow-doctors are Panamanian, two Puerto Rican. One went to medical school in Belgium, two in Spain, one in Mexico.

He wishes he could know his patients better, the way Dad does. It's a hit-and-run sort of doctoring. Ah, but here is one he knows, can even call by name!

The man is an East Indian. There used to be a large

group from India among the Canal employees, so many Singhs that they were carried on the lists by numbers, Singh Number One, Singh Number Two, and so on up to at least twelve, but now most of them have gone. This patient, though only about Dr. Howard's age, seems old. He has a serious ailment and about twelve children, the youngest only three. Too bad, thinks Howard, the poor fellow couldn't have Dad for a doctor. He wouldn't be just rushed through a clinic, shuttled off to some other clinic or department, given a perfunctory and impersonal treatment, sent away to be forgotten until he turns up again—if he doesn't die first. Anyway, to be forgotten.

Thinking of Dad, Dr. Howard takes a little extra time which he really should not spare, inquires about the twelve children and especially the little one. Perhaps he should bring him in soon for a checkup. Remember, the clinic is always here to serve. And if there is ever anything he himself can do to help, not just as a doctor but as a friend . . . .

Sunday mornings are cool in Vermont, blessedly cool after the oven of a troop carrier in Guantanamo or the mugginess of a Virginia air base. Rolling out of bed, still drugged with sleep, young Dr. Howard Pritham (Howie) drinks deeply of the heady New England air. A pity to have to get up so early six days out of seven! Early, did he say? "Judas priest," he can hear Grandpa hoot, "you call six o'clock early!" Though Grandma writes that since he turned ninety, Doc has been humoring himself a bit, getting up later sometimes, five o'clock instead of four.

Howie bathes and dresses hastily, then steals a minute to look in at sleeping David, age three, and to gloat over the diminutive Ellen Jean, born on July 23. Too bad not to spend more time with them. Perhaps this Sunday, his only day off, they can all go on a picnic, the kind Grandma used to plan for him and Merrie. Heavens, what a chore it must have been for her, he and Freddie and Merrie all barging in on her, year after year, to spend the summer! But how they all loved it! And if they were a burden, she certainly never let on.

Going downstairs to the hearty breakfast Ellen insists on preparing, he feels a surge of prideful ownership in this big old house. He is glad they could not afford anything in Hanover or Norwich and that nothing of more modern vintage was available. He has always wanted an old house to fix up, and this one in the tiny town of Wilder, population less than 500, sure qualifies. It's at least a hundred years old, and it certainly needs fixing, as much as Grandpa's six decades ago. It has no special style of architecture, just a big two-story wooden old house. Ellen calls it "early Wilder," and he suspects that she would prefer "late suburbia." But, always the good sport, here she is painting and papering like mad, and, thank heaven, she shares his preference for country life and outdoor sports like skiing. Wonderful to be back here in God's country, within easy access of ski slopes and clean lakes and mountain trails—yes, and not too far from good old Moosehead and duck hunting over in the salt marshes by Freeport!

He drives the four miles to Hanover, just across the Connecticut River in New Hampshire, where he is beginning a four-year surgical residency at Mary Hitchcock Hospital, affiliated with the Dartmouth College Medical School. As every morning, six days a week, he goes on duty at seven. First he makes rounds with the other residents and interns, examining patients, checking charts, writing new orders for the day. Since this is an operating morning, he then goes to the O.P. room and scrubs for an eight A.M. case. This month he is on Neurosurgical Service. There is a heavy load of operating today, four cases with complications. No lunch. It is mid-afternoon when he gets out of the operating room, and there is just time to pick up a hasty cup of coffee and a bun in the cafeteria.

Next, to the problems that have come up during the day which need his attention. He visits his more critical patients, makes rounds again with the chief resident or attending physician. Then he is notified by the operator of the new admissions which have come in during the afternoon. After the intern has taken the history and done a complete physical on the patient, it is his job as resident to give a more thorough examination, making a preliminary diagnosis and prescribing treatment. There is more than the usual number of admissions today, and it is seven o'clock when he has finished, a normal hour for getting through.

Now, thank goodness, since he is not on call tonight and there are no emergencies, he can go home! There is still a lot of day left. After dinner, which Ellen will have kept warm in the oven, he can romp for a half-hour with David, then get in a couple of hours' work on the house. It has been a busy, grueling, but satisfying work day. Even Grandpa, he feels sure, wouldn't think he had done too badly.

"I wish Grandpa could see this case," he thinks sometimes as he goes about his work. Or—"I wonder what Grandpa would think of this new treatment." Or, more often—"I'd like to know what Grandpa would say to this patient you know is dying—or to this psychotic—or to this cantankerous old vixen."

"Grandpa would do this . . . or that," Ellen has heard him say many times. Then he might rush back to the hospital after hours to see a patient, or deny himself an extra hour of skiing to play with David, or even make an important decision determining their whole future.

They live in different worlds, different eras, the old and the young Dr. Prithams. Instead of four short terms with no college preparation, it has already taken Howie eight years of college and medical school to train. After these four years of residency he will probably go to some big city for two more years of training in chest surgery. Fourteen years, plus the three in naval service. Like Grandpa before him, he wants the best training possible for the job he has chosen. Yet he knows he will be lucky if, in his time and place, he can render half as skilled and dedicated service.

A city, yes, but not to stay. He chose Mary Hitchock because of its unique status as a complete medical center in a rural area. And not for him a high-pressure scramble for any $50,000 salary. He wants just enough for a good life for himself and his family. And what's a good life? Some fine hospital to work in, of course, like Mary Hitchcock, but close to slopes for skiing, woods and lakes and bays and mountains for hunting and other outdoor enjoyment. A country home, preferably, with lots of acreage and, maybe, horses. Yes, and independence, freedom, not from hard work, but to use all his skill and energy to the limit of their capacity, and yet be his own boss.

In other words, just as he decided even before he was twelve, to be as much like Grandpa as possible.

Big or little, that world of old Doc Pritham's? How can it be measured? Not by time or space. Its boundaries cannot be found on a map of Maine. And already it encompasses three generations.

About the Author

Dorothy Clarke Wilson has acquired a large following through the years with her inspirational fiction and non-fiction. Her books *Dr. Ida, Take My Hands, Ten Fingers for God, Handicap Race,* and *Palace of Healing* are still reaching a wide readership; and her last book, *Lone Woman: The Story of Dr. Elizabeth Blackwell* (1970), has been exceptionally well received. A native of Maine, Mrs. Wilson is the wife of a retired minister and lives in Orono, Maine. She has traveled extensively in India, the Bible lands, and most recently the Indian country of Nebraska researching her fictional biography in progress, *Bright Eyes.*

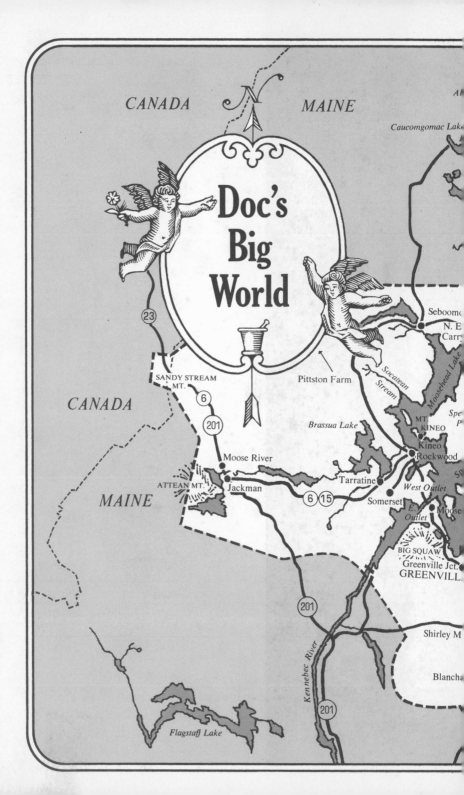